THE OLD TESTAMENT AND CHRISTIAN SPIRITUALITY

Society of Biblical Literature

International Voices in Biblical Studies

General Editors
Monica J. Melanchthon
Louis C. Jonker

Editorial Board
Eric Bortey Anum
Ida Fröhlich
Jione Havea
Hisako Kinukawa
Sam P. Mathew
Néstor Míguez
Nancy Nam Hoon Tan

Number 2
THE OLD TESTAMENT AND
CHRISTIAN SPIRITUALITY

THE OLD TESTAMENT AND CHRISTIAN SPIRITUALITY

Christo Lombaard

Society of Biblical Literature
Atlanta

Copyright © 2012 by the Society of Biblical Literature

All rights reserved. No part of this work may be reproduced or published in print form except with permission from the publisher. Individuals are free to copy, distribute, and transmit the work in whole or in part by electronic means or by means of any information or retrieval system under the following conditions: (1) they must include with the work notice of ownership of the copyright by the Society of Biblical Literature; (2) they may not use the work for commercial purposes; and (3) they may not alter, transform, or build upon the work. Requests for permission should be addressed in writing to the Rights and Permissions Office, Society of Biblical Literature, 825 Houston Mill Road, Atlanta, GA 30329, USA.

Library of Congress Cataloging-in-Publication Data

Lombaard, Christo.
 The Old Testament and Christian spirituality : theoretical and practical essays from a South African perspective / by Christo Lombaard.
   p. cm. — (Society of Biblical Literature. International voices in biblical studies ; v. 2)
 Includes bibliographical references.
  ISBN 978-1-58983-652-5 (paper binding : alk. paper) — ISBN 978-1-58983-653-2 (electronic format)
 1. Spirituality—Biblical teaching. 2. Bible. O.T.—Criticism, interpretation, etc. 3. Theology—South Africa. I. Title.
  BS1199.S7L66 2012
  248—dc23
                    2012004259

Table of Contents

Introduction ... vii

The Old Testament in Christian Spirituality: Perspectives on the Undervaluation of the Old Testament in Christian Spirituality ... 1

Four South African Proposals for a Central Theme to "Scriptural Spirituality" ... 27

Four Recent Books on Spirituality and the Psalms: Some Contextualising, Analytical, and Evaluative Remarks ... 53

Genealogies and Spiritualities in Genesis 4:17–22, 4:25–26, 5:1–32 ... 83

What Is Biblical Spirituality? Perspectives from a Minor Genre of Old Testament Scholarship ... 111

Table of Contents

Betwixt Text and Nature, God and Evolution:
Biblical Reception and Creationism at the Creation Museum
in Cultural-Anthropological Perspective   139

Exegesis and Spirituality   171

About the Author   191

Introduction

This volume is a collection of previously published journal articles and chapters in books. For a number of reasons, none of which are good, the academic wheels in South Africa turn not on books, as is the international convention, but on articles in refereed journals. One of the results of this South African habit is that sustained projects by scholars often do not appear in print together. I am very grateful therefore to the publisher, the Society of Biblical Literature, for assisting with, in this case at least, rectifying that situation. I also thank the editors of the International Voices in Biblical Studies series for taking up this volume in their series. Special mention must be made of Louis Jonker and Leigh Andersen in this respect, for their patience and tireless efforts.

The fact that most of the studies collected here have been published in South African journals, has limited the international reach of the scholarship. That some of these studies were first read as congress papers in Europe hardly remedies this situation. With the strong growth currently experienced in the field of Spirituality Studies in general, and Biblical Spirituality in particular, this volume makes these studies more accessible to a wider audience, in the hope of providing some further impetus to the multiple fields of study which combine to form the academic discipline of Biblical Spirituality, or more specifically in this case, Old Testament Spirituality. (What is meant by this terminology is made clear in Chapter 5.)

In a way it is not strange that, relatively speaking, Biblical Spirituality should experience such strong growth as it has in South Africa. On the one hand, South African theologians tend to have a very acute critical sense of the way the Bible is employed, because of the country's socio-political history during particularly the second half of the twentieth century. On the other hand, earlier, while the Western theological world was making sense of historical-critical methodologies of exegesis and trying to digest the implications thereof, South Africans were involved in the various colonialisms—on the receiving end, that is. By the time the full implications of historical criticism reached the highly active broader theological community of scholars on the southern-most tip of Africa, much of the modernist assumptions that had initially underpinned it implicitly had been appreciated and pointed out. Bible scholars who cared to do so could thus fully employ such exegetical approaches without losing the faith, which is ever the great fear in church and some academic circles in South Africa.

It is thus not all that surprising that, to my knowledge, the first professorial chair in Biblical Spirituality has been established at a South African university, namely at the University of the Free State in Bloemfontein. The incumbent, Pieter de Villiers, and my recently retired colleague for Christian Spirituality at the University of South Africa, Celia Kourie, both initially New Testament scholars, have been instrumental in establishing the broader discipline of Christian Spirituality and the narrower discipline of Biblical Spirituality within the country and outside its borders.

In acknowledgement of their giant efforts in this regard, I dedicate this volume to them.

These South African initiatives found much international nourishment from the Titus Brandsma Institute for Spirituality at Radboud University, Nijmegen, the Netherlands, in particular from Kees Waaijman, Jos Huls and Huub Welzen there, and from such eminent figures in the field as David Perrin in Canada (and through him the Society for the Study of Christian Spirituality) and Sandra Schneiders in the United States of America. At different times and in different ways, words of interest and encouragement on their part have meant—in a somewhat more literal way than is the customary use of this phrase—the world to us, as we develop these disciplines in South Africa.

To colleague Petra Dijkhuizen, my thanks and admiration for her work on the technical aspects of this text. My thanks too to

Reichard Taljaard for designing the graphic presentation on page eighteen of this volume.

I would also like to express my thanks to the publications concerned for giving permission for the re-publication of the studies here. Those involved with the often thankless and always tiring work of editing academic journals and volumes may not realise the appreciation for what they in fact mean for our pursuits of scholarly understanding.

The publications I refer to here, in alphabetical order, are *Acta Theologica*, *Ekklesiastikos Pharos*, *Hervormde Teologiese Studies* and from 2001 *HTS Teologiese Studies/Theological Studies*, *Tydskrif vir Semitistiek/Journal for Semitics*, the *Journal of Theology for Southern Africa*, *Scriptura*, *Verbum et Ecclesia*, and then: H. Blommestijn, C. Caspers, R. Hofman, F. Mertens, P. Nissen and H. Welzen, eds., *Seeing the Seeker. Explorations in the Discipline of Spirituality* (Festschrift for Kees Waaijman; *Studies in Spirituality,* Supplement 19; Louvain, Belgium: Peeters, 2008). Again, I express my sincere thanks to the respective editors for granting their blessing to have my work from their publications used in this collection. The essays from these volumes have, apart from the technical presentation here and minor changes in formulation and bibliographical updates, been left largely unchanged, to the point that cross references between the different essays have been left in their original form and have not been altered to refer to this text also.

Christo Lombaard
Pretoria, South Africa
24 April 2012

The Old Testament in Christian Spirituality: Perspectives on the Undervaluation of the Old Testament in Christian Spirituality[*]

ABSTRACT
Christian spirituality draws strongly on the Bible. Yet it is the New Testament that almost without exception features most prominently. Ten possible reasons are offered why the Old Testament takes on such a disproportionally diminutive role in the practice and study of spirituality: (1) textual complexity/critical scholarship/theological education; (2) modern popular pieties; (3) the cultural gaps between the Old Testament worlds and our worlds; (4) theological difficulties/Christian sensibilities; (5) fear of "boundary-less" interpretations; (6) the reference to Scripture by writers on spirituality; (7) the notion of progressive revelation; (8) theological diversity within the Old Testament; (9) OT : NT = law : grace; (10) the long and the short of textual units.

1. Faith as Life and the Book of Life

Spirituality is like dancing; play; sex and pleasure;[1] taste and touch and the other senses;[2] beauty;[3] breath and the wind;[4] in *this* sense: it is better experienced than described. Words do not succeed, here

---

[*] This essay was initially presented as a paper at the congress of the Southern African Society for Biblical and Religious Studies, in September 2002, at the University of Stellenbosch, South Africa.
[1] Cf. C. Kourie, "Towards a Spirituality of the Ordinary" (Paper read at the *Ecumenical Pastoral Institute in Cape Town* [EPIC] meeting at the University of Pretoria, 2001), 4.
[2] T. Gorringe, *The Education of Desire. Towards a Theology of the Senses*. (London: SCM, 2001), 1–27.
[3] B. Thijs, *Geloven Uit de Kunst? Een Pleidooi voor Geloofsverbeelding in de Gemeente* ('s-Gravenhage: Meinema, 1990), 57–67.
[4] A. E. McGrath, *Christian Spirituality: An Introduction* (Oxford: Blackwell, 1999), 1–2.

as in many other spheres of life,[5] in portraying adequately the dimensions of these primary states of being, these "sensations" of being human. Hence the variety of expressions and definitions employed to explain what is meant by the term "spirituality," and consequently also the varied domains of religion or faith which are described with this term.[6]

From an existentialist perspective,[7] it could be said that faith *is* life. *Credo ergo sum*. For believers, life without faith is non-life,[8] both in this world (psychologically, at least) and in the next. "Christian spirituality is not just one dimension of the Christian

---

[5] See C. J. S. Lombaard, "Taal: Kuns of Kêns? Nóg Losse, nóg Vaste Woorde oor Woorde," *Tydskrif vir Letterkunde* 39, no. 1/2 (2001): 60–61; see also J. Kagan, *Surprise, Uncertainty and Mental Structures* (Cambridge, Mass.: Harvard University Press, 2002).

[6] Cf. K. Waaijman, "Toward a Phenomenological Definition of Spirituality," *Studies in Spirituality* 3 (1993): 5–57; D. Marmion, *A Spirituality of Everyday Faith: A Theological Investigation of the Notion of Spirituality in Karl Rahner* (Louvain Theological and Pastoral Monographs 23; Louvain: Peeters Press, 1998), 3–40; M. Downey, *Understanding Christian Spirituality* (New York: Paulist Press, 1997), 5–29; D. J. Smit, "Kan Spiritualiteit Beskryf Word?" *Ned. Geref. Teologiese Tydskrif* 30, no. 1 (1989): 85–92; J. W. Oostenbrink, "Gereformeerde Spiritualiteit as Korporatiewe Spiritualiteit," *In die Skriflig* 33, no. 3 (1999): 367–83; Kourie, "Spirituality of the Ordinary," 3–7.

[7] Interestingly, referring very positively to Rossouw (see H. W. Rossouw, *Klaarheid en Interpretasie. Enkele Probleemhistoriese Gesigspunte in verband met die Leer van die Duidelikheid van die Heilige Skrif* [D.Th. proefskrif, VU; Amsterdam: Drukkerij en uitgeverij Jacob van Campen N.V., 1963]), Jonker also indicates the strongly existentialist character of the spirituality of the Reformation (see W. D. Jonker, "Die Eie-aard van die Gereformeerde Spiritualiteit," *Ned. Geref. Teologiese Tydskrif* 30, no. 3 [1989]: 292).

[8] This is the sort of idea that underlies the thinking of e.g. Taylor, though in an unnecessarily alarmist way (see J. V. Taylor, *A Matter of Life and Death* [London: SCM, 1986], 17–34). Evangelical and missiological inclinations of an alarmist kind are probably counter-productive in our time; cf. C. J. S. Lombaard, "'Oortuiging' en Prediking—Woordspel op 'n 'Hartsaak,'" *Skrif en Kerk* 21, no. 3 (2000): 614.

life; it *is* the Christian life."[9] For the faithful, faith is a *"way of life"*; faith *is* life.[10]

---

[9] Downey, *Understanding Christian Spirituality*, 71; cf. H. Berkhof, *Christelijk Geloof. Een Inleiding tot de Geloofsleer* (Zesde, bijgewerkte druk; Nijkerk: Callenbach, 1990), 1–2.

[10] See L. S. Cunningham and K. J. Egan, *Christian Spirituality: Themes from the Tradition* (New York: Paulist Press, 1996), 9; see also McGrath, *Christian Spirituality*, 3. From this perspective, "religion" is the broader category and "spirituality" is the way in which one expresses one's faith—for our purposes here, one's Christian faith. Often in both popular and academic circles, this order is reversed, e.g. Nel: "... spirituality should be seen as the most basic human principle of ultimate meaning-seeking and ... religion should be seen as the most prominent parameter" (see J. P. Nel, "Spirituality and Religion: A Challenge to Near Eastern Studies," *Journal for Semitics/Tydskrif vir Semitistiek* 10, no. 1/2 [2001]: 10).

In order to clear up this confusion between a phenomenological or a humanities approach and what might be termed a confessional or a Christian theological approach to spirituality/religion/faith, I would suggest a categorisation from the broadest to the most personal category as: (1) existential quest(ion)s/"the depth dimension of all human existence" (Downey, *Understanding Christian Spirituality*, 14; italics added) → (2) religions and philosophies → (3) expressions of commitments (in various social spheres of differing size and importance) within each of the former → (4) personal experiences and expressions of faith. The latter is not an isolated and insular piety; "holistic spirituality" includes the dimensions of society, politics and church—be it directly or indirectly; see Marmion, *Spirituality of Everyday Faith*, 2; L. Kretzschmar, "What is Holistic Spirituality and Why Is It Important for the Church Today?" in *Towards a Holistic, Afro-centric and Participatory Understanding of the Gospel of Jesus Christ* (ed. D. Hoffmeister and L. Kretzschmar; Johannesburg: Baptist Convention of South Africa, 1995), 31–44; L. Kretzschmar, "The Three Journeys: A Functional Model of Holistic Spirituality," in *Towards a Holistic, Afro-centric and Participatory Understanding of the Gospel of Jesus Christ* (ed. D. Hoffmeister and L. Kretzschmar; Johannesburg: Baptist Convention of South Africa, 1995), 45–54; cf. Downey, *Understanding Christian Spirituality*, 24–25; Cunningham and Egan, *Christian Spirituality*, 18–21; A. B. du Toit, "Lewensgemeenskap met God as Essensie van Bybelse Spiritualiteit," *Skrif en Kerk* 14, no. 1 (1993): 39–40; C. J. S. Lombaard, "The Bible in the Apartheid Debate," in *1948 + 50 Years. Theology, Apartheid and Church: Past, Present and Future* (ed. J. W.

The Old Testament, for its part, has often been described as the "Book of Life." Against the (perceived) centredness on Christ and faith alone in the New Testament, the Old Testament is experienced as of a more "earthy" order: what are considered the "normal aspects" of life is to a greater extent encountered in the first two thirds of the Bible. This includes the birth and death of ordinary people; their customs, laws and rituals; the animals, plants, seasons, and other aspects of nature they encounter; friendship, love, and even erotica;[11] violence and murder; politics and family matters; rural and urban contexts; epic journeys of survival; God's words—bearing both good news and bad—and human responses to those words—both positive and negative... (cf. the subtitles to Preuß's double volume of Old Testament theology: respectively *JHWHs erwählendes und verpflichtendes Handeln* and *Israels Weg mit JHWH*).[12]

Hofmeyr, C. J. S. Lombaard and P. J. Maritz; Perspectives on the Church/Perspektiewe op die Kerk, Series 5, Vol. 1; Pretoria: IMER [Institute for Missiological and Ecumenical Research], University of Pretoria, 2001), 85–86; Smit, "Kan Spiritualiteit Beskryf Word?" 85; L. D. Hulley, "Spirituality and Ethics: Do They Belong Together?" in *Christian Spirituality in South Africa* (ed. C. Kourie and L. Kretzschmar; Pietermaritzburg: Cluster Publications, 2000), 55–65; A. Nolan, *Biblical Spirituality* (Springs: The Order of Preachers [Southern Africa], 1982), 7–11.

My references to spirituality in the rest of this paper refer to the last two of these four "levels" or "spheres" in interaction. The academic study of spirituality, although related to all four of these levels and hence not "objective" in any positivistic sense, takes "a step away" in order to analyse, compare, and theorise these phenomena, and to consider meta-issues.

Refer to Addendum 1 at the end of this article for a graphic presentation of the "levels" or "spheres" of spirituality.

[11] Cf. J. A. Loader, "Exegetical Erotica to Canticles 7:2–6," *Journal for Semitics/Tydskrif vir Semitistiek* 10, vol. 1/2 (2001): 98–111.

[12] See H. D. Preuß, *Theologie des Alten Testaments, Band 1: JHWHs erwählendes und verpflichtendes Handeln* (Stuttgart: Kohlhammer, 1991) and H. D. Preuß, *Theologie des Alten Testaments, Band 2: Israels Weg mit JHWH* (Stuttgart: Kohlhammer, 1992).

On the face of it, then, it would seem that "faith as life" and the "Book of Life" would be an easy match. Not so, though. The Old Testament is only infrequently drawn from for spiritual exercises, and continues to play a much less substantial role in the church than its proportions in the Bible would suggest. Even when the Old Testament is referred to, it is often only done in a more or less metaphorical sense, rather than exegetically or theologically, and then all too briefly too, with the Old Testament references enclosed by ample references to New Testament texts.[13] This should be of concern particularly to church traditions, such as Calvinism,[14] that stress the equal inspiration and value of all parts of Scripture.[15] In Roman Catholicism too, even though it offers us the deepest roots of the modern interest in and practice and study of spirituality,

---

[13] See e.g. Cunningham and Egan, *Christian Spirituality*, 9–14; cf. S. D. Snyman, "Spiritualiteit—'n Perspektief uit die Ou Testament," *In die Skriflig* 31, no. 4 (1997): 376–77. This is the case in general; there are of course exceptions, e.g. Cunningham and Egan, *Christian Spirituality*, 144–48. The thematic approach of McGrath (*Christian Spirituality*, 35–81, 88–108) goes about employing the Bible in a different way; here too though the New Testament features more prominently. The two studies which have come to my attention that give the most promising direction for the use of the Old Testament within Spirituality are by the New Testament scholar Du Toit ("Lewensgemeenskap met God," 28–46), who takes the *praesentia Dei* as central moment, and the Old Testament scholar Snyman ("Spiritualiteit—'n Perspektief uit die Ou Testament," 375–87), who takes life *coram Deo* as central moment (cf. also John Barton, "Biblical Roots: The Old Testament," in *The Study of Spirituality* [ed. C. Jones, G. Wainwright and E. Yarnold; London: SPCK, 2000], 55–56). Nolan (*Biblical Spirituality*, 29–41) employs "justice" as the central spiritual theme of the Old Testament, and "love" as that of the New, which leads him to "Kingdom Spirituality" (Nolan, *Biblical Spirituality*, 43–58)—concepts which were very fruitful for his anti-apartheid theology, yet too narrow to do justice to the diversity of theologies, ethics and spiritualities within the Bible (cf. A. Nolan, *God in South Africa* [Cape Town: David Philip, 1988]; Lombaard, "The Bible in the Apartheid Debate," 81–86).

[14] Cf. Jonker, "Die Eie-aard van die Gereformeerde Spiritualiteit," 294–95.

[15] Cf. P. C. Potgieter, *Skrif, Dogma en Verkondiging* (Kaapstad: Lux Verbi, 1990), 25–26.

there is the strong sense that all modern spiritualities go back to the spiritualities of the four Gospels and the spirituality of Paul.[16] The emphasis remains on the New Testament.[17]

The purpose of this contribution is to outline some of the reasons for the difficult fit of "faith as life" and the "Book of Life," that is, of spirituality and the Old Testament.

2. Ten Possible Reasons

I propose ten possible reasons for the less than ideal reference the Old Testament finds within the theory and practice of Christian spirituality. These ten reasons are given as an overview and do not purport to be an exhaustive historical overview or, for that matter, a full digest of current developments and trends.[18] Like most writing on spirituality, the ten reasons suggested here are based on a personal sense informed by various forms of individual experiences, academic readings, and intellectual reflection guided by a range of influences. Taken together, though, these ten reasons seek to elucidate the undervaluation of the Old Testament in the practice and study of Christian spirituality.

---

[16] Cf. Marmion, *Spirituality of Everyday Faith,* 25. An interpretation that relays spirituality to Scripture only would be too superficial: expressions of spirituality naturally draw from the Bible, but do so within certain ecclesial, social and political circumstances, reacting upon these too, as acknowledged by Marmion, *Spirituality of Everyday Faith,* 26; cf. also Downey, *Understanding Christian Spirituality,* 46–48; D. J. Smit, "Wat Is Gereformeerde Spiritualiteit?" *Ned. Geref. Teologiese Tydskrif* 29, no. 2 (1988): 191–92; Smit, "Kan Spiritualiteit Beskryf Word?" 91.

[17] See in addition the registers in Smit, "Wat Is Gereformeerde Spiritualiteit?" 184–85 and Smit, "Kan Spiritualiteit Beskryf Word?" 93–94, and the relative length of the discussion in the adjoining chapters in Jones et al., eds., *The Study of Spirituality, viz.* Barton, "Biblical Roots: The Old Testament," 47–57 and C. P. M. Jones, "Biblical Roots: The New Testament," 58–89.

[18] For a historical and modern international overview of spirituality, cf. the essays collected in *The Study of Spirituality* (ed. C. Jones, G. Wainwright and E. Yarnold; London: SPCK, 2000).

2.1 Textual complexity/critical scholarship/theological education

The text of the Old Testament is not a simple text.[19] The long history of its development, which historical-critical scholarship has indicated, yet on which there seems to be no consensus,[20] makes the Hebrew Bible a book that is often ignored for the purposes of spiritual enrichment. The concomitant repetitions, contradictions and inconsistencies found in the texts of the Old Testament have not helped to endear this part of the Scriptures to the Bible-reading public. Important to note here is, however, that the historical scholarship of the Old Testament does not in essence stand at odds with Spirituality scholarship,[21] since the latter is to a great extent historically oriented.[22] This shared focus on the past, along with

---

[19] For a historical overview of what is meant philosophically by the "text" of Scripture within circles concerned with spirituality, cf. D. S. Pacini, "Reading Holy Writ: the Locus of Modern Spirituality," in *Christian Spirituality III. Post-Reformation and Modern* (ed. L. Dupré and D. E. Saliers; New York: Crossroads, 1991), 174–210.

[20] The Pentateuch theories are a case in point: cf. Wellhausen 1963⁴ *versus* Blum 1990 *versus* Van Seters 1994 *versus* Braulik 1991 *versus* Otto 2000, to name some of the main players. Jones mentions the parallel problems historical-critical scholarship has created regarding the New Testament (see Jones, "Biblical Roots: The New Testament," 60).

[21] On the relationship between spirituality and theology in general, cf. e.g., P. Sheldrake, *Spirituality and Theology: Christian Living and the Doctrine of God* (London: Darton, Longman & Todd Ltd, 1998), 3–34, 183–95; Marmion, *Spirituality of Everyday Faith,* 29–39; McGrath, *Christian Spirituality,* 27–33; interestingly, Greshake places spirituality as the primary category over theology (see G. Greshake, "Zum Verhältnis von Theologie und Spiritualität," *Studies in Spirituality* 10 (2000), 21–32.

[22] Cf. e.g., Downey, *Understanding Christian Spirituality,* 54–72, 126–27; McGrath, *Christian Spirituality,* 135–72; Cunningham and Egan, *Christian Spirituality,* 7; M. Casey, "Bernard's Biblical Mysticism. Approaching Sermons on the Song of Songs 74," *Studies in Spirituality* 4 (1994), 12–30; U. T. Holmes, *A History of Christian Spirituality. An Analytical Introduction* (New York: Seabury Press, 1981), 14–157.

the implied, yet still unexplored, shared interests in the philosophy of history, hermeneutics and so forth, should make these two disciplines if not twins, then at least siblings who share a special bond. The place at which to start such inter-disciplinary interaction is already during the education of clergy and others interested in religion, at tertiary education institutions.[23] The breach between the disciplines of Old Testament Science and Spirituality with which most of us grew up theologically, would thus in time be closed in both the theory and practice of spirituality.

2.2 Modern popular pieties

To a great extent the modern Christian church is characterised by pieties that may be described as "Jesus only" or, particularly in more charismatic expressions, "Spirit centeredness."[24] Spirituality traditionally draws on Christ, the Spirit, and the church.[25] Although the importance of neither Jesus nor the Holy Spirit in Christian theology is to be diminished, the role of the First Person in the Trinity deserves greater attentiveness in the church,[26] hence opening the door to the Old Testament to a greater extent. My call is thus for a more clearly theocentric, that is Trinitarian, sensitivity in the church.[27] Interestingly, even when others[28] stress the Trinity

---

[23] Cf. E. H. Peterson, *Subversive Spirituality* (Grand Rapids: Eerdmans, 1997), 54–60.

[24] On the latter cf. e.g., K. Runia, "Towards a Biblical Theology of Experience," in *Christian Experience in Theology and Life* (ed. I. H. Marshall; Edinburgh: Rutherford House Books, 1988), 181–85; Jonker, "Die Eie-aard van die Gereformeerde Spiritualiteit," 293, 298.

[25] Marmion, *Spirituality of Everyday Faith,* 26.

[26] See also C. Kourie, "What Is Christian Spirituality?" in *Christian Spirituality in South Africa* (ed. C. Kourie and L. Kretzschmar; Pietermaritzburg: Cluster Publications, 2000), 17–18; Kourie, "Spirituality of the Ordinary," 7.

[27] Sheldrake, *Spirituality and Theology,* 47–62, 75–83; cf. G. D. Fee, *Listening to the Spirit in the Text* (Grand Rapids: Eerdmans, 2000), 24–32.

[28] See e.g., Downey, *Understanding Christian Spirituality,* 44–45, 79–80.

Undervaluation of the Old Testament in Christian Spirituality 9

and the Bible, the resulting references are in no greater extent to the Old Testament. This stands, to some degree at least, in the tradition of systematic theologians too, who employ the New Testament substantially more than the Old, and better, in considering the central tenets of the Christian faith, to which the doctrine of the Trinity belongs.

2.3 The cultural gaps between the Old Testament worlds and our worlds

It takes only a brief encounter with the Old Testament for us to experience the practices and traditions we encounter there as "strange." This holds true for readers from both primarily Western and primarily traditional African backgrounds.[29] From whichever cultural matrix one encounters the Old Testament, one could easily misunderstand matters that seem familiar and reject matters that seem outlandish. In order to aid the bridging of such divergence, the study of the greater context of the ancient Near East and its implications for our understanding of the Old Testament and the spiritualities one finds reflected there, should not be underestimated. Such study may indeed open some doors to appropriating aspects of these ancient spiritualities we encounter to spiritualities[30] in our times.[31] The cultural gaps between the Old Testament worlds and our worlds do not have to be only estranging, but may also be enriching.

---

[29] On the former, cf. Barton, "Biblical Roots: The Old Testament," 48–49; on the latter, cf. J. N. Kudadjie, "African Spirituality," in *Spirituality in Religions. Profiles and Perspectives* (ed. C. W. du Toit; Pretoria: Research Institute for Theology and Religion, University of South Africa, 1996), 66–78.

[30] The plural "spiritualities" is used advisedly—cf. e.g., Cunningham and Egan, *Christian Spirituality,* 15–16; McGrath, *Christian Spirituality,* 8–24; Du Toit, "Lewensgemeenskap met God," 29.

[31] Nel, "Spirituality and Religion: A Challenge to Near Eastern Studies," 3–5.

2.4 Theological difficulties/Christian sensibilities

Throughout the Christian centuries, the sensitivity of the faithful to the violence, sanctioned by God, that we encounter in the Old Testament, has often rendered this part of the Bible to the margins of active Christian literature. How could a loving God be so cruel and violent? Features such as the attribution of such acts to God by writers centuries after the recounted events would have occurred, in order to make a theological or political point, long realised by Old Testament scholars, do not make much popular impact, because they do not fit well with popular notions of scriptural inspiration. However, the humanistic legacy of Reformation figures such as Desiderius Erasmus includes that the Bible can at once be treated as wholly human literature and as holy, that is, divinely inspired Scriptures.[32] The Bible critically studied and the Bible spiritually nourishing are not two notions at odds.[33] Education of lay believers on both inspiration theory and the less direct (i.e., non-applicationary) ways in which aspects of the Old Testament world unacceptable to modern sensibilities should be seen, is a prerequisite for the Book of Life finding adequate expression in the spiritual lives of believers.

2.5 Fear of "boundary-less" interpretations

Particularly the clergy and the *doctores* of the modern church have developed an aversion to ways of reading the Bible that are unscientific, that is, without a thoroughly scientific method—be it historical criticism, structuralist methodologies, or literary

---

[32] J. D. Tracy, "*Ad fontes*: The Humanist Understanding of Scripture as Nourishment for the Soul," in *Christian Spirituality II. High Middle Ages and Reformation* (ed. J. Raitt; New York: Crossroad, 1989), 255–58.
[33] S. M. Schneiders, "Scripture in Spirituality," in *Christian Spirituality I. Origins to the Twelfth Century* (ed. B. McGinn and J. Meyendorff; London: Routledge & Kegan Paul, 1989), 19.

analyses.[34] The earlier traditions of biblical interpretation, such as allegorical readings, are now severely frowned upon, for the reason that they could be so free as to allow almost any exposition. Biblical interpreters in our time who employ these techniques soon find themselves outside the main streams of interpretation, not only because of the uncontrolled exegesis, but also because of the theological implications such methods have for the view of Scripture. The Old Testament with its at times violent contents—to name again this one among the many difficulties people often raise—tended for these very reasons to fall prey more easily to interpretative techniques such as allegory.[35] Reading the Bible with a view to spiritual enrichment creates the impression for many that it comes just too close for comfort to these unacceptable interpretative techniques.[36] A "higher" or "deeper" meaning, an "eternal truth," a spiritually and at times emotionally moving result from such readings seem to leave the door ajar for uncontrolled, even plainly wild, interpretations to become acceptable. The fact that, for instance, classic historical-critical readings from the Old Testament can be employed fruitfully in spiritual reflections,[37] since both are contextually oriented,[38] lies outside the field of experience of many, and thus remains largely unknown.

---

[34] Cf. e.g., H.-J. Kraus, *Geschichte der historisch-kritischen Erforschung des Alten Testaments* (3., erw. Auflage; Neukirchen-Vluyn: Neukirchener Verlag, 1982); W. Richter, *Exegese als Literaturwissenschaft. Entwurf einer alttestamentliche Literaturtheorie und Methodologie* (Göttingen: Vandenhoeck & Ruprecht, 1971); Robert Alter, *The Art of Biblical Narrative* (New York: Basic Books, 1981), respectively.
[35] Cf. Rossouw, *Klaarheid en Interpretasie*, 48–87.
[36] Cf. Holmes, *A History of Christian Spirituality*, 12; J. L. Houlden, "Bible, Spirituality of the," in *Westminster Dictionary of Spirituality* (ed. G. S. Wakefield; Philadelphia: Westminster, 1983), 48; Schneiders, "Scripture in Spirituality," 8–19.
[37] See Schneiders, "Scripture in Spirituality," 19.
[38] Nolan, *Biblical Spirituality*, 22–27.

2.6 The reference to Scripture by writers on spirituality

Writers on spirituality habitually insist on the importance of the Bible[39] to the point that Houlden could formulate: "What else is the Bible if not spirituality?"[40] Scripture is one of the "constitutive disciplines" of Spirituality as an academic discipline, as Schneiders, among others, indicates.[41] She continues to point out that "[t]he scholar of Christian spirituality, therefore, needs a ... deep familiarity with the content and dynamics of this literature and a methodological competence that will allow her or him to handle biblical material responsibly."[42] Then follows the by now unexpected statement: that no specialist knowledge is required; one merely "must be shaped by the great biblical motifs."[43] This stands at odds with the demands made by the complexity of particularly the literature of the Old Testament referred to above. What is more, living from Scripture becomes thus, in a sense, only at a distance, not close-up, with the minutiae of biblical literature providing the unexpected riches that would feed both the exercise and the academic discipline of Spirituality. In the history of Christian spirituality there has in general been given "no attention to the variety of background, historical period and authorship"[44] of the biblical texts. Hence, for the most part, spirituality scholars will study others' use of Scripture[45] or propose hermeneutical

---

[39] See e.g., B. P. Holt, *A Brief History of Christian Spirituality* (Oxford: Lion Publishing, 1993), 28; Kourie, "What Is Christian Spirituality?" 14.
[40] Houlden, "Bible, Spirituality of the," 48.
[41] S. M. Schneiders, "The Study of Christian Spirituality: Contours and Dynamics of the Discipline," *Studies in Spirituality* 8 (1998), 43.
[42] Ibid.
[43] Ibid.
[44] Houlden, "Bible, Spirituality of the," 48
[45] See e.g. Casey, "Bernard's Biblical Mysticism," 12–30

approaches,[46] but tend not to engage in exegesis primarily. Old Testament science is the poorer for this.[47]

2.7 The notion of progressive revelation

Both in academic theology and in popular faith the notion of a progressive, that is, a continuing, "ever better" divine revelation in the Bible is quite common. This concept inevitably accords greater stature to the New Testament than to the Old. Even when the Bible as source for spirituality is discussed in a sensitive, well-informed, and careful manner,[48] one cannot escape the nagging sense that the Old Testament is read as though through New Testament spectacles. At times the idea that the New Testament is more advanced than the Old, is quite pronounced;[49] hence the New Testament is referred to much more frequently than the Old Testament.[50] The idea of progressive revelation is, however, difficult to relate to the conviction, in some Christian churches at least, of the equal authority of all parts of Scripture.[51] In addition, reversing the idea of progressive revelation while employing its terminology, Loader has indicated a way in which the Old Testament provides a "corrective" to the New.[52] Lastly, neither the Old Testament nor the New can properly be interpreted other than in the other's light.[53] On the basis of these three points, my petition here is for bifocals: for us to accord both Testaments full integrity

---

[46] See e.g. K. Waaijman, "A Hermeneutic of Spirituality," *Studies in Spirituality* 5 (1995), 5–39.
[47] Cf. Fee, *Listening to the Spirit in the Text,* 3–15; Schneiders, "Scripture in Spirituality," 19.
[48] See e.g. Cunningham and Egan, *Christian Spirituality,* 35–41.
[49] Nolan, *Biblical Spirituality,* 61.
[50] Ibid., 43–72.
[51] Cf. Potgieter, *Skrif, Dogma en Verkondiging,* 25–26.
[52] See J. A. Loader, "'Theologia Religionum' from the Perspective of Israelite Religion—An Argument," *Missionalia* 13, no. 1 (1985): 14–15 in particular.
[53] See Schneiders, "Scripture in Spirituality," 4.

2.8 Theological diversity within the Old Testament

The theological diversity within the Old Testament relates not only to the different theologies found in the Old Testament (which is examined within Old Testament Science in the sub-discipline of Old Testament Theology),[54] but also to the different "group religions" within Israel[55] that could at the same time support different theological traditions which may or may not have been mutually exclusive.[56] This diversity of theologies in the Old Testament is not as clearly distinguished as are the different theologies in the New Testament. Hence, for instance, the different expressions of Yahwism in the Old Testament are more difficult to identify and to come to terms with than the different representations of Jesus that we find: in the New Testament (in Matthean, Markan, Lukan, Johannine, Pauline and Petrine theology);[57] in the church (e.g. in Roman Catholic, Anglican, Orthodox, Reformation, Charismatic/Pentecostal and Third World institutionalised churches);[58] and across churches (e.g. in

---

[54] Cf. e.g. Preuß, *Theologie des Alten Testaments, Band 1,* 1–27 for an overview.
[55] Cf. e.g. Rainer Albertz, *Religionsgeschichte Israels in alttestamentlicher Zeit* (vol. 1; Göttingen: Vandenhoeck & Ruprecht, 1992), 40–43.
[56] Cf. K. Weippert, "Synkretismus und Monotheismus," in *Kultur und Konflikt* (ed. J. Assman, and D. Harth; Frankfurt: Suhrkamp Verlag, 1990), 150–60; Albertz, *Religionsgeschichte Israels,* 40–43; K. van der Toorn, *Family Religion in Babylonia, Syria and Israel: Continuity and Change in the Forms of Religious Life* (Leiden: Brill, 1996), 181–205; Z. Zevit, *The Religions of Ancient Israel: A Synthesis of Parallactic Approaches* (London: Continuum, 2001), 643–46.
[57] Cf. Du Toit, "Lewensgemeenskap met God," 29.
[58] Cf. e.g., respectively, D. Maruca, "Roman Catholic Spirituality," in *Westminster Dictionary of Spirituality* (ed. G. S. Wakefield; Philadelphia:

"liberation spirituality"[59] and "feminist spirituality"[60]). Yet, if the theological diversity within the Old Testament were mastered to a greater extent, these would both enrich the different spiritualities prominent in our time and, because of a greater sense of shared heritage and identity, enhance the possibilities of communication between these contemporary traditions.

2.9 OT : NT = law : grace

Often in the churches and among their members the relationship between the Old Testament and the New is still seen as one of law in opposition to grace (alternatively, as promise *versus* fulfilment[61]). A strong tendency thus remains to equate the Old Testament with "law," as opposed to the New Testament containing "grace" that, in Pauline language, frees us from the

---

Westminster, 1983), 336–39; F. Cull, "The Anglican Way: A School for Beginners," in *Christian Spirituality in South Africa* (ed. C. Kourie and L. Kretzschmar; Pietermaritzburg: Cluster Publications, 2000), 100–124; S. Lash, "Orthodox Spirituality," in *Westminster Dictionary of Spirituality* (ed. G. S. Wakefield; Philadelphia: Westminster, 1983), 283–85; H. L. Rice, *Reformed Spirituality: An Introduction for Believers* (Louisville: Westminster John Knox, 1991); P. Russel-Boulton, "A Pentecostal Spirituality," in *Christian Spirituality in South Africa* (ed. C. Kourie and L. Kretzschmar; Pietermaritzburg: Cluster Publications, 2000), 125–37; S. Tshelane, "The Spirituality of the African Initiated Churches," in *Christian Spirituality in South Africa* (ed. C. Kourie and L. Kretzschmar; Pietermaritzburg: Cluster Publications, 2000), 138–56.

[59] Cf. Marmion, *Spirituality of Everyday Faith,* 336–46; J. Sobrino, *Spirituality of Liberation: Toward Political Holiness* (Maryknoll: Orbis, 1988).

[60] Cf. Marmion, *Spirituality of Everyday Faith,* 346–57; U. King, *Women and Spirituality. Voices of Protest and Promise* (London: Macmillan Education Ltd, 1989); Y. Dreyer, "Vroue-ervaring en Spiritualiteit," *Hervormde Teologiese Studies* 44, no. 2/3 (1999): 360–79; S. Rakoczy, "Living Life to the Full: Reflections on Feminist Spirituality," in *Christian Spirituality in South Africa* (ed. C. Kourie and L. Kretzschmar; Pietermaritzburg: Cluster Publications, 2000), 69–91.

[61] Cf. e.g. Paul J. Achtemeier and Elizabeth R. Achtemeier, *The Old Testament Roots of Our Faith* (Philadelphia: Fortress, 1962).

law.[62] We are left with the deduction that we are thus "freed" from the Old Testament, returning to it only to see how we were enslaved to or by law, or—always somewhat awkwardly—to find ways of now expressing gratitude to God for receiving grace. In this way, for instance, Nolan employs "justice" as the central spiritual theme of the Old Testament and "love" as that of the New.[63] This creates a false sense with many that the "Old" in "Old Testament" refers to that which no longer applies, since something better has come along.[64] It is a "false sense," however, since God as a God of wrath and mercy is found in both Testaments of the Bible.[65] Neither law nor grace, neither promise nor fulfilment are restricted to the Hebrew or Greek sections of the Bible. More radically: read closely, the laws in the Old Testament *are* expressions of grace. The "law" against which Paul reacts and which often informs the recurring aversion among some Christians to the Hebrew Bible, is not the Old Testament as a book, but the practice of some of Paul's contemporaries (which they on their part had related to certain interpretations of certain parts of the Hebrew Bible). To apply such exegetically inaccurate and theologically unsound categories as these to the Old Testament, and then on those grounds to dismiss two thirds of the Bible as unworthy of our spiritual consideration, stands no one in good stead.

2.10   The long and the short of textual units

In practice, Christians find it easier to read small sections from the New Testament—mere verses often—to "take something from it," than is the case with sections from the Old Testament. A parable, a bare sentence from the Sermon on the Mount, or a single Pauline

---

[62] Cf. Jonker, "Die Eie-aard van die Gereformeerde Spiritualiteit," 298.
[63] See Nolan, *Biblical Spirituality*, 29–41.
[64] E. Zenger, *Einleitung in das Alte Testament* (3. Auflage; Berlin: Kohlhammer, 1998), 12–18.
[65] See e.g. Holt, *A Brief History of Christian Spirituality*, 31.

injunction seems more manageable than the Joseph novella, an Isaian prophecy or even a Psalm or Proverb which can at times turn out to be treacherously taxing just before bed time. This, though popular, is of course a false perception: reading a single verse from the New Testament leaves one as vulnerable to misinterpretation as reading a single verse from the Old Testament. Yet, the perception persists, so that except for a courageous few, the New Testament is preferred for a "quick read." This leaves the Old Testament, or at least the greatest part of it, under-utilised in the spiritual life of the church as a whole and in that of individual believers.

The case here is not that the Old Testament finds no place at all within spirituality. However, these ten reasons offer some explanations for the tradition within the Christian churches that the New Testament nourishes us spiritually, while the Old Testament remains in the spiritual shadows, so to speak. Even when the Old Testament is employed, only two *loci* from it figure with any given frequency: most beloved, the Psalms,[66] and second, the concept of *imago Dei* (Gen 1:27). In both cases, better readings are often required,[67] though there are some exceptions that take historical-critical exegesis seriously.[68] By and large, then, the Old Testament

---

[66] Holt, *A Brief History of Christian Spirituality,* 29; Houlden, "Bible, Spirituality of the," 48–49; G. S. Wakefield, "The Psalms," in *Westminster Dictionary of Spirituality* (ed. G. S. Wakefield; Philadelphia: Westminster, 1983), 322–23; cf. G. Sklar-Chik, "Prayer: Praying the Psalms," in *Christian Spirituality in South Africa* (ed. C. Kourie and L. Kretzschmar; Pietermaritzburg: Cluster Publications, 2000), 195–208.

[67] Sklar-Chik, for example, reads Psalm 57 as Davidic; and the idea of humanity created in God's image is often so loaded with modern meanings that one can hardly refer to such interpretations as exegesis (see Sklar-Chik, "Prayer: Praying the Psalms," 204–7; cf. Lombaard, "The Bible in the Apartheid Debate," 78–80).

[68] W. Brueggemann, *Spirituality of the Psalms* (Minneapolis: Fortress, 2002); C. Stuhlmueller, *The Spirituality of the Psalms* (Collegeville, Minn.: Liturgical Press, 2002).

plays a much smaller role in spirituality than its proportions in the Christian Scriptures would suggest. This is the case within churches, for individual believers, and where the Bible is a source for instruction.

3. Conclusion

Investigating the relationship between the Old Testament and spirituality is no one-sided quest for relevance on the part of the former, though no doubt being relevant to church, society, and individual believers is incumbent upon us.[69] The Bible remains, first of all, a book of faith, but then always with its *immediate* implications for the broader contexts in which believers find themselves.[70] To change somewhat the imagery of Gorringe,[71] this is like the tango dance, which consists of two steps. Anyone who takes one step only falls over. The second step follows automatically and very rapidly on the first. This too is part of the interactive essence of Christian spirituality: that the Bible will be one step of the dance of life, and Christian practice the other—with neither step taken in half measures.

---

[69] Cf. Nel, "Spirituality and Religion: A Challenge to Near Eastern Studies," 2–3.
[70] Lombaard, "The Bible in the Apartheid Debate," 85–86.
[71] See Gorringe, *The Education of Desire,* 106.

ADDENDUM 1:
"LEVELS" / "SPHERES" OF SPIRITUALITY

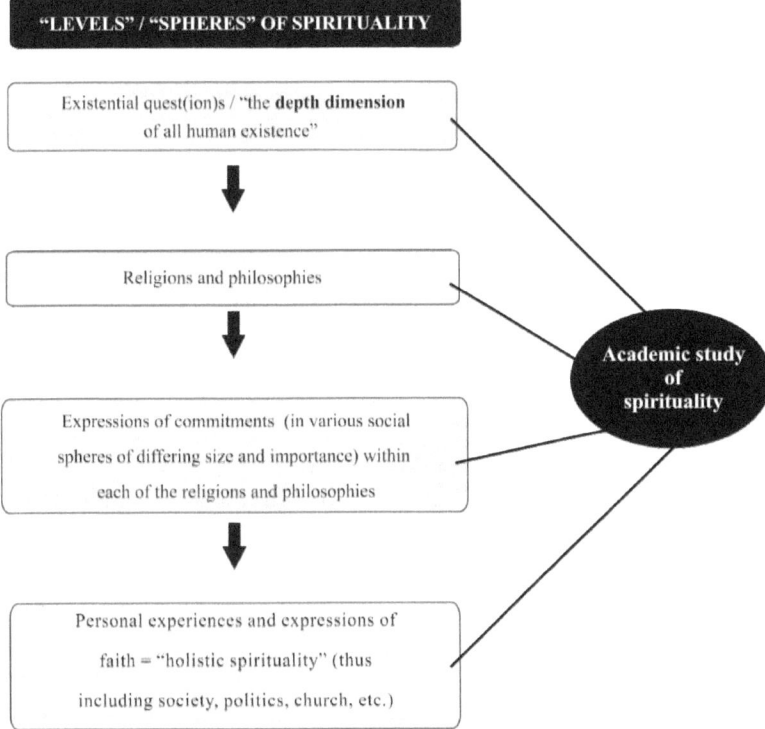

BIBLIOGRAPHY

Achtemeier, Paul J., and Elizabeth R. Achtemeier. *The Old Testament Roots of Our Faith*. Philadelphia: Fortress, 1962.

Albertz, Rainer. *Religionsgeschichte Israels in alttestamentlicher Zeit*. Vol. 1. Göttingen: Vandenhoeck & Ruprecht, 1992.

Alter, Robert, *The Art of Biblical Narrative*. New York: Basic Books, 1981.

Barton, John. "Biblical Roots: The Old Testament." Pages 47–57 in *The Study of Spirituality*. Edited by C. Jones, G. Wainwright and E. Yarnold. Student edition. London: SPCK, 2000.

Berkhof, H. *Christelijk Geloof. Een Inleiding tot de Geloofsleer*. Zesde, bijgewerkte druk. Nijkerk: Callenbach, 1990.

Blum, E. *Studien zur Komposition des Pentateuch*. Berlin: De Gruyter, 1990.

Braulik, G. *Die deuteronomischen Gesetze und der Dekalog: Studien zum Aufbau von Deuteronomium 12–26*. Stuttgart Katholisches Bibelwerk, 1991.

Brueggemann, W. *Spirituality of the Psalms*. Minneapolis: Fortress, 2002.

Casey, M. "Bernard's Biblical Mysticism: Approaching Sermons on the Song of Songs 74." *Studies in Spirituality* 4 (1994): 12–30.

Cull, F. "The Anglican Way: A School for Beginners." Pages 100–124 in *Christian Spirituality in South Africa*. Edited by C. Kourie and L. Kretzschmar. Pietermaritzburg: Cluster Publications, 2000.

Cunningham, L. S. and K. J. Egan. *Christian Spirituality: Themes from the Tradition*. New York: Paulist Press, 1996.

Du Toit, A. B. "Lewensgemeenskap met God as Essensie van Bybelse Spiritualiteit." *Skrif en Kerk* 14, no. 1 (1993): 28–46.

Dreyer, Y. "Vroue-ervaring en Spiritualiteit." *Hervormde Teologiese Studies* 44, no. 2/3 (1999): 360–79.

Downey, M. *Understanding Christian Spirituality*. New York: Paulist Press, 1997.
Fee, G. D. *Listening to the Spirit in the Text*. Grand Rapids: Eerdmans, 2000.
Gorringe, T. *The Education of Desire. Towards a Theology of the Senses*. London: SCM, 2001.
Greshake, G. "Zum Verhältnis von Theologie und Spiritualität." *Studies in Spirituality* 10 (2000): 21–32.
Holmes, U. T. *A History of Christian Spirituality: An Analytical Introduction*. New York: Seabury Press, 1981.
Holt, B. P. *A Brief History of Christian Spirituality*. Oxford: Lion Publishing, 1993.
Houlden, J. L. "Bible, Spirituality of the." Pages 48–51 in *Westminster Dictionary of Spirituality*. Edited by G. S. Wakefield. Philadelphia: Westminster, 1983.
Hulley, L. D. "Spirituality and Ethics: Do They Belong Together?" Pages 55–65 in *Christian Spirituality in South Africa*. Edited by C. Kourie and L. Kretzschmar. Pietermaritzburg: Cluster Publications, 2000.
Jones, C. P. M. "Biblical Roots: The New Testament." Pages 58–89 in *The Study of Spirituality*. Edited by C. Jones, G. Wainwright and E. Yarnold. Student edition. London: SPCK, 2000.
Jones, C., G. Wainwright and E. Yarnold, eds. *The Study of Spirituality*. Student edition. London: SPCK, 2000.
Jonker, W. D. "Die Eie-aard van die Gereformeerde Spiritualiteit." *Ned. Geref. Teologiese Tydskrif* 30, no. 3 (1989): 288–99.
Kagan, J. *Surprise, Uncertainty and Mental Structures*. Cambridge, Mass.: Harvard University Press, 2002.
King, U. *Women and Spirituality. Voices of Protest and Promise*. London: Macmillan Education Ltd, 1989.
Kourie, C. "What Is Christian Spirituality?" Pages 9–33 in *Christian Spirituality in South Africa*. Edited by C. Kourie and L. Kretzschmar. Pietermaritzburg: Cluster Publications, 2000.

———. "Towards a Spirituality of the Ordinary." Paper read at the *Ecumenical Pastoral Institute in Cape Town* (EPIC) meeting at the University of Pretoria, 23 March 2001.

Kraus, H.-J. *Geschichte der historisch-kritischen Erforschung des Alten Testaments*. 3., erw. Auflage. Neukirchen-Vluyn: Neukirchener Verlag, 1982.

Kretzschmar, L. "What is Holistic Spirituality and Why Is It Important for the Church Today?" Pages 31–44 in *Towards a Holistic, Afro-centric and Participatory Understanding of the Gospel of Jesus Christ*. Edited by D. Hoffmeister and L. Kretzschmar. Johannesburg: Baptist Convention of South Africa, 1995.

———. "The Three Journeys: A Functional Model of Holistic Spirituality." Pages 45–54 in *Towards a Holistic, Afro-centric and Participatory Understanding of the Gospel of Jesus Christ*. Edited by D. Hoffmeister and L. Kretzschmar. Johannesburg: Baptist Convention of South Africa, 1995.

Kudadjie, J. N. "African Spirituality." Pages 62–79 in *Spirituality in Religions. Profiles and Perspectives*. Edited by C. W. du Toit. Pretoria: Research Institute for Theology and Religion, University of South Africa, 1996.

Lash, S. "Orthodox Spirituality." Pages 283–85 in *Westminster Dictionary of Spirituality*. Edited by G. S. Wakefield. Philadelphia: Westminster, 1983.

Loader, J. A. "Exegetical Erotica to Canticles 7:2–6." *Journal for Semitics/Tydskrif vir Semitistiek* 10, no. 1/2 (2001): 98–111.

———. "'Theologia Religionum' from the Perspective of Israelite Religion—An Argument." *Missionalia* 13, no. 1 (1985): 14–32.

Lombaard, C. J. S. "'Oortuiging' en Prediking—Woordspel op 'n 'Hartsaak.'" *Skrif en Kerk* 21, no. 3 (2000): 607–20.

———. "Taal: Kuns of Kêns? Nóg Losse, nóg Vaste Woorde oor Woorde." *Tydskrif vir Letterkunde* 39, no. 1/2 (2001): 60–61.

———. "The Bible in the Apartheid Debate." Pages 69–87 in *1948 + 50 Years. Theology, Apartheid and Church: Past, Present and Future*. Edited by J. W. Hofmeyr, C. S. J. Lombaard and P. J. Maritz. Perspectives on the Church/Perspektiewe op die Kerk, Series 5: Vol. 1. Pretoria: IMER (Institute for Missiological and Ecumenical Research), University of Pretoria, 2001.

Marmion, D. *A Spirituality of Everyday Faith: A Theological Investigation of the Notion of Spirituality in Karl Rahner*. Louvain Theological and Pastoral Monographs 23. Louvain: Peeters Press, 1998.

Maruca, D. "Roman Catholic Spirituality." Pages 336–39 in *Westminster Dictionary of Spirituality*. Edited by G. S. Wakefield. Philadelphia: Westminster, 1983.

McGrath, A. E. *Christian Spirituality. An Introduction*. Oxford: Blackwell, 1999.

Nel, P. J. "Spirituality and Religion: A Challenge to Near Eastern Studies." *Journal for Semitics/Tydskrif vir Semitistiek* 10, no. 1/2 (2001): 1–19.

Nolan, A. *God in South Africa*. Cape Town: David Philip, 1988.

Oostenbrink, J. W. "Gereformeerde Spiritualiteit as Korporatiewe Spiritualiteit." *In die Skriflig* 33, no. 3 (1999): 367–83.

Otto, E. *Das Deuteronomium im Pentateuch und Hexateuch. Studien zur Literaturgeschichte von Pentateuch und Hexateuch im Lichte des Deuteronomiumrahmens*. Forschungen zum Alten Testament 30. Tübingen: J.C.B. Mohr (Paul Siebeck), 2000.

Pacini, D. S. "Reading Holy Writ: The Locus of Modern Spirituality." Pages 174–210 in *Christian Spirituality III. Post-Reformation and Modern*. Edited by L. Dupré and D. E. Saliers. New York: Crossroads, 1991

Peterson, E. H. *Subversive Spirituality*. Grand Rapids: Eerdmans, 1997.

Potgieter, P. C. *Skrif, Dogma en Verkondiging*. Kaapstad: Lux Verbi, 1990.

Preuß, H. D. *Theologie des Alten Testaments, Band 1: JHWHs erwählendes und verpflichtendes Handeln.* Stuttgart: Kohlhammer, 1991.

———. *Theologie des Alten Testaments, Band 2: Israels Weg mit JHWH.* Stuttgart: Kohlhammer, 1992.

Rakoczy, S. "Living Life to the Full: Reflections on Feminist Spirituality." Pages 69–91 in *Christian Spirituality in South Africa.* Edited by C. Kourie and L. Kretzschmar. Pietermaritzburg: Cluster Publications, 2000.

Rice, H. L. *Reformed Spirituality: An Introduction for Believers.* Louisville: Westminster John Knox, 1991.

Richter, W. *Exegese als Literaturwissenschaft. Entwurf einer alttestamentliche Literaturtheorie und Methodologie.* Göttingen: Vandenhoeck & Ruprecht, 1971.

Rossouw, H. W. *Klaarheid en Interpretasie. Enkele Probleemhistoriese Gesigspunte in verband met die Leer van die Duidelikheid van die Heilige Skrif.* D.Th. proefskrif, Vrije Universiteit. Amsterdam: Drukkerij en uitgeverij Jacob van Campen N.V., 1963.

Runia, K. "Towards a Biblical Theology of Experience." Pages 175–98 in *Christian Experience in Theology and Life.* Edited by I. H. Marshall. Edinburgh: Rutherford House Books, 1988.

Russel-Boulton, P. "A Pentecostal Spirituality." Pages 125–37 in *Christian Spirituality in South Africa.* Edited by C. Kourie and L. Kretzschmar. Pietermaritzburg: Cluster Publications, 2000.

Sheldrake, P. *Spirituality and Theology: Christian Living and the Doctrine of God.* London: Darton, Longman & Todd Ltd, 1998.

Schneiders, S. M. "Scripture in Spirituality." Pages 1–20 in *Christian Spirituality I. Origins to the Twelfth Century.* Edited by B. McGinn and J. Meyendorff. London: Routledge & Kegan Paul, 1989.

———. "The Study of Christian Spirituality. Contours and Dynamics of the Discipline." *Studies in Spirituality* 8 (1998): 38–57.

Sklar-Chik, G. "Prayer: Praying the Psalms." Pages 195–208 in *Christian Spirituality in South Africa*. Edited by C. Kourie and L. Kretzschmar. Pietermaritzburg: Cluster Publications, 2000.

Smit, D. J. "Wat Is Gereformeerde Spiritualiteit?" *Ned. Geref. Teologiese Tydskrif* 29, no. 2 (1988): 182–93.

―――. "Kan Spiritualiteit Beskryf Word?" *Ned. Geref. Teologiese Tydskrif* 30, no. 1 (1989): 83–94.

Snyman, S. D. "Spiritualiteit—'n Perspektief uit die Ou Testament." *In die Skriflig* 31, no. 4 (1997): 375–87.

Sobrino, J. *Spirituality of Liberation. Toward Political Holiness*. Maryknoll: Orbis, 1988.

Stuhlmueller, C. *The Spirituality of the Psalms*. Collegeville, Minn.: Liturgical Press, 2002.

Taylor, J. V. *A Matter of Life and Death*. London: SCM, 1986.

Thijs, B. *Geloven Uit de Kunst? Een Pleidooi voor Geloofsverbeelding in de Gemeente*. 's-Gravenhage: Meinema, 1990.

Tracy, J. D. "*Ad fontes*: The Humanist Understanding of Scripture as Nourishment for the Soul." Pages 252–67 in *Christian Spirituality II. High Middle Ages and Reformation*. Edited by J. Raitt. New York: Crossroad, 1989.

Tshelane, S. "The Spirituality of the African Initiated Churches." Pages 138–56 in *Christian Spirituality in South Africa*. Edited by C. Kourie and L. Kretzschmar. Pietermaritzburg: Cluster Publications, 2000.

Van Buren, M. L. "Spirituality in the Dialogue of Religions." In *Spirituality in Ecumenical Perspective*. Edited by G. E. Hinson. Louisville: Westminster John Knox, 1993.

Van der Toorn, K. *Family Religion in Babylonia, Syria and Israel. Continuity and Change in the Forms of Religious Life*. Leiden: Brill, 1996.

Van Seters, J. *The Life of Moses: The Yahwist as Historian in Exodus-Numbers*. Louisville: Westminster John Knox, 1994.

Waaijman, K. "Toward a Phenomenological Definition of Spirituality." *Studies in Spirituality* 3 (1993): 5–57.
———. "A Hermeneutic of Spirituality." *Studies in Spirituality* 5 (1995): 5–39.
Wakefield, G. S. "The Psalms." Pages 322–23 in *Westminster Dictionary of Spirituality*. Edited by G. S. Wakefield. Philadelphia: Westminster, 1983.
Weippert, K. "Synkretismus und Monotheismus." Pages 143–79 in *Kultur und Konflikt*. Edited by J. Assman and D. Harth. Frankfurt: Suhrkamp Verlag, 1990.
Wellhausen, J. *Die Composition des Hexateuchs und der historischen Bücher des Alten Testaments*. 4. unveränd. Auflage. Berlin: De Gruyter, 1963.
Zenger, E. *Einleitung in das Alte Testament*. 3. Auflage. Berlin: Kohlhammer, 1998.
Zevit, Z. *The Religions of Ancient Israel: A Synthesis of Parallactic Approaches*. London: Continuum, 2001.

Four South African Proposals for a Central Theme to "Scriptural Spirituality"*

ABSTRACT
In this contribution, the proposals made by four South Africans towards a viable central theme for "Scriptural spirituality"—that is, a spirituality which seeks explicitly to centre on the Bible—are taken under review. These proposals have been made in:
- Du Toit, A. B. "Lewensgemeenskap met God as Essensie van Bybelse Spiritualiteit." *Skrif en Kerk* 14, no. 1 (1993): 28–46.
- Louw, D. J. "Spiritualiteit as Bybelse Vroomheid in die Teologie en die Gemeentelike Bediening." *Praktiese Teologie in Suid-Afrika* 4, no. 2 (1989): 1–17.
- Nolan, A. *Biblical Spirituality*. Springs: The Order of Preachers (Southern Africa), 1982.
- Snyman, S. D. "Spiritualiteit—'n Perspektief uit die Ou Testament." *In die Skriflig* 31, no. 4 (1997): 375–87.

Each of these proposals is briefly described. The problems related to identifying such a central theme are briefly indicated by means of a well-advanced debate within the sub-discipline of Old Testament Theology on the validity of identifying a "Mitte." In closing, a few remarks are made on the context within which these suggestions on spirituality have been made. This raises questions on the "universalising"/"extrapolation" possibilities inherent in all work on spirituality. Are all remarks on spirituality—be they expressions of piety or scholarly contributions (though, naturally, these dimensions are not unrelated)—not always inescapably individualistic, yet thoroughly embedded contextually, and precisely because of these two features, pregnant with "universalising"/"extrapolation" possibilities, if done sensitively and dialogically?

---

* This essay was initially presented as a paper at the congress of the Spirituality Association of South Africa, in January 2004, at the University of Stellenbosch, South Africa.

1. The Bible and Spirituality

In what follows, the proposals made by four South Africans regarding a viable central theme for what may be called "Scriptural spirituality"—that is, a spirituality which seeks explicitly to centre on the Bible—are taken under review. These proposals have been made in three articles and a concise book (which is actually a collection of a lecture series), each seeking to indicate a theme or concept with which to sum up the spirituality we find either in the Bible as a whole or in one of the two Testaments.

The characteristic concern of Christian spirituality, that it takes its most important source to be the Bible, remains remarkable, and is a concern I share.[1] Faith, the church, and the mission of the church (widely defined) would be the poorer—theologically and practically—if the Bible were afforded a less central place.[2] However, to this statement, I propose four provisos be appended:

- That the Bible not be misused in the service of whatever ideological, political or socio-cultural programme. It is easy to criticise the way the Bible was used to promote, for instance, Nazism,[3] or apartheid,[4] but it is much more difficult to criticise the way the Bible is used to promote ideals we now regard as positive, even sacred, such as

---

[1] Cf. also W. D. Jonker, "Die Eie-aard van die Gereformeerde Spiritualiteit," *Ned. Geref. Teologiese Tydskrif* 30, no. 3 (1989): 290.

[2] Cf. C. J. S. Lombaard, "Ecumenism and the Bible," in *Essays and Exercises in Ecumenism* (ed. C. J. S. Lombaard; Pietermaritzburg: Cluster Publications, 1999), 34–35.

[3] Cf. e.g. S. Heschel, "Nazifying Christian Theology: Walter Grundmann and the Institute for the Study and Eradication of Jewish Influence on German Church Life," *Church History* 63 (1994): 587–605.

[4] See e.g. G. Cronjé, Wm. Nicol and E. P. Groenewald. *Regverdige Rasse-apartheid* (Stellenbosch: Die Christen-studenteverenigingmaatskappy van Suid-Afrika, 1947).

democracy or reconciliation.⁵ My point here is not for moral neutrality, in different guises, or against faithful/theological engagement with societal agendas, but that any form of piety with which we approach the Bible remain critically analysed. The following three points expand on this.

- That the Bible be used with integrity. "We do not find a consistent system of theological propositions in the Bible";⁶ the concept "theological propositions" may as well be transposed with concepts such as "ethical positions" and "political values." In addition, apart from the evolution (that is, the development of themes) we find in the Bible, the reality of parallel, even contradictory biblical texts and traditions (which can be called on to support parallel, even contradictory modern concerns),⁷ should not be ignored— such would be schizophrenic⁸ faith. Harmonising the

---

⁵ See e.g., C. Gunton, ed., *The Theology of Reconciliation* (London: T&T Clark, 2003); J. W. de Gruchy, *Reconciliation: Restoring Justice* (Cape Town: David Philip, 2002); cf. E. B. Farisani, "The Use of Ezra-Nehemiah in a Quest for a Theology of Renewal, Transformation and Reconstruction" (Ph.D. thesis, Pietermaritzburg: University of Natal, 2002).

⁶ K. Nürnberger, *Theology of the Biblical Witness. An Evolutionary Approach* (Theologie: Forschung und Wissenschaft, Band 5; Münster: LIT Verlag, 2002), v.

⁷ Cf. J. H. le Roux, "Two Possible Readings of Isaiah 61," in *Liberation Theology and the Bible* (ed. P. G. R. de Villiers; Pretoria: University of South Africa, 1987), 31–44; J. H. le Roux, *Whose Side Is God on?/Aan Wie se Kant is God?* (Pretoria, Unisa: CB Powell-Bybelsentrum, 1992); C. J. S. Lombaard, "The Bible in the Apartheid Debate," in *1948 + 50 Years. Theology, Apartheid and Church: Past, Present and Future* (ed. J. W. Hofmeyr, C. J. S. Lombaard and P. J. Maritz; Perspectives on the Church/Perspektiewe op die Kerk, Series 5: Vol. 1; Pretoria: IMER [Institute for Missiological and Ecumenical Research], University of Pretoria, 2001), 61.

⁸ I use "schizophrenic" in its correct technical sense of losing contact with reality (in this case the reality of what the Bible is: a book which is also historically situated), and not in its popular sense of a "split personality."

parallels and contradictions in Scripture is always fruitless: it takes leave of the text; it leaves us with a bland artefact; it attends some sort of power play. In short: the Bible is a complex text. With a compositional history of over ten centuries, and thus with a *Wirkungsgeschichte*/interpretational history of over thirty centuries, it could be no other way. The ways in which the Bible is used to nurture faith—that is, "Scriptural spirituality"—should take this into account, and do so in detail. More is required than that we simply "be shaped by the great biblical motifs."[9] The complexity of the Bible must come home in personal devotions, church services, and societal involvement. Theoretical and exegetical integrity—a studied awareness of the issues and an informed navigation through the possibilities—is required, if the Bible is to be truly afforded the centrality to which we so easily confess.

- That engagement with the Bible is dialogically critical. The paragraph above was concerned with what we bring to the text. However, the process is reciprocal: the concept of the hermeneutical circle incorporates that the reader remains open to be "talked to," to be addressed/(in)formed/changed by the text.[10] Such "conversing" would exclude none of the possibilities: theoretical, exegetical, existential, functional.... That the Bible and the reader converse in many ways is a confession and experience Christian spirituality cannot do without. The text "reads" the reader

---

[9] S. M. Schneiders, "The Study of Christian Spirituality. Contours and Dynamics of the Discipline," *Studies in Spirituality* 8 (1998): 43; C. J. S. Lombaard, "The Old Testament in Christian Spirituality: Perspectives on the Undervaluation of the Old Testament in Christian Spirituality," *HTS Teologiese Studies/Theological Studies* 59, no. 2 (2003): 440.

[10] Cf. A. C. Thiselton, *New Horizons in Hermeneutics* (Grand Rapids: Zondervan, 1992), 31–54.

critically too. Conversing and conversion (broadly defined) remain always-related possibilities.

- That different spiritualities are allowable.[11] The two paragraphs prior to this one, taken together, implicitly make the case for a pluralism of expressions of Christian spirituality in any given context. What the reader(s) bring(s) to the biblical text(s) and what the biblical text(s) bring(s) to the reader(s) are so varied that one can hardly expect all to express their faith similarly.[12] Yet, in different contexts and times, one or more expressions of the Christian faith[13] may come to be more powerful than others. In addition, the most strongly competing spiritualities in any given context may together also constitute a force of sorts that dominates other spiritualities. I am cynical that this will ever change in practice to some idyllic scenario; nor do I think that any and all spiritualities are to be evaluated as equally valid expressions of the Christian faith. I do however judge the existence of a diversity of Christian spiritualities to be a healthy state of affairs. A monochrome spirituality from as colourful a book as the Bible can only result from highly controlled circumstances, which would be repressive. Multiple spiritualities and not only tolerance, but active appreciation

---

[11] This paragraph has direct implications for ecumenism. Spirituality and ecumenism offer us a most interesting intersection; cf. also the remarks by Smit (see D. J. Smit, "Kan Spiritualiteit Beskryf Word?" *Ned. Geref. Teologiese Tydskrif* 30, no. 1 [1989]: 83–84).

[12] Perhaps it is on this point that religious conservatism and religious liberalism differ most.

[13] Van der Merwe (see H. van der Merwe, "Biblical Spirituality," *Ned. Geref. Teologiese Tydskrif* 30, no. 4 [1989]: 468) in his opening paragraph echoes many of the different pieties mentioned in Jonker, "Die Eie-aard van die Gereformeerde Spiritualiteit," 299. The parallels seem too close to be coincidental; however, no references that would clear up this curiosity are indicated.

of the diversity resulting from the Christian Sourcebook are indicative of a mature, informed situation.[14]

With the above as a broad framework of orientation, let us now turn to the four proposals for centres to Scriptural spirituality.

2. The Assembled Group

The group of scholars I have chosen[15]—because their particular writings under discussion below drew my interest in the way the Bible is used (this time related to the discipline of Spirituality)—are in some senses diverse, in some senses alike. Three are Dutch Reformed Church academics: Du Toit is a retired University of Pretoria New Testament scholar, Louw is a Stellenbosch Philosopher and Practical Theologian (at the time of writing, Dean of the Faculty of Theology), and Snyman a professor of Old Testament at the University of the Free State. Nolan is a Catholic (Dominican: Order of Preachers) theologian, an academic and a journalist—I think it would be safe to gather all of his professional activities under the heading of "liberation theologian"— who is at the time of writing based in Johannesburg. All are committed churchmen, yet all but Louw at times in their careers have had to face accusations of political and/or theological "liberalism" (placed in quotation marks here, because such a term can mean almost anything in the mouth of an accuser). All have an interest in the academic discipline of Spirituality; Nolan is however the most prolific on this terrain, not only in his publications, but also, for instance, in leading retreats. All have in their writings shown strong concern for linking academic theology with, on the one

---

[14] Cf. Smit, "Kan Spiritualiteit Beskryf Word?" 83–84.
[15] I have not included Van der Merwe's article (see above note 13) in my discussions here: despite the title holding promise for the theme here, the nature of his article is such that it provides something of a select overview of what may be termed biblical theology.

A Central Theme to "Scriptural Spirituality"

hand, personal piety,[16] and on the other hand, broader societal issues.[17]

What binds these four figures most closely together for the purposes here, though, is that all four have written on the topic of the Bible and spirituality. In these writings, each has suggested a central theme for what may be called "Scriptural spirituality"—that is, a spirituality that seeks explicitly to centre on the Bible. Each of these proposals is briefly described and evaluated below.

2.1 Du Toit: Living in the presence of God

Du Toit takes as the essence of spirituality that one lives in communion with God ("lewensgemeenskap met God").[18] The *Praesentia Dei* forms for him a centralising concept. In the Old Testament, with specific reference to the Psalms, this comes to the fore even when God is experienced as hidden, or when people live as though God does not exist.[19] The face of God is a significant symbol of this presence or of a meeting with God, in life generally

---

[16] See e.g., A. B. du Toit, *Room van Romeine: 'n Bybelkorrespondensie-kursus* (Wellington: Bybelkor, 1984); D. J. Louw, *Illness as Crisis and Challenge* (Halfway House: Orion, 1995); A. Nolan, *The Service of the Poor and Spiritual Growth* (Catholic Institute for International Relations justice papers. Trâocaire: Canadian Catholic Organization for Development and Peace, 1985); F. Snyman, *In die Begin: Bybelstudie vir Huisgodsdiens of Stiltetyd met Besprekingsvrae vir Groepe oor Genesis 1–4* (Wellington: Bybelkor, 1988).

[17] See e.g., C. Breytenbach and A. B. du Toit, *Eenheid en Konflik: Eerste Beslissinge in die Geskiedenis van die Christendom* (Pretoria: NG Kerkboekhandel Transvaal, 1987); D. J. Louw, *Versoening in Geweld: 'n Pleidooi om Vrede in Suider-Afrika* (Stellenbosse Teologiese Studies 15; Kaapstad: N.G. Kerkuitgewers, 1987); A. Nolan, *The Bible and the Struggle for Democracy* (Durban: Diakonia, 1989); S. D. Snyman, *Geweld, die Ou Testament en 'n Nuwe Suid-Afrika* (Bloemfontein: Universiteit van die Oranje-Vrystaat, 1992).

[18] A. B. du Toit, "Lewensgemeenskap met God as Essensie van Bybelse Spiritualiteit," *Skrif en Kerk* 14, no. 1 (1993): 29.

[19] Ibid.

but most particularly in the cult.[20] Pss 42 and 84 therefore present us with "biblical spirituality at its purest."[21] Motifs to do with God living among the people of Israel, also in the tabernacle or Shekinah, are additional expressions of the *Praesentia Dei*, though the act of praying is not limited to such special places.[22] The latter is even more the case in the New Testament. The motif of living is now intensified: congregation and body become God's temple; Jesus lives among people; God lives with the faithful in the new Jerusalem.[23]

The living communion with God is relational. The metaphor of the covenant is significant in Jesus's communion words (a *new* covenant), in Pauline language, and in the book of Hebrews. Here, as in the Old Testament covenants, God's initiative is most prominent in creating the life of communion. Marriage provides the second, related, metaphor with which to express both God's initiative (Ezek 16; Eph 5 and Rev 17, 21, 22, most particularly) and consistent love (Hosea) for those who are loved by God.[24] A third metaphor is that of the *familia Dei*: in love, God takes the initiative, and cares intimately for the child (e.g., Jer 3:19 and 31:9, but especially Jesus's prayer).[25] The Bible thus always places the individual's experience of faith within the corporate character of spirituality, though the New Testament allows for a somewhat greater emphasis on the individual.[26]

Other metaphors expressing the *Praesentia Dei* are "knowing God/Christ," particularly found with the prophets and Paul; with specific reference to the Old Testament: "walking with God," and

---

[20] Ibid., 29–30.
[21] Ibid., 30 (translation from the Afrikaans).
[22] Ibid.
[23] Ibid., 31, 40.
[24] Ibid., 31–32.
[25] Ibid., 33.
[26] Ibid., 32–33.

"friendship";[27] with specific reference to the New Testament: the Pauline and Johannine literature both refer to an indicative and an imperative, that is, the relationship with God that is, in Christ, at once a given and a command—something that exists, and yet should be worked on ("heiligmaking," which may be translated as "becoming more holy" or "sanctification"). This again involves knowing God, indicating not a mystic union, but a personal relationship.[28]

Biblical spirituality, Du Toit points out, expresses itself in certain moments of meeting, in which one experiences the closeness of God in a concentrated manner.[29] Such moments include, in ecstatic form, prophetic and apocalyptic encounters, but consist more usually of receiving the word of God within cultic or personal prayer contexts. The Psalms express such meetings-in-prayer particularly grippingly, while in New Testament times the connection with the Holy Spirit becomes crucial, still with the emphasis on prayer. In addition, acknowledging one's transgressions and, hence, humility, are most typical of biblical spirituality. Of further importance are intercession on behalf of others, the courage of faith ("geloofsmoed") to dare confrontations with God, and—a theme running through much of Du Toit's writing since Du Toit 1965—joy.[30]

Du Toit emphasises that spirituality can never be only inward-looking; strong ethical implications characterise the life style and practice of the faithful. Communion with God implies responsibility to God; life *coram Dei* implies obeying God, with

---

[27] Ibid., 34–36.
[28] Ibid., 37.
[29] Ibid., 37–39.
[30] See A. B. du Toit, *Der Aspekt der Freude im urchristlichen Abendmahl* (D.Th. diss., Basel; Winterthur: Keller, 1965); cf. Du Toit, "Lewensgemeenskap met God," 37–39.

John 15, an important text in this regard. Cultic experiences build ethics into the personal piety of the believer's daily life.[31]

The brokenness of our experience of God now, will— referring to the Isaiah apocalypse (Isa 25:6–12) and Jesus's foundation of the Holy Communion meal—become whole in the *eschaton*. This will be the ultimate experience of the *Praesentia Dei*.[32] "True biblical spirituality therefore always has an eschatological crown."[33]

These thoughts are highly typical of the spirituality of Du Toit as I have come to know him, too: though he experiences the closeness of God very personally and intensely, it comes over in a highly intellectualised, finely formulated way. Emotions are never to the fore, though one cannot but sense the refined sentiments, even passion, that lies behind the academic style. This is a passion that strongly involves the individual, the church, and the broader society, and is critical, yet remains loyal. Certainly in Du Toit's case, his identification of the *Praesentia Dei* as the core of biblical spirituality parallels his own faith experience precisely.

2.2 Louw: Godliness in faith and life

For Louw, spirituality and revelation through Scripture cannot be separated.[34] The Bible is the source of the contents of the believers' faith, feeding the ways their faith finds practical expression. This biblical piety ("Bybelse vroomheid") may be hampered by the academic practice of theology, if faith were to be

---

[31] Du Toit, "Lewensgemeenskap met God," 39–40, 45 n. 58.
[32] Ibid., 40.
[33] Ibid., 41 (translation from the Afrikaans).
[34] D. J. Louw, "Spiritualiteit as Bybelse Vroomheid in die Teologie en die Gemeentelike Bediening," *Praktiese Teologie in Suid-Afrika* 4, no. 2 (1989): 3.

A Central Theme to "Scriptural Spirituality" 37

simply cognitised, intellectualised, objectivised.[35] Such a danger is inherent to Reformed spirituality.[36]

This risk can, however, be overcome from Scripture itself,[37] because the Holy Spirit works through Scripture, giving rise to existential commitments[38]—which by their very nature are more than intellectual commitments only—and practical, corporate consequences.[39] This fundamental existential commitment is for Louw encapsulated in the Pauline concept of εὐσέβεια (often given in Bible translations as "godliness"), with specific reference to the New Testament First Letter to Timothy. Louw traces εὐσέβεια back to Old Testament wisdom's *principium interpretatio*, namely the יִרְאַת יְהוָה,[40] which he summarises as "geloof in aksie" ("faith in action")[41] or "*belewe/ervaar* ... geregtigheid en wysheid" ("experience ... justice and wisdom").[42] However, Louw does not argue precisely how he came to decide on the term εὐσέβεια—he seems to have taken it over from Jonker,[43] who mentions εὐσέβεια only briefly—nor the precise relationship of εὐσέβεια with the concept of the יִרְאַת יְהוָה. Nevertheless, the μυστήριον of the (biblical) revelation creates the quality of the practical and the

---

[35] Ibid., 5, 13; cf. Steenkamp concerning a similar sentiment with Nolan (see A. W. Steenkamp, "Evangelie-as-Inkarnasie—Aspekte van 'n Kontekstuele Teologie in Suider-Afrika met Spesifieke Verwysing na Albert Nolan en Takatso Mofokeng" [Ph.D. proefskrif, Universiteit van Stellenbosch, 1995]).

[36] Jonker, in "Die Eie-aard van die Gereformeerde Spiritualiteit," 293, indicates the flipside, namely the danger of the (emotional) experiential side coming to dominate Reformed spirituality.

[37] Louw, "Spiritualiteit as Bybelse Vroomheid," 5.

[38] Ibid., 5, 13.

[39] Ibid., 8, 12.

[40] Ibid., 7; cf. C. J. S. Lombaard, "Elke Vertaling is 'n Vertelling. Opmerkings oor Vertaalteorie, Geïllustreer aan die hand van die Chokmatiese *ratio interpretationis*," *Old Testament Essays* 15, no. 3 (2002): 756.

[41] Louw, "Spiritualiteit as Bybelse Vroomheid," 7, 10.

[42] Ibid., 13.

[43] Jonker, "Die Eie-aard van die Gereformeerde Spiritualiteit," 288.

experiential aspects of faith as εὐσεβεία.⁴⁴ This is equally important for ordained and lay believers.⁴⁵

Strong parallels to the thoughts expressed here by Louw can be found in an article of two years earlier by the Bloemfontein theologian Strauss.⁴⁶ Louw gives no evidence of having read Strauss's article, though, which would support the deduction that we find here separate but similar expressions of thoughts on spirituality in the Dutch Reformed Church in the late 1980s.

Louw's article includes frequent references to dogmatological and practical-theological themes. Interestingly, Louw employs the Bible not as an exegete would, trying to determine in greater detail what, for instance, the concept εὐσεβεία would mean. Louw's interest is in the here and now: what leading a godly life means for believers today. εὐσεβεία is for Louw a key word from which a series of thoughts spring (the mode of the philosopher) and which must find expression in the lives (the mode of the practical theologian) of those who have faith in Christ.⁴⁷

2.3 Nolan: Old Testament justice + New Testament love = Kingdom spirituality

Nolan has the rare gift (which I have experienced personally, at a short retreat led by him) of combining historical-critical exegesis⁴⁸

---

[44] Louw, "Spiritualiteit as Bybelse Vroomheid," 8.
[45] Ibid., 13–15.
[46] See S. A. Strauss, "'n Geheiligde Lewe: Oefening in die Toewyding aan God," *Fax Theologica* 7, no. 1 (1987): 20–38.
[47] Louw, "Spiritualiteit as Bybelse Vroomheid," 7.
[48] See e.g., A. Nolan, *Jesus before Christianity. The Gospel of Liberation* (London: Dartwood, Longman & Todd, 1977), 10–19; A. Nolan, *Jesus before Christianity* (2d ed.; Cape Town: David Philip, 1986), 10–19; J. Draper, "Old Scores and New Notes: Where and What Is Contextual Exegesis in the New South Africa?" in *Towards an Agenda for Contextual Theology. Essays in Honour of Albert Nolan* (ed. M. T. Speckman and L. T. Kaufmann;

A Central Theme to "Scriptural Spirituality" 39

with contemporary application, that is, an application that includes both personal piety and wider societal dimensions. It is for the latter that he has become most famous.[49] For Nolan himself, though, Bible, spirituality and social awareness cannot be separated: "a Biblical spirituality would have to include a very serious attempt *to read the signs of our times.*"[50] Nolan recognises with appreciation the hermeneutical circle of context and text when we read the texts of the Bible.[51]

Interestingly, even though Nolan's *Biblical Spirituality* includes substantial reflection on "The Spirit of the Prophets,"[52] the New Testament is afforded decisive priority over the Old.[53] The reason for this is not quite clear.

Pietermaritzburg: Cluster Publications, 2001), 149; Steenkamp, "Evangelie-as-Inkarnasie," 69, 94–100.

[49] Cf. A. Nolan, *God in South Africa* (Cape Town: David Philip, 1988); A. Nolan and R. F. Broderick, eds., *"To Nourish Our Faith": The Theology of Liberation in Southern Africa* (Hilton: The Order of Preachers [Southern Africa], 1987), 1–80.

[50] A. Nolan, *Biblical Spirituality* (Springs: The Order of Preachers (Southern Africa), 1982), 22.

[51] A. Nolan, "The Theology of Liberation and the Bible," in *"To Nourish Our Faith": The Theology of Liberation in Southern Africa* (ed. A. Nolan and R. F. Broderick; Hilton: The Order of Preachers [Southern Africa], 1987), 30, 32–33, 38; cf. Draper, "Old Scores and New Notes," 149; Steenkamp, "Evangelie-as-Inkarnasie," 71–77.

[52] See Nolan, *Biblical Spirituality,* 13–27.

[53] In the opening paragraph of the closing chapter of *Biblical Spirituality,* titled "Gospel Values," Nolan writes: "The great leap forward from the Old Testament to the New Testament can be described as a leap from the external observance of *laws* to the internalisation of *values*, from the letter of the law to the freedom of the Spirit. At some stage in our spiritual lives we will have to make a similar leap forward to freedom" (Nolan, *Biblical Spirituality,* 61). Here "the idea that the New Testament is more advanced than the Old, is quite pronounced" (see Lombaard, "The Old Testament in Christian Spirituality," 441). Stated more generally, I would rather argue that "'(t)he 'law' against which Paul reacts and which often informs the recurring aversion among some Christians to the Hebrew Bible, is not the Old Testament as a book, but the practice of some of

Nolan places *justice* (מִשְׁפָּט and צְדָקָה) central to the Old Testament, and *love* (ἀγάπη) central to the New Testament. He stresses, however, that in the New Testament love and justice are intimately related.[54] This love, Nolan argues, goes beyond or deepens justice, interiorising it as compassion.[55] Precisely this is "Kingdom spirituality"[56]—the "*destiny* of the human race,"[57] "based upon a concern for the salvation of the whole world."[58]

Thus, the Old Testament is about מִשְׁפָּט and צְדָקָה: "righteousness, uprightness, integrity, honesty or judgement."[59] "The God of the Old Testament... puts wrongs right and he wants his people to put wrongs right in every area of life."[60] The text of 1 John provides for Nolan a bridge between the two Testaments, but he does not employ it overtly as such: he states that the analysis of love in 1 John 4:7–8 is specifically paralleled with the analysis of justice in 1 John 2:29, conclusively tying these two concepts together—with the text in 1 John 2:29 repeating ideas

---

his contemporaries" (ibid., 443). When the apostle Paul's rhetoric against religious legalism is employed too generally in our times, it leads to an undervaluation of the Old Testament in the contemporary practice and study of spirituality (ibid., 433–50). Nolan at one stage (in Nolan, *Biblical Spirituality*, 62) comes very close to accepting that not the Old Testament itself, but the way it was interpreted and lived in the society to which Jesus responded, was all about laws and superficiality. The concern there is with secular values ancient and modern, rather than religious practice, so he never quite follows the argument through. (I admit freely, though, that my Calvinistic concern for the equal inspiration and authority of all parts of Scripture lies at the base of this argument of mine. This non-Roman Catholic issue is mine, and not Nolan's.)

[54] See Nolan, *Biblical Spirituality*, 29, 36. A question that could be raised here is whether this is not equally the case in the Old Testament.
[55] Ibid., 36–39; cf. Nolan, *Jesus before Christianity*, 141
[56] Ibid., 43–58; the Kingdom of God is explored more extensively in Nolan, *Jesus before Christianity*, 44–49.
[57] Ibid., 46.
[58] Ibid., 48.
[59] Ibid., 29.
[60] Ibid., 32.

found in Jer 22:16. The two Testaments are thus tied together in different ways: not only by the linked concepts of justice and love, but also by liberation as a theme running through and, by implication, unifying the Hebrew and Greek sections of the Bible.[61]

The only reason one can construe from *Biblical Spirituality* the sense that the New Testament is given priority over the Old, is Nolan's statement that God's "revelation of new things *ended* with Jesus and the last book of the Bible."[62] Elsewhere, though, he writes more clearly on this matter: that we must understand the Old Testament and the God of the Old Testament patriarchs the way Jesus understood them.[63] It seems that, for Nolan, Jesus, as laid bare historically-critically, is the key. Whatever queries one might have about this way of relating the two Testaments,[64] for Nolan *justice* is the foundation to the Old Testament, and *love* to the New. "Biblical spirituality is Kingdom spirituality";[65] and specifying both parts of that sentence: "The message of the gospel is the message of freedom."[66]

---

[61] Most explicitly in Nolan, *Biblical Spirituality*, 53–54 and Nolan, "The Theology of Liberation and the Bible," 36–38; most extensively in Nolan, *God in South Africa*, 106–33; cf. Nolan, "The Theology of Liberation and the Bible," 30.

[62] Nolan, *Biblical Spirituality*, 22.

[63] See Nolan, *Jesus before Christianity*, 137; *Jesus before Christianity*[2], 10–19.

[64] See the argument followed in footnote 53. More importantly here, though, one might critique Nolan's optimism at being able to find (the real thoughts of) the real Jesus behind the New Testament texts. The different waves of research into the historical Jesus have borne many results, but none definitive. All researchers tend to find their own Jesus (by now a well-known point)—an insight that has important implications not only for the philosophy of science, but also for thinkers on spirituality: see the fourth section of this essay titled "Context, individuality and extrapolation." (To be clear: my problem is not with the historical-critical methodology; that I find positive. My problem is with the too optimistic outlook that often accompanies such research.)

[65] Nolan, *Biblical Spirituality*, 57.

[66] Ibid., 58.

Nolan's concern for the political scene in pre-1994 apartheid South Africa and his interpretation of the Bible echo each other precisely. Justice and love are neither socio-political concerns alone nor a biblical affair alone. These two are linked together inextricably in the way Nolan reads the Bible and lives his life.

2.4 Snyman: Living before God

Snyman regards *coram Deo* as the expression that would come closest to formulating what the Old Testament—his particular focus—would understand as spirituality.[67] He employs the tripartite division of the Old Testament into Torah, Prophets and Writings in order to present brief samples relevant to explaining what spirituality in the Old Testament is.[68]

Spirituality starts, for Snyman, with God,[69] and with God crafting a relationship with people, beginning with the revelation of his Name (Exod 3:14–25). אֶהְיֶה אֲשֶׁר אֶהְיֶה denotes, with reference to a range of Old Testament theologies, God as the always present. God's essence is in fact his presence. This is a line that runs through the whole of the Old Testament, and continues into the New ("Immanuel" in Matthew; "I am…" in John). In the Old Testament we thus find that spirituality means living one's life "in the continued presence of God."[70]

In the Torah, this presence centres around the concept of the covenant, which extends to both the cultic and non-cultic life, and stresses love, obedience, and gratitude.[71]

---

[67] S. D. Snyman, "Spiritualiteit—'n Perspektief uit die Ou Testament," *In die Skriflig* 31, no. 4 (1997): 376; cf. Smit, "Kan Spiritualiteit Beskryf Word?" 85.
[68] Ibid., 377.
[69] Ibid., 377–78; cf. Jonker, "Die Eie-aard van die Gereformeerde Spiritualiteit," 293–94.
[70] Ibid., 378 (translation from the Afrikaans).
[71] Ibid., 379.

A Central Theme to "Scriptural Spirituality"

The prophets emphasise turning back to a life in close communion with God, which implies faithfulness to Yahweh and social justice. The prophets however also struggle with God (e.g., Jeremiah and Habakkuk), in the event indicating that God and God's answers at times remain incomprehensible, but that at other times the conversation with God is in itself enough.[72] "Spirituality in the Old Testament is ... living in the presence of God even if realities and the incomprehensibility thereof speak against it ... living as people who see God ...."[73] Lastly, the prophets also find themselves astounded before the mystery of God, as expressed in the prophetic doxologies.[74]

Among the Writings, the Psalms receive particular attention, and most specifically Ps 42: life *coram Deo* is an attractive theme even when experiencing God's absence, be it individually or corporately.[75] Prov 4:23 addresses the more personal piety: one's thoughts influence one's whole life.[76] Living one's life according to Old Testament wisdom's *principium interpretatio*, the יִרְאַת יְהוָה referred to above,[77] is typical of Old Testament spirituality. Such is the "art of life."[78]

In Snyman's broadly analytical article, expressions of Old Testament spirituality are thus indicated as including living with an awareness of God's presence, within a covenant that elicits obedience to the Torah, yet involves dilemmas, because of God also being *Deus absconditus*, with precisely such dilemmas inducing in the believer awe and a sense of mystery.[79]

---

[72] Ibid., 380–82.
[73] Ibid., 381 (translation from the Afrikaans).
[74] Ibid., 382.
[75] Ibid., 382–83. Note, however, that for Nolan the absence of God in Ps 42 is the question with which the oppressor taunts the oppressed (see Nolan, *God in South Africa*, vi; cf. Steenkamp, "Evangelie-as-Inkarnasie," 67.
[76] Snyman, "Spiritualiteit—'n Perspektief uit die Ou Testament," 384.
[77] See §2.2; cf. Lombaard, "Elke Vertaling is 'n Vertelling," 756.
[78] Ibid., 5 (translation from the Afrikaans).
[79] Ibid., 385.

2.5 The assembled "themes"

To summarise: Du Toit places the *Praesentia Dei* central to the spirituality we find in Scripture as a whole; for Louw, the concept of εὐσεβεία sums up the (mostly) New Testament faith; Nolan combines Old Testament justice and New Testament love into a full biblical "Kingdom spirituality"; whereas Snyman finds *coram Deo* a useful concept with which to characterise (mostly) Old Testament faith.

Interestingly, all take the Bible extremely seriously, both for their own lives of faith and for their deliberations on what spirituality is, biblically speaking. All insist that the faith we find in the Bible has undeniable practical implications. All refer to both Testaments, though some offer us a more equivalent view than others. All show keen awareness of philosophical hermeneutics: the interaction between text-in-context and reader-in-context. All state that they offer in their respective publications only an initial view, and that much more remains to be said. All are aware that many spiritualities exist, and that these expressions of the Christian faith configure different aspects of their shared religion differently. Thus, in many respects, what these authors say and how they say it overlap, despite their choosing four different "centrepieces."

However, our four authors are not identical. This shows up most clearly when each respective author's contribution is taken under review, and when one finds at least some parallels, or at times, very strongly shared traits between the author's own faith and what he finds to be central to the Bible.

These two observations—that different authors seem to find different (though, of course, not entirely unrelated) spiritual "centrepieces" to the Bible, despite so many similarities between them, and that what each finds to be the centrepiece so strongly reflects his own spiritual identity—brings to the fore two questions:

A Central Theme to "Scriptural Spirituality" 45

- Is it at all possible to identify a spiritual centre to the Bible that would show stability across different contexts? Or,
- Could it be that it is not possible to extrapolate a spirituality from one context to another?

It is these two questions that will be touched upon very briefly in the two closing points below.

3. The Matter of a Spiritual "Mitte" to Scripture

Identifying a spirituality central to the Bible is not without its problems, it seems. Most importantly, one might object, different researchers tend to find different results—admittedly, not entirely unrelated results; nevertheless, results dissimilar enough to warrant some questioning.

A parallel to this problem is an issue that has beset Old Testament scholarship involved with the sub-discipline of Old Testament Theology for some time. Many suggestions have been made for a central theme, theology, centre, foundation (the list of synonyms goes on…)—the usual term is the German "Mitte"—to the Old Testament,[80] around which all the rest of the Old Testament can be systematised. Some of the main problems with choosing such a "Mitte"[81] are:

- Choosing a "Mitte" is reductionist: though great parts of the Old Testament could fit well into such a central theme,

---

[80] Cf. H. D. Preuβ, *Theologie des Alten Testaments, Band 1: JHWHs erwählendes und verpflichtendes Handeln* (Stuttgart: Kohlhammer, 1991), 25–26 for an overview.

[81] Cf. e.g., Preuβ, *Theologie des Alten Testaments Band 1*, 25–27; Nürnberger, *Theology of the Biblical Witness*, 3–4, 70–85; W. Brueggemann, *Old Testament Theology. Essays on Structure, Shape, and Text* (Minneapolis: Fortress, 1992), 1–44; M. Welker, Biblische Theologie II: Fundamentaltheologisch (RGG⁴, Band 1 A-B, 1998), 1549–53.

much of the Old Testament will have to be forced into a frock that fits it poorly. The Old Testament is simply too diverse a book for one neat cover.
- Choosing a "Mitte" is exclusionist: keeping one's eyes on this one theme has the effect of blinding one to some parts of the Old Testament (the Wisdom literature has most often been neglected in such instances). The Old Testament is, again, simply too diverse a book to allow for "centralising."
- To choose a "Mitte" that would be broad enough as to truly incorporate the whole of the Old Testament, would result in something so vague as to be practically meaningless. The content of the Old Testament is simply too wide-ranging to be summed up in one concept or theme.
- Western systematising is given to ontological statements (i.e., "God is…"), usually related to a concept, which is foreign to the ancient Near Eastern thought world (where "God does…" fits better).
- Similarly, choosing a "Mitte" from outside the Old Testament (usually from Systematic Theology) with which to organise/simplify/systematise it, could never do justice to the nature of the Old Testament and the world from which it sprang.
- A "Mitte" would tend to be a static item, whereas the Old Testament has grown through serial rewriting and forth-writing.

Each of the references to the Old Testament here may be substituted with the term "spirituality": the exact same problems apply. The same despair that Albertz[82] has expressed about the viability of Old Testament Theology, *inter alia* because of the

---

[82] R. Albertz, *Religionsgeschichte Israels in alttestamentlicher Zeit 1* (Grundrisse zum Alten Testament; Ergänzungsreihen, ATD Band 8/1; Göttingen: Vandenhoeck & Ruprecht, 1992), 17–38.

problems listed above, may befall the discipline of Spirituality if such a "Mitte" for biblical spirituality is sought and not found.

However, another way may be found: if the search for a universal "Mitte" is given up, but the possibility is left open for individuals or groups to give expression to their contextually experienced Bible-based spiritualities, more may be gained than lost here.

4. Context, Individuality and Extrapolation

An individual's spirituality is always the outcome—though not in a deterministic manner!—of a range of factors:[83] philosophical, historical, socio-economic, cultural, dogmatological, ecclesiological, practical, psychological…. Nobody's spirituality is wholly individual; influences abound. Yet everybody's spirituality is their own. No two believers, despite a range of similarities, configure the different aspects of their faith identically. Any description of spirituality is always "subjective, perspectival, contextual."[84] Is this not perhaps the most fruitful insight to be drawn from the analysis of the four proposals above?

I would suggest that a point of orientation to guide us through different proposals, such as the four discussed above, could be that faith knows no exact replicas or—in a modern idiom—clones. Within all the faith-related impulses exerting influence on me, *I* believe. *My* faith and *our* faith, though similar enough to constitute an "our," are not one and the same. "We believe" and "I believe" always exist together—tangled (mutually influential), yet not indistinguishable, and with the measure of identification never wholly clear, never quite static.

---

[83] Cf. Jonker, "Die Eie-aard van die Gereformeerde Spiritualiteit," 289–90; Smit, "Kan Spiritualiteit Beskryf Word?" 88; Lombaard, "The Bible in the Apartheid Debate," 86.

[84] Smit, "Kan Spiritualiteit Beskryf Word?" 83, 86.

Still, given the interaction/mutual influence of the individual with the context, such individualism is no licence for extreme pietistic tendencies. Taking the four authors discussed above seriously, this must be a *giving* individualism: my spirituality has something to contribute to the circles in which I move. Not only am I who I am by means of other people (the South African *ubuntu* ideology);[85] I also am who I am *for* other people. Every "I" influences "us," contributing to constituting our faith.

In such a multitude of Christian spiritualities, all related to one another in different and ever-changing measures, one of the elements supporting the Christian nature of these spiritualities, would be the Bible. Not the Bible over-simplified, as it could so easily turn into whenever the Bible becomes a rallying point for some cause, but in adherence to the four points made under the first heading ("The Bible and Spirituality") of this essay. On this point, then, it holds true that "[i]n the last instance it is not the subjective sincerity with which spirituality is practiced, but the basis thereof that is of decisive meaning."[86]

The possibilities of "universalising" or "extrapolating" to other situations any contribution on biblical spirituality—be they expressions of personal piety or scholarly contributions (though, naturally, these dimensions are not unrelated)—should respect the twin features that each contribution is inescapably individualistic, yet thoroughly embedded contextually. It is precisely because of these two features taken together, that a contribution on spirituality remains pregnant with "universalising"/"extrapolation" possibilities, providing it is done sensitively and dialogically.

---

[85] Cf. e.g. A. Shutte, *Ubuntu: An Ethic for a New South Africa* (Pietermaritzburg: Cluster Publications, 2001).

[86] Jonker, "Die Eie-aard van die Gereformeerde Spiritualiteit," 290 (translation from the Afrikaans).

BIBLIOGRAPHY

Albertz, R. *Religionsgeschichte Israels in alttestamentlicher Zeit 1*. Grundrisse zum Alten Testament, Ergänzungsreihen, ATD Band 8/1. Göttingen: Vandenhoeck & Ruprecht, 1992.

Breytenbach, C. and A. B. du Toit. *Eenheid en Konflik: Eerste Beslissinge in die Geskiedenis van die Christendom*. Pretoria: NG Kerkboekhandel Transvaal, 1987.

Brueggemann, W. *Old Testament Theology. Essays on Structure, Shape, and Text*. Minneapolis: Fortress, 1992.

Cronjé, G., Wm. Nicol and E. P. Groenewald. *Regverdige Rasse-apartheid*. Stellenbosch: Die Christen-studentevrenigingmaatskappy van Suid-Afrika, 1947.

De Gruchy, J. W. *Reconciliation: Restoring Justice*. Cape Town: David Philip, 2002.

Draper, J. "Old Scores and New Notes: Where and What Is Contextual Exegesis in the New South Africa?" Pages 148–68 in *Towards an Agenda for Contextual Theology. Essays in Honour of Albert Nolan*. Edited by M. T. Speckman and L. T. Kaufmann. Pietermaritzburg: Cluster Publications, 2001.

Du Toit, A. B. *Der Aspekt der Freude im urchristlichen Abendmahl*. D.Th. diss., Basel. Winterthur: Keller, 1965.

———. *Room van Romeine: 'n Bybelkorrespondensie-kursus*. Wellington: Bybelkor, 1984.

———. "Lewensgemeenskap met God as Essensie van Bybelse Spiritualiteit." *Skrif en Kerk* 14, no. 1 (1993): 28–46.

Farisani, E. B. "The Use of Ezra-Nehemiah in a Quest for a Theology of Renewal, Transformation and Reconstruction." Ph.D. thesis, Pietermaritzburg: University of Natal, 2002.

Gunton, C. ed. *The Theology of Reconciliation*. London: T&T Clark, 2003.

Heschel, S. "Nazifying Christian Theology: Walter Grundmann and the Institute for the Study and Eradication of Jewish Influence on German Church Life." *Church History* 63 (1994): 587–605.
Jonker, W. D. "Die Eie-aard van die Gereformeerde Spiritualiteit." *Ned. Geref. Teologiese Tydskrif* 30, no. 3 (1989): 288–99.
Le Roux, J. H. "Two Possible Readings of Isaiah 61." Pages 31–44 in *Liberation Theology and the Bible*. Edited by P. G. R. de Villiers. Pretoria: University of South Africa, 1987.
———. *Whose Side Is God On?/Aan Wie se Kant is God?* Pretoria, Unisa: CB Powell-Bybelsentrum, 1992.
Lombaard, C. J. S. "Ecumenism and the Bible." Pages 26–41 in *Essays and Exercises in Ecumenism*. Edited by C. J. S. Lombaard. Pietermaritzburg: Cluster Publications, 1999.
———. "The Bible in the Apartheid Debate." Pages 69–87 in *1948 + 50 Years. Theology, Apartheid and Church: Past, Present and Future*. Edited by J. W. Hofmeyr, C. S. J. Lombaard and P. J. Maritz. Perspectives on the Church/Perspektiewe op die Kerk, Series 5: Vol. 1. Pretoria: IMER (Institute for Missiological and Ecumenical Research), University of Pretoria, 2001.
———. "Elke Vertaling is 'n Vertelling. Opmerkings oor Vertaalteorie, Geïllustreer aan die hand van die Chokmatiese *ratio interpretationis*." *Old Testament Essays* 15, no. 3 (2002): 754–65.
———. "The Old Testament in Christian Spirituality: Perspectives on the Undervaluation of the Old Testament in Christian Spirituality." *HTS Teologiese Studies/Theological Studies* 59, no. 2 (2003): 433–50.
Louw, D. J. *Versoening in Geweld: 'n Pleidooi om Vrede in Suider-Afrika*. Stellenbosse Teologiese Studies 15. Kaapstad: N.G. Kerkuitgewers, 1987.

———. "Spiritualiteit as Bybelse Vroomheid in die Teologie en die Gemeentelike Bediening." *Praktiese Teologie in Suid-Afrika* 4, no. 2 (1989): 1–17.

———. *Illness as Crisis and Challenge*. Halfway House: Orion, 1995.

Nolan, A. *Jesus before Christianity. The Gospel of Liberation*. London: Dartwood, Longman & Todd, 1977.

———. *Biblical Spirituality*. Springs: The Order of Preachers (Southern Africa), 1982.

———. *The Service of the Poor and Spiritual Growth*. Catholic Institute for International Relations justice papers. Trâocaire: Canadian Catholic Organization for Development and Peace, 1985.

———. *Jesus before Christianity*. Second edition. Cape Town: David Philip, 1986.

———. "The Theology of Liberation and the Bible." Pages 30–41 in *"To Nourish Our Faith": The Theology of Liberation in Southern Africa*. Edited by A. Nolan and R. F. Broderick. Hilton: The Order of Preachers (Southern Africa), 1987.

———. *God in South Africa*. Cape Town: David Philip, 1988.

———. *The Bible and the Struggle for Democracy*. Durban: Diakonia, 1989.

——— and R. F. Broderick, eds. *"To Nourish Our Faith": The Theology of Liberation in Southern Africa*. Hilton: The Order of Preachers (Southern Africa), 1987.

Nürnberger, K. *Theology of the Biblical Witness. An Evolutionary Approach*. Theologie: Forschung und Wissenschaft, Band 5. Münster: LIT Verlag, 2002.

Preuß, H. D. *Theologie des Alten Testaments, Band 1: JHWHs erwählendes und verpflichtendes Handeln*. Stuttgart: Kohlhammer, 1991.

Schneiders, S. M. "The Study of Christian Spirituality. Contours and Dynamics of the Discipline." *Studies in Spirituality* 8 (1998): 38–57.

Shutte, A. *Ubuntu: An Ethic for a New South Africa*. Pietermaritzburg : Cluster Publications, 2001.
Smit, D. J. "Kan Spiritualiteit Beskryf Word?" *Ned. Geref. Teologiese Tydskrif* 30, no. 1 (1989): 83–94.
Snyman, F. *In die Begin: Bybelstudie vir Huisgodsdiens of Stiltetyd met Besprekingsvrae vir Groepe oor Genesis 1–4*. Wellington: Bybelkor, 1988.
Snyman, S. D. *Geweld, die Ou Testament en 'n Nuwe Suid-Afrika*. Bloemfontein: Universiteit van die Oranje-Vrystaat, 1992.
———. "Spiritualiteit—'n Perspektief uit die Ou Testament." *In die Skriflig* 31, no. 4 (1997): 375–87.
Steenkamp, A. W. "Evangelie-as-Inkarnasie—Aspekte van 'n Kontekstuele Teologie in Suider-Afrika met Spesifieke Verwysing na Albert Nolan en Takatso Mofokeng." Ph.D. proefskrif, Universiteit van Stellenbosch, 1995.
Strauss, S. A. "'n Geheiligde Lewe: Oefening in die Toewyding aan God." *Fax Theologica* 7, no. 1 (1987): 20–38.
Thiselton, A. C. *New Horizons in Hermeneutics*. Grand Rapids: Zondervan, 1992.
Van der Merwe, H. "Biblical Spirituality." *Ned. Geref. Teologiese Tydskrif* 30, no. 4 (1989): 468–76.
Welker, M. Biblische Theologie II: Fundamentaltheologisch, *RGG*[4], Band 1 A-B, 1998: 1549–53.

Four Recent Books on Spirituality and the Psalms: Some Contextualising, Analytical, and Evaluative Remarks[*]

ABSTRACT
In the four years from 2002 to 2005, four new books on the Psalms and spirituality were published. These are:
- Stuhlmueller, C. *The Spirituality of the Psalms.* Collegeville, Minn.: Liturgical Press, 2002.
- Brueggemann, W. *Spirituality of the Psalms.* Minneapolis: Fortress, 2002.
- Waaijman, K. *Mystiek in de Psalmen.* Baarn: Ten Have, 2004.
- Firth, D. G. *Hear, o Lord. A Spirituality of the Psalms.* Calver: Cliff College Publishing, 2005.

In this essay, brief remarks on the context within which this publication trend takes place are made. Each of the works is then briefly described, and general evaluative remarks conclude the essay.

1. Introduction

The turn to spirituality in our time, much to the surprise of those who had earlier predicted a religionless future for humanity, still begs adequate sociological explanation. Although some explanations have been offered—such as a reaction to a dehumanising technocratic age—these are of course only partial explanations. Some have ventured to ascribe the growth of interest in spirituality in Christian circles to an anti-intellectual turn, and though there may be truth to this criticism in some instances, it certainly does not hold true in any universal sense. The blossoming

---

[*] This essay was initially presented as a paper at the congress of the Spirituality Association of South Africa, in January 2006, at the University of Stellenbosch, South Africa.

of interest in Biblical Spirituality goes to prove this point: here is a discipline that does not seek less rigorous critical exegetical work and hermeneutical reflection, but asks for more. This "more" is that the usual scholarly exegesis of a biblical text be related contextually (that is historically)[1] to its interpreters through the ages (the *wirkungsgeschichtliche* approach to exegesis), up to and including the lives of the faithful of today.[2] The *communio sanctorum* thus find themselves, through their relationship in faith, facilitated by a particular text, related to one another—a choir of voices singing not necessarily in harmony, but at least from the same sheets. Ancient oral traditions, becoming texts, edited, placed within literary contexts, canonised, read and applied through the ages by individuals and communities, up to our time—all within concrete socio-historical circumstances: such is the acrobatic tumble of meaning.

This interest in Biblical Spirituality is demonstrated by a series of four books that were published from 2002 to 2005 with the title indicating a direct focus on the spirituality of the Psalms. The four publications are:

- Stuhlmueller, C. *The Spirituality of the Psalms*. Collegeville, Minn.: Liturgical Press, 2002.
- Brueggemann, W. *Spirituality of the Psalms*. Minneapolis: Fortress, 2002.
- Waaijman, K. *Mystiek in de Psalmen*. Baarn: Ten Have, 2004.

---

[1] Cf. P. G. R. de Villiers, "The Psalms and Spirituality," *Old Testament Essays* 12, no. 3 (1999): 423–25.

[2] Cf. J. F. Craghan, *Love and Thunder. A Spirituality of the Old Testament* (Collegeville, Minn.: The Order of St. Benedict, Inc., 1983), 2; L. C. Bezuidenhout, "Perspektiewe uit die Psalms wat Lig Werp op die Wese van die Geloofsgemeenskap," *Hervormde Teologiese Studies* 51, no. 3 (1995): 714–15; S. D. Snyman, "Spiritualiteit—'n Perspektief uit die Ou Testament," *In die Skriflig* 31, no. 4 (1997): 382–83.

- Firth, D. G. *Hear, o Lord. A Spirituality of the Psalms.* Calver: Cliff College Publishing, 2005.

A brief description of each of these contributions is presented below, with some analytical remarks, upon which follows an interpretative overview.

2. Stuhlmueller's Historical Spirituality of the Psalms

Carrol Stuhlmueller, Passionist priest and Old Testament scholar at the Catholic Theological Union in Chicago until his death in 1994, left among his possessions an almost completed manuscript titled *The Spirituality of the Psalms*. The University of Portland Old Testament scholar Carol Dempsey subsequently edited and updated this manuscript, appending to it as closing chapters earlier work by the deceased author on Pss 1 and 2 (Stuhlmueller 1983), and published this work in 2002 under Stuhlmueller's name alone.[3]

The opening pages of this book seek to place the Psalms collection within its broader biblical framework; it does so, however, by referring only to some New Testament Psalm quotations.[4] Nonetheless, in the rest of the book wide-ranging and, more importantly, well-considered references to pertinent texts from both Testaments are amply added.[5] This broad inner-biblical referencing technique, one senses, serves within the North American context to carefully undermine certain knee-jerk

---

[3] See C. Stuhlmueller, *The Spirituality of the Psalms* (Collegeville, Minn.: Liturgical Press, 2002) and C. Stuhlmueller, *Psalms 1 and 2* (Message of Biblical Theology series; Old Testament Message 21 and 22; Wilmington: Michael Glazier, 1983). One is left slightly at a loss, here and there, whether to ascribe stylistic variations in the text of this book to the writing technique of Stuhlmueller or to the editing by Dempsey.

[4] See Stuhlmueller, *Spirituality of the Psalms*, 1, 8. Are the opening pages thus one instance where one may suspect Dempsey's hand?

[5] Ibid., 95–101; cf. 38–41.

reactions to historical readings of the Psalms, namely to make the employment of Psalm references by New Testament texts normative for modern exegesis.[6] The ambience of committed faith within which this is clearly done by the author,[7] renders this book a valuable tool to convey the faith-building value of historical-critical renderings of the Bible texts.

Stuhlmueller's approach is what may be termed existential-romantic: he tries to enter into the life world of the ancient Psalm singers. By noticing the very fine details of everyday life reflected in a Psalm, one can "meet, with solicitude and openness, an ancient culture and people."[8] By not in the first instance "evaluating their usefulness or importance," we meet the Psalms/Psalmists "on their own grounds."[9] It is therefore important to take seriously the oral and redactional processes, both ancient (found in the Hebrew, Septuagint and Vulgate texts) and modern (in different translations), behind the Psalm collection as we have it, and the history that influenced such processes.[10] The Deutero- and Trito-Isaiah texts are frequently, if briefly, indicated as parallels of sorts to ancient redactional work on the Psalm collections.

Using Ps 95 as example, Stuhlmueller then illustrates how a passage could be read at once as historical, literary and prayer text.[11] By combining close attention to the text with the reader's imagination,[12] the ancient tradition as it had already been actualised in the text itself, in the church through the centuries, and

---

[6] Ibid., 18–20; cf. 71ff.

[7] See I. Nowell, "Review of *The Spirituality of the Psalms* by Carrol Stuhlmueller," *Worship* 77, no. 5 (2003): 479; cf. e.g. Stuhlmueller, *Spirituality of the Psalms,* 23–24.

[8] Stuhlmueller, *Spirituality of the Psalms*, 3 (cf. 13, xx).

[9] Ibid.

[10] Ibid., 3–8.

[11] Ibid., 9–24.

[12] Cf. Stuhlmueller, *Spirituality of the Psalms*, 77–78, where he combines the work of De Vaux with imagination (see R. de Vaux, *Ancient Israel. Its Life and Institutions* [trans. J. McHugh; London: Darton, Longman & Todd, 1961]).

Spirituality of the Psalms

in the individual's own life, gains a fuller meaning. Without indicating it, Stuhlmueller here combines tradition-historical exegesis, classically *à la* Von Rad,[13] with the more modern reception-historical approach (the latter not in the philosophical hermeneutical sense,[14] but in the *wirkungsgeschichtliche* sense,[15] thus creating a chain of meaning to which the reader of the Psalm may now be linked. Inner-Testamental and inter-Testamental quotations, allusions and debates, references by the church fathers, and the interpretations of leading spiritual lights through the centuries, find acknowledgement alongside modern exegetical scholarship.[16] In this, Stuhlmueller is fully a child of *Vaticanum II*.[17]

Within such a framework, it is possible, for instance, for Stuhlmueller to address, within fortifying sections on hymns of praise, the sensitive historical issue of the polytheistic background to the Old Testament, or to use the J and P textual layers of the Exodus account of the first plague to describe how secular history becomes faith history.[18] Thus, grouping the Psalms thematically (i.e., praise; the Lord as King and Creator; the royal Psalms; lament, both communal and individual; illness and death; rejection and resolution; wisdom; and thanksgiving), Stuhlmueller not only discusses the range of life experiences reflected in the Psalms, but also relates these to issues and experiences of modern life.[19]

---

[13] See explicitly, Stuhlmueller, *Spirituality of the Psalms*, 49, and G. von Rad, *Theologie des Alten Testaments, Band 1: Die Theologie der geschichtlichen Überlieferungen Israels* (Fünfte, durchgesehen Auflage; München: Chr. Kaiser Verlag, 1962).

[14] Cf. A. C. Thiselton, *New Horizons in Hermeneutics* (Grand Rapids: Zondervan, 1992), 80–141.

[15] Cf. G. Grimm, *Rezeptionsgeschichte. Grundlegung einer Theorie* (München: Wilhelm Fink, 1977).

[16] Stuhlmueller, *Spirituality of the Psalms*, 21–24.

[17] Ibid., 23–24.

[18] Ibid., 25–38, 42–47.

[19] Ibid., 25–202.

Stuhlmueller thus succeeds in combining a reading of the text of the Psalms which is unequivocally historically-oriented with a spiritual life that is indisputably related to God. Context ancient meets context modern in a fulfilling interaction between ancient Scripture and modern reader. To my sensibilities, this is the model for interaction with the Scriptures by individuals and the church which holds the greatest promise for a theologically and intellectually sustainable interface.

3. Brueggemann's Analysis of the Psalms

Since, most particularly, his Genesis commentary,[20] Walter Brueggemann (Columbia Theological Seminary Old Testament scholar and Presbyterian church leader) has been known for his ability to translate complex technical exegesis into a more popular mode, so as to be accessible to readers not well versed in the necessary scholarly apparatus of exegetes. Brueggemann has developed a style of academic writing which may be described as "analytical," "conceptual," or "paradigmatic."[21] This entails, with all the necessary introductory exclusions and limitations, the use of certain concepts, often combined opposites, with which to analyse a text or body of texts—an approach again to be seen in his *Theology of the Old Testament*.[22] Though it may leave much about the texts unsaid, this approach has the benefit that new thematic relationships between texts can be discovered, in a concise and accessible—"eminently practical"[23]—way. Certain concepts are

---

[20] W. Brueggemann, *Genesis* (Interpretation: A Bible Commentary for Teaching and Preaching; Atlanta: John Knox, 1982).

[21] But not in the sense of Kuhn (see T. S. Kuhn, *The Structure of Scientific Revolutions* (2d ed.; Chicago: University of Chicago Press, 1970).

[22] W. Brueggemann, *Theology of the Old Testament: Testimony, Dispute, Advocacy* (Minneapolis: Fortress, 1997).

[23] See Craghan, *Love and Thunder*, 125; cf. W. Brueggemann, *Spirituality of the Psalms* (Minneapolis: Fortress, 2002), vii–viii; Craghan here refers to W. Brueggemann, "Psalms and the Life of Faith: A Suggested Typology of

employed as analytical frameworks with which to read the texts of the Bible, often with a view to comment on modern social, political and ecclesial concerns. Thus, this style of writing has led to Brueggemann's works being highly valued by ministers/pastors/priests, theologians in other fields of specialisation, and the broader church public. This, in part, explains Brueggemann's sustained popularity, productivity, and influence.

Brueggemann's *Spirituality of the Psalms* is a popular work in the sense that it is a booklet written with no academic purposes in mind.[24] However, it has strong academic precursors in earlier publications by Brueggemann.[25] The 1984 work, *The Message of the Psalms*, was adapted,[26] with individual Psalm discussions now omitted, to become *Spirituality of the Psalms* (2002). Here, as there,[27] a three-part analytical framework is used with which to categorise the Psalms—and human life—as reflecting orientation,

---

Function," *Journal for the Study of the Old Testament* 17 (1980): 3–32, the direct precursor to W. Brueggemann, *The Message of the Psalms. A Theological Commentary* (Minneapolis: Augsburg, 1984), culminating in W. Brueggemann, *Spirituality of the Psalms* (Minneapolis: Fortress, 2002); see also below.

[24] This booklet is, however, not meant for uneducated readers, as scattered references to leading lights in the fields of sociology, philosophy and psychology (cf. e.g. Brueggemann, *Spirituality of the Psalms*, ix, 14, 42 respectively) would indicate.

[25] Cf. Brueggemann, "Psalms and the Life of Faith," 30–32; W. Brueggemann, *Praying the Psalms* (Winoa: St Mary's Press, 1982); W. Brueggemann, *Israel's Praise. Doxology against Idolatry and Ideology* (Philadelphia: Fortress, 1988); W. Brueggemann, *The Psalms and the Life of Faith* (Minneapolis: Fortress, 1995); W. Brueggemann, *Abiding Astonishment: Psalms, Modernity and the Making of History* (Literary Currents in Biblical Interpretation; Louisville: Westminster John Knox, 1991); and most notably, W. Brueggemann, *The Message of the Psalms. A Theological Commentary* (Minneapolis: Augsburg, 1984).

[26] Cf. H. W. Ballard, "Review of *Spirituality of the Psalms* by Walter Brueggemann," *Journal of Hebrew Scriptures* 4 (2002/2003). Online: http://www.arts.ualberta.ca/JHS/reviews/review050.htm.

[27] Brueggemann, *Message of the Psalms*, 25–167.

disorientation, and new orientation.[28] He relates this to the work of God in Christ ("crucifixion and resurrection") in a paradigmatic way, as a Christian—though not a christological—interpretative strategy.[29] In the church this crucifixion-resurrection pattern is reflected in the ritual of baptism, and in the Old Testament in the history of Jerusalem and the exile, as a pattern of "loss" and "gift."[30] In modern life, Brueggemann seeks in this way to counter the relentless optimism that Western/American popular culture demands of its subjects.[31] What is more, the orientation-disorientation-new orientation interpretative matrix Brueggemann adopts is a dialogical exegetical approach, that is: sensitive to the internal debate of the Psalms; and dynamic, that is: sensitive to the movement in people's lives from one circumstance to the other.

The value of the Psalms, reflects Brueggemann, lies in the breadth of experience that they give voice to, both in ancient Israel and for later believers.[32] The problems of modern writings on the Psalms are that devotionals are often pious but naïve, whereas scholarship frequently offers academic understanding without being "belief-full" perception.[33] Rather, Brueggemann would have it, scholarship and discipleship should enrich one another.[34] Gunkel,[35] Mowinckel,[36] and Westermann[37] must meet the soul.[38]

---

[28] Brueggemann, *Spirituality of the Psalms*, viii, x, 8–13
[29] Ibid., x, 12–13.
[30] Ibid., xi.
[31] Ibid., xii–xiii, 14–15, 26.
[32] Ibid., 1–2.
[33] Ibid., 7.
[34] Ibid., 2–5.
[35] See G. Gunkel, *Die Psalmen* (Göttinger Handkommentar zum Alten Testament, II.2; Göttingen: Vandenhoeck & Ruprecht, 1926⁴); G. Gunkel and J. Begrich, *Einleitung in die Psalmen: Die Gattungen der religiosen Lyrik Israels* (Göttinger Handkommentar zum Alten Testament, 2; Göttingen: Vandenhoeck & Ruprecht, 1933).
[36] See S. Mowinckel, *Psalmenstudien, I–VI* (Kristiania: J. Dybwad, 1922–1924); and S. Mowinckel, *The Psalms in Israel's Worship* (Oxford: Blackwell, 1962).

Spirituality of the Psalms 61

This requires what Brueggemann terms "a postcritical reading of the Psalms,"[39] for which Paul Ricoeur's "second naïveté"[40] would perhaps be a more generally recognisable term.

The Psalms of orientation, as the first part of Brueggemann's analytical framework, reflect stability in the relationship between those praying and God.[41] God's acts of creation and maintenance offer theological and social certainties, and these Psalms both reflect and create that reality liturgically. Hence, these Psalms reflect the values of a powerful social class and may for them serve purposes of dominance. For those dominated, these Psalms may, however, express hope, even eschatological expectations. Four kinds of Psalms fall into this orientation dimension: *creation* (Pss 8, 33, 104, 145), *Torah* (Pss 1, 15, 19, 24, 119), *wisdom* (Pss 14, 37) and *well-being* (Pss 131, 133).

In the Psalms of disorientation active faith within negative circumstances is found.[42] Realism, in facing the world as it is, meets with belief in God despite the circumstances. This is not pop theology, civil religion, nor even the church's spirituality. Here, God does change, as do the circumstances of life. Yet trust in God remains: it is indeed Yahweh that is spoken to, even if in derogatory or disrespectful ways. Surprisingly, positive sentiments (assurance of relief) are often reflected here too. Such Psalms of disorientation may be personal (Pss 13, 35, 86) or communal (Pss 74, 79, 137).

A new orientation is found in Pss 30, 34, 40, 138 (on personal thanksgiving), 65, 66, 124, 129 (on communal thanksgiving), 29,

---

[37] C. Westermann, *Lob und Klage in den Psalmen* (5., erw. Aufl.; Göttingen: Vandenhoeck & Ruprecht, 1977).
[38] Brueggemann, *Spirituality of the Psalms*, 3–7.
[39] Ibid., 7; cf. 3
[40] Cf. S. M. Schneiders, "Scripture and Spirituality," in *Christian Spirituality: Origins to the Twelfth Century* (ed. B. McGinn, J. Meyendorff and J. Leclerq; London: SCM, 1985), 19.
[41] Brueggemann, *Spirituality of the Psalms*, 16–24.
[42] Ibid., 24–45.

47, 93, 97, 98, 99, 114 (on kingship), and 100, 103, 113, 117, 135, 146–50 (on praise). These are characterised by the unexpected grace of God, and a newly found well-being, nurtured through the previous difficulties.[43]

This three-in-one spirituality that Brueggemann finds reflected in the Psalms is certainly true to life; hence the enduring influence of the Psalms. Interesting is Brueggemann's greater emphasis on the second dimension, disorientation, as is his continued interest in the use of the Psalms for social justice in the last section of the publication.[44] This indicates where for him lies the spiritual centre of the Psalms: theodicy.

The Psalms, and Christianity, are not only individualistic. Justice mediates communion, which implies fairness before God. In the Psalms, theodicy is not only a question of God's love versus God's power (i.e. against evil), but also—drawing on Thomas Merton and José Miranda—a social concern: who is in power in such a way as to define legal, economic and political balances, and present these as the will of God? Theodicy thus combines religion and society within revolution, in latter-day societies as well as in the Psalmic language: of the wicked and righteous, and of God's just sovereignty. Hence, both sociologically and in the Psalms, either an unacceptable system and its legitimating God may be rejected, or God is called on to sabotage the unacceptable social system.

Thus, Brueggemann indicates, a spirituality of orientation will in essence be pro status quo; whereas a spirituality of disorientation will tend to be revolutionary; and a spirituality of new orientation will seek to construct a new consensus.[45] The Psalms are therefore historically contingent, and cannot be read

---

[43] Ibid., 46–57.
[44] Ibid., 58–69.
[45] Ibid., 69–74.

Spirituality of the Psalms 63

uncontextually, without social relevance.[46] Praying the Psalms is at once an act of committed faith and an act of critical justice.

4. Waaijman's Spirituality and Theology of the Psalms

Kees Waaijman, Carmelite priest, director of the Titus Brandsma Instituut and professor of Spirituality at Radboud Universiteit (until recently called the Katholieke Universiteit Nijmegen) is the foremost figure in Spirituality scholarship internationally, with his *Spiritualiteit: Vormen, Grondslagen, Methoden* (2000;[47] and multiple translations of it) the most comprehensive resource in the field. After some four decades of working on Spirituality and as a Psalms specialist,[48] he offers his readers a depth of insight into biblical, historical, and contemporary spirituality. The same is the case again here in *Mystiek in de Psalmen*,[49] though it is an altogether different kind of work to *Spiritualiteit: Vormen, Grondslagen, Methoden*. Where in the 2000 publication he wrote about spirituality, in the 2004 work Waaijman writes spirituality. Perhaps this is why he personally regards *Mystiek in de Psalmen* as his crowning work.

Similar to much of his other writings, the approach in *Mystiek in de Psalmen* is what may be termed "thematic" or "idea-logical":

---

[46] "... the spirituality of the Psalms is shaped, defined and characterised in specific historical, experiential categories and shuns universals" (ibid., 73).
[47] K. Waaijman, *Spiritualiteit: Vormen, Grondslagen, Methoden* (Gent: Carmelitana, 2000).
[48] See K. Waaijman, *Psalmen over Recht en Onrecht : Psalmen 3, 4, 5, 7, 11, 17, 23, 26, 27, 57, 63* (Kampen: Kok, 1980); K. Waaijman, *Psalmen by Ziekte en Genezing* (Kampen: Kok, 1981); K. Waaijman, *Psalmen over de Uittocht : Het Lied van Mirjam, het Lied van Mozes, Psalmen 66, 68, 77, 78, 80, 81, 95, 105, 106, 114, 135* (Kampen: Kok, 1983); K. Waaijman, *Psalmen over de Schepping : Psalmen 8, 29, 33, 65, 74, 104, 136, 139, 147, 148* (Kampen: Kok, 1989).
[49] K. Waaijman, *Mystiek in de Psalmen* (Serie Mystieke Teksten en Thema's, 22; Baarn: Ten Have, 2004).

one after another, certain topics from the history and practice of religion/philosophy/spirituality are selected and explicated. The progression in the argument does not follow a hard, step-by-step logic, but rather, certain ideas imply others, in a variety of ways, with the progression of thought driven by texts and themes from within the interdisciplinary field that is Spirituality. Although such a writing style may lead to a thoroughly philosophically oriented spirituality, Waaijman's exegetical grounding (he frequently refers to standard exegetical works such as Zenger and Westermann)[50] prevents this, and renders this a biblical spirituality. In addition, Waaijman has a linguistic register that gives him access to wide-ranging written spirituality sources, which he draws on extensively. Clearly, he is also the most versed of the authors under discussion here in the classic literature of Spirituality. Interestingly, apart form his direct subject matter here—the Psalms—the most influential other source on Waaijman's thinking are the writings of Martin Buber.[51]

In *Mystiek in de Psalmen*, Waaijman seeks to deduce from his study of the Psalms the contours of the mystery of God ("godsmystiek"). The Psalms' mystic language covers a range of possibilities.[52] Dominant, though, is "the Name" through which in prayer humanity and divinity meet,[53] and which therefore becomes

---

[50] See E. Zenger, *Psalmen Auslegungen, 1* (Freiburg: Herder, 2003); C. Westermann, *Genesis 1–11* (Biblischer Kommentar Altes Testament 1/1; Neukirchen-Vluyn: Neukirchener Verlag, 1983[3)]; cf. Waaijman, *Mystiek in de Psalmen,* 9, 21.

[51] Cf. C. J. Waaijman, *De Mystiek van Ik en Jij: Een Nieuwe Vertaling van "Ich und Du" van Martin Buber met Inleiding en Uitleg en een Doordenking van het Systeem dat Eraan ten Grondslag Ligt* (Proefschrift, Katholieke Universiteit Nijmegen; Utrecht: Bijleveld, 1976); K. Waaijman, *De Mystiek van Ik en Jij. Een Nieuwe Vertaling van "Ich und Du" van Martin Buber* (Kampen: Kok, 1990).

[52] Waaijman, *Mystiek in de Psalmen,* 10–12.

[53] Ibid., 13–14; cf. Snyman's take on the Name (see Snyman, "Spiritualiteit—'n Perspektief uit die Ou Testament," 377–78).

Spirituality of the Psalms 65

a repetitive theme throughout *Mystiek in de Psalmen*. To signify God, Waaijman mostly utilises the term "Wezer"—"He who is"/"That which is," among other connotations—a term loaded with both biblical-revelatory and existential-philosophical connotations.

Among the three mystical starting points—the self, the other, and the Other—it is the latter which defines the former two.[54] This happens in concrete contexts, through a dialogical immediacy ("dialogische onmiddellijkheid")[55] which elicits response-ability ("antwoordelijkheid"/"responsibilité"), that is, giving oneself over in trust, resulting in creative re-formation.[56] In this sense, the Psalms are mystically dialogical.[57]

With wide-ranging references to Christian, Jewish, and Muslim mystics and to Scripture, the latter with the most detailed focus on sections from the Psalms, Waaijman discusses a variety of topics in Spirituality. These are: creation,[58] being saved from death,[59] forgiveness and re-creation,[60] fear, trust and meeting God anew,[61] one's own life's journey,[62] respect for/fear of the Lord,[63] good and evil,[64] God's Name, interestingly connected with liberation,[65] God

---

[54] Waaijman, *Mystiek in de Psalmen*, 14–16.
[55] Ibid., 18.
[56] Ibid., 19–20.
[57] Wölber (see H.-O. Wölber, "Der Königsweg der Spiritualität. Gedanken zur Frömmigkeit aus der Bibel," *Evangelische Kommentare* 9/12 [1976]: 727), drawing on Küng (see H. Küng, *Christ sein* [München: R. Piper, 1974]), makes the point that the Bible is not only a book that talks about God, but also with God—an insight which is also full of dialogical possibilities (cf. Bezuidenhout, "Perspektiewe uit die Psalms," 713–14, 718).
[58] Waaijman, *Mystiek in de Psalmen*, 21–31.
[59] Ibid., 32–42.
[60] Ibid., 43–54.
[61] Ibid., 55–67.
[62] Ibid., 68–78.
[63] Ibid., 79–89.
[64] Ibid., 90–100, 101–11.
[65] Ibid., 112–23.

and Israel,[66] God as king,[67] pilgrimage,[68] Torah/(wisdom) teaching,[69] justice and protection,[70] and life and death.[71]

Frequent descriptions of real-life experiences affecting all people prevent this spirituality from becoming esoteric,[72] as do many Hebrew word analyses,[73] along with indications of historical dating and events.[74] Universal human life circumstances form the backdrop to which Psalm sections are analysed. In addition, traditional theological themes such as sin and redemption[75] also find their place.

In this way, Waaijman is in essence writing theology—a theology of the Psalms, to be sure, but something quite different to the tradition that has developed within Old Testament science with the sub-genre of scholarship called Old Testament Theology.[76] The differences lie not only in the deliberately more restricted subject matter, namely with the focus on the Psalms, but also in the span of sources drawn on. These are not exclusively Christian, but are selected in order to place certain aspects or verses from a Psalm within a wider, more illuminating framework. This results in an outcome that is sensitively inter-religious Christian theology-in-the-making, and as such may be of great interest also to scholars in

---

[66] Ibid., 124–34.
[67] Ibid., 135–46, 147–57.
[68] Ibid., 158–68.
[69] Ibid., 169–79.
[70] Ibid., 180–90.
[71] Ibid., 191.
[72] See e.g. Waaijman, *Mystiek in de Psalmen*, 34–42.
[73] Ibid., 68.
[74] Ibid., 135–57.
[75] Ibid., 43–54.
[76] Cf. B. C. Ollenburger, E. A. Martens and G. F. Hasel, eds., *The Flowering of Old Testament Theology. A Reader in Twentieth-Century Old Testament Theology, 1930–1990* (Surveys in Biblical and Theological Study 1; Winona Lake: Eisenbrauns, 1992); P. Adam, *Hearing God's Words. Exploring Biblical Spirituality* (New Studies in Biblical Theology 16; Downers Grove: InterVarsity, 2004), 42–44.

Spirituality of the Psalms

the fields of missiology, science of religion, and inter-religious dialogue.

It must be noted, though, that reading this book will be an intellectually more profitable exercise if one has read some of Waaijman's other works. His reference to the soul ("ziel"),[77] for instance, becomes more lucid if one has read an earlier explication of his on this term.[78]

5. The Way in Which Firth Hears the Lord

The contribution by David Firth (2005),[79] a Baptist originally from Australia, who taught the Old Testament also in Zimbabwe, South Africa, and the United Kingdom (he has recently moved to St. John's College, Nottingham), is introduced with a theoretical orientation which explains his approach to the Psalms. Apart from placing the Psalms centrally in his own faith development, the Psalms are also central to his academic life[80] and the life of his faith community.[81] In addition, Firth places his reading of the Psalms within the research history on these texts.[82] In broad outlines, he sketches the development of Psalm studies from the traditional phase (where Davidic authorship is more or less accepted), to the historical-critical and therefore cult-oriented

---

[77] Waaijman, *Mystiek in de Psalmen*, 28–30.
[78] See e.g. K. Waaijman, "The Soul as Spiritual Core Concept," *Spiritus* 6 (1996), 5–19.
[79] D. G. Firth, *Hear, o Lord. A Spirituality of the Psalms* (Cliff College Academic Series. Calver: Cliff College Publishing, 2005).
[80] Cf. D. G. Firth, "Responses to Violence in Lament Psalms of the Individual" (Ph.D. diss., University of Pretoria, 1996); D. G. Firth, "Stages of Prayer through the Psalms," *South African Baptist Journal of Theology* 10 (2001), 1–9; D. G. Firth, *Surrendering Retribution in the Psalms: Responses to Violence in the Individual Complaints* (Paternoster Biblical Monographs-PBM; Carlisle: Paternoster, 2005).
[81] Firth, *Hear, o Lord*, 1–3.
[82] Ibid., 4–13.

phase (with Gunkel and Mowinckel most influential),[83] to the latest, that is, the literary-oriented phase. Firth argues that the latter approach is the most productive, *exegetically*, because it replaces the uncertainties of historical reconstructions with the greater certainties of thematic-compositional activities of the Psalms' compilers, and *spiritually*, because it holds the greatest promise for modern-day application. However, in practice Firth is not averse to considering historical possibilities.[84]

Firth credits Brueggemann as the leading light of this literary-oriented approach, and draws strongly on the latter's orientation-disorientation-new orientation matrix of Psalm analysis, noted above, but renames them as order, disorder, and reorder. However, Firth adds greater emphasis to the Royal Psalms than Brueggemann does,[85] because he takes as his primary binary stance the cooperative distinction between pain and praise that one encounters in the Psalms,[86] which translates as experience and eschatology in the Royal Psalms.[87]

The Psalms of the ordered world, with which Firth starts his analysis,[88] reflect God's nature as orderly, which thus characterises creation, to which the faithful should orient their lives in prayer.[89] The Torah Psalms (1, 19, 119) and those that invite entering the community of faith (Pss 15 and 24) are, within this scheme, complementary, combining respectively the internal and the external; alternatively, the individual and the context. A faith ordered to God's presence will seek to impart that presence to the world, since creation is ordered, something Pss 8 and 147–48

---

[83] For their works, see footnotes 35 and 36 respectively.
[84] See e.g. Firth, *Hear, o Lord,* 24, 56, 74.
[85] Ibid., 11, 101–22, 128; cf. Brueggemann, *Spirituality of the Psalms,* x.
[86] Firth, *Hear, o Lord,* 3.
[87] Ibid., 11, 128.
[88] Ibid., 15–38.
[89] Ibid., 17–24.

celebrate,[90] and which the Psalms both praise and trust in (respectively, Pss 29, 93, 104, 146 and 46, 23, 121).[91]

The Psalms of the disordered world reflect the negative experiences of life.[92] Individual penitence (Ps 51) and communal confession (Pss 90 and 106) seek the cause for this disorder within; external sources of pain threaten, again, a single believer (Pss 7, 139, 3, 56, 69) or the group (Ps 79).[93] At times, God creates the disorder, either through punishment or absence—Pss 6 and 88, relating to the individual, and 60 and 83, relating to the communal.[94]

In the Psalms of the reordered world, God answers prayers, indicating Divine reign, and resulting in testimonies and thanksgiving for particular acts, which in turn elicit encouragement and undertakings.[95] Thus, the individual experiences forgiveness (Ps 32), healing (Ps 30) and deliverance (Pss 92 and 138), along with a renewed relationship with God (Ps 73), which also relates to the community.[96]

Firth's discussions of the different Psalms are characterised by brief analyses of the contents of each text, divided into pericopes (which parallels the approach in Brueggemann, *Message of the Psalms*). Interwoven throughout the discussion of the Psalms, Firth remarks on the question his order-disorder-reorder matrix naturally raises, namely theodicy.[97] The problem of the goodness of God

---

[90] Ibid., 24–27.
[91] Ibid., 29–38.
[92] Ibid., 39–42.
[93] Ibid., 49–65.
[94] Ibid., 65–77.
[95] Ibid., 79–82.
[96] Ibid., 82–99.
[97] Reacting to the closing chapter of Brueggemann, *Message of the Psalms*, Firth (in *Hear, o Lord,* 127) is ill at ease with applying the term "theodicy" to the Psalms. He argues that, taken as a whole, the Psalms already know the "reordering"/hope (so too Brueggemann, *Spirituality of the Psalms,* xii), and hence the negative view implicit in the term "theodicy" is inappropriate for use

70   *The Old Testament and Christian Spirituality*

versus the evil experienced in life, touched on in many Psalms, and a central question of the human spirit (if perhaps not universally, then at least in all thought influenced by ancient Greek philosophy), is remarked on frequently and sensitively. The difficult questions are not shirked from, nor are the easy answers accommodated. It is in this thread of discussion that runs throughout Firth's tri-partite matrix that the title of this book finds, to my mind, its major justification. Further justification is found in the perspectives offered subsequently on how this philosophical-theological issue, theodicy, relates to prayer.[98]

On the Royal Psalms, Firth argues as follows: in the post-exilic period of Israel's history these Psalms gain messianic connotations, namely as prayers of hope for the future, based on what had been in the past. The New Testament employs the Psalms in the same way, Firth indicates, expecting God's kingdom yet to arrive in its fullness.[99] The scheme of order-disorder-reorder hope is then used by Firth with reference to Pss 2, 89, 132, 20, 67 and 117, to demonstrate such a manner of praying.[100] In this and other ways, therefore, the Psalms may be said to shape the prayers of the faithful, whichever kinds of prayers are prayed. Past *and* future shape our present spirituality.[101] Firth's stress on the close relationship between individuality and communality in the

---

relating to the Psalms. This fits well with the view Firth expresses repeatedly, that even when experiencing the "disorder," the faithful already have hope, since they have experience of the "order." This is a valid and valuable theological and pastoral argument. However, if one defines the term "theodicy" slightly broader, as I do here—"the problem of the goodness of God versus the evil experienced in life"—it too contains this positive element, and thus remains a handy shorthand-term to describe this involved matter.

[98] Firth, *Hear, o Lord*, 101–29.
[99] Ibid., 101–5.
[100] Ibid., 105–20.
[101] Ibid., 127–29.

Spirituality of the Psalms

Psalms,[102] in contra-distinction to the individualism characteristic of our times, thus fits well into this argument.

6. Taken Together

These four books contribute, no doubt, to breaking the relative silence on biblical spirituality.[103] All the more so because, taken together, these four works show some appealing parallels, but also some notable differences.

Interestingly, none of these books are fully academic books in the manner one would expect from a scholarly monograph. At the same time, none is "unacademic": an informed reader can detect between the lines the exegetical work, the theories and the authors underpinning what is being said. This approach, combined with, in all four works, the simplicity of writing style, render them all valuable educational tools.

More foundationally, all four publications taken in review here stress the communal aspect of spirituality: the Christian faith *has* a social conscience. However, the way in which this point is driven home differs in noticeable ways. The liberal[104] Presbyterian Brueggemann draws on social-scientific theory with which to analyse both biblical text and modern context; the Catholic exegete Stuhlmueller enriches the biblical text by thick referencing to other biblical texts, thus building a directly Bible-based case; the Catholic spiritualist Waaijman draws on existential thought to place ordinary aspects of life in a wider, faith-full dimension; the Baptist, former missionary, Old Testament scholar Firth draws on vignettes from his personal experience to demonstrate the

---

[102] Ibid., 12

[103] Cf. Adam, *Hearing God's Words*, 15.

[104] "Liberal" should not be understood here in the classical sense, of the rationalist and moralist exegesis of for instance nineteenth-century Europe, but in the sense in which it is employed in American politics, which is mirrored strongly in the fault lines of the American ecclesial geography.

concreteness of Psalmic contextual spirituality. In this way we find ourselves presented with a prism of possibilities, each deeply felt and with solid academic, philosophical and personal integrity. Here too, it seems, then, my earlier points remain applicable: that one always tends to find one's own spirituality back in Scripture, not by design, but as an inescapable matter of an individual's frame of reference, and, thus, that spirituality remains always intensely personal.[105] These distinctive faith configurations are, however, strongly communally formed: the natural influences of faith and life that (in)forms each person's own faith and life. It is, furthermore, precisely this collection of personal pieties that, we find, enriches and (in)forms one another in various ways, rendering spirituality thus, in a circular way, at the very same time again inescapably communal.

Having said this, the differing text-theoretical/hermeneutical/exegetical approaches must be noted. It is on this point that a critical evaluation must be offered, in the hope that it will stimulate debate and lead to clarity on the different approaches. It is Firth in particular who offers us with his opening methodological pages a strong stimulus to consider not only what is being done in Biblical Spirituality, but also how it is done.[106]

---

[105] See C. J. S. Lombaard, "Four South Africans' Proposals for a Central Theme to 'Scriptural Spirituality,'" *Scriptura* 88, no. 1 (2005): 147–48.

[106] Firth is, of course, correct in that he finds himself part of the new wave in Psalm research, which seeks out the links between the different units (Psalms/Psalm collections/Psalm genres) within this literary body, and posits for these theological intent in the compositional process. However, as is the case with all a-historical approaches, this line of reasoning errs, in my view, in two ways: it overstates its own possibilities, and it understates the possibilities of the historical approaches against which it mirrors itself (cf. C. J. S. Lombaard, "The Old Testament between Diachrony and Synchrony: Two Reasons for Favouring the Former," in *South African Perspectives on the Pentateuch between Synchrony and Diachrony* [ed. J. H. le Roux and E. Otto; New York: T&T Clark, 2007], 61–70).

For one, to state that investigating the editorial linkages between the units of this literary body is a literary process, and not a historic one, does not take into account that these editorial processes took place in very specific historical circumstances. The editors had a point to make, and as with all writings, these points were made in the face of concrete circumstances. To ignore the contextuality of editorial work is to ignore a vital aspect of this communicative process (cf. De Villiers, "The Psalms and Spirituality," 432).

In practice, though, Firth (*Hear, o Lord,* 103) does indicate a firm dating for such editorial activities, *viz.* post-exilic. It is precisely because certain Psalms are late compositions, drawing on earlier traditions, argues Stuhlmueller (*Spirituality of the Psalms,* 68–70), that they are useful today. The relationship between the text-as-literature approach and the historical approach remains, always, more than a little unclear.

Second, all literary interpretations of whichever texts are uncertain, and often reflect much of the analysts' own concerns (cf. Lombaard, "Four South Africans' Proposals," 139–50). Naturally, this does not make such interpretations invalid; it is very difficult to prove, though, that these interpretations existed within the texts themselves—as difficult as proving the cultic or historical background to an individual Psalm to which the a-historical approaches object. The nigh impossibility of certainty of interpretation is thus not escaped by the new wave of Psalm interpretations. The focus may have shifted to the body of Psalms as a whole, rather than the individual Psalms, and as such it constitutes a valuable contribution; however, the results are no less uncertain. They remain reconstructions; the hermeneutical circle *à la* Schleiermacher still applies as much with one exegetical approach as with the other (cf. R. P. Knierim, *The Task of Old Testament Theology. Substance, Method, and Cases* [Grand Rapids: Eerdmans, 1995], 269).

This is not meant as a criticism of either historical or literary approaches to the text of the Old Testament in general and the Psalms in particular. This is a remark from the philosophy of science. It has long been accepted that the choice for rationalism is of itself irrational; in more modern times, this climaxed in the insight that method does not bring us scientific truth (cf. H.-G. Gadamer, *Wahrheit und Methode: Grundzuge einer philosophischen Hermeneutik* [Tubingen: Mohr, 1975]).

Scholarship, that is, intellectually satisfying interaction with one's subject matter, is in itself an ideal (cf. C. J. S. Lombaard, "South African Perspectives on the Communication of the Bible in Church and Society" [Ph.D. diss., North-West University, Potchefstroom Campus, 2004], 7–9). What is more, it is at once a highly individualistic and a thoroughly social process. The fact that it is the texts of the Bible which we have chosen as our subject matter, is a choice already deeply rooted in spirituality, which finds its roots in the Old Testament itself—cf. Knierim, *The Task of Old Testament Theology*, 269–97 for an attempt

The three-fold matrix employed by Brueggemann and Firth also invites further comment. With both authors, their use of this interpretative matrix is meant at least in part as a reaction against unsophisticated popular impressions of the Psalms, namely as songs of praise only. The middle dimension of their matrix highlights the negative. This, I would suggest, is apt: it is often in the most negative of circumstances where faith becomes most concrete. The kinds of biblical spirituality[107] cannot be restricted, though, since the ways of the Spirit cannot be defined.[108] At the same time, this highlighting of the middle dimension of their matrix by Brueggemann and Firth is intended to subvert the one-sided "power of positive thinking"-culture[109] of our times. Positively, the stress that God's presence ought to be experienced within the negative experiences of life, must be lauded. It adds a depth to popular theology that is much needed. With the works by Stuhlmueller and Waaijman, such a "social intent" with the writing of their works is less overt, partly due to their interpretative frame not being made clear as directly. Still, they make much the same point in different, less paradigmatic, ways. This more subtle approach indicates again the variety of ways in which the intent of a book may be reached.

---

to deduce the meaning of spirituality within the Old Testament, coloured, though, as it is by his structuralist approach to reading biblical texts. This approach is ill-suited to teasing out spiritualities which are thoroughly contextually, that is, historically conditioned. Harper, too briefly to be successful, employs a thematic approach (see J. S. Harper, "Old Testament Spirituality," in *Exploring Christian Spirituality. An Ecumenical Reader* [ed. K. J. Collins; Grand Rapids: Baker, 2000], 311–26).

[107] Cf. J. C. Endres, "Psalms and Spirituality in the 21st Century," *Interpretation* 56 (2002): 147–49.

[108] Wölber, "Der Königsweg der Spiritualität," 725.

[109] This term was popularised by the title of the book by Peale (see N. V. Peale, *The Power of Positive Thinking* [New York: Simon & Schuster Adult Publishing, 1952]), with its success being attributable both to playing to the American cultural "can do"-milieu and success theology as an integral part of that milieu.

7. Conclusion

Quite naturally, the Scriptures form an integral part of Christian spirituality.[110] However, two matters should be kept in mind in relation to this: first, that the ancient spiritual experiences we encounter in the Bible were human incidents,[111] but also, second, that they were, theologically speaking, not only brought about by humans. Hence, the Bible itself is a spiritual occurrence. Biblical spirituality thus implies a life of faith that draws daily on the Bible[112]—this holds true both for individuals and the church.[113] The Word of God itself acknowledges in its pages different forms of spirituality.[114] This we note here again, with these four books taken in review. The spirituality of the Psalms combines for all four authors exegesis *and* faith.[115]

Though faith may at times be described as simple, simplicity should not be expected to characterise this hermeneutical process. The complexity of the texts of the Bible, as texts[116] and

---

[110] C. Kourie, "What Is Christian Spirituality?" in *Christian Spirituality in South Africa* (ed. C. Kourie and L. Kretzschmar; Pietermaritzburg: Cluster Publications, 2000), 14–18; J. T. Claassen, "Christelike Spiritualiteit as Kommunikatiewe Handeling" (M.Th. verhandeling, Unisa, Pretoria, 2003), 115.
[111] Cf. Craghan, *Love and Thunder,* xii, 1.
[112] The distinction by Sorg between objective and subjective spirituality of the Psalms, that is, respectively, between the faith we find *reflected in* the Bible and the faith of the latter-day believer *(in)formed by* the Bible, deserves to be taken up and developed further (see R. Sorg, "The Spirituality of the Psalms," in *Orate Fratres* 22.12, 1948, 529–33).
[113] Wölber, "Der Königsweg der Spiritualität," 725.
[114] See e.g. Harper, "Old Testament Spirituality," 312.
[115] Claassen, "Christelike Spiritualiteit as Kommunikatiewe Handeling," 13; Wölber, "Der Königsweg der Spiritualität," 725.
[116] Cf. e.g. F. E. Deist, *Witnesses to the Old Testament* (The Literature of the Old Testament, Vol. 5; Pretoria: NG Kerkboekhandel, 1988); And as Craghan (in *Love and Thunder,* vii) exclaims: "The text is the thing!"...

hermeneutically,[117] is well established. Equally, the spirituality of the modern Bible reader is situated within an involved, complex contextuality.[118] The fact remains that the way in which Scripture is read, directly affects the lives of faith of those readers.[119] This is one of the reasons that Biblical Spirituality is such an important field of study, combining as it does scholarly exegesis with the "more" (cf. the opening paragraph of this essay) of critical faith interaction.

It is a little strange, though, that when reference is made to Spirituality and the Old Testament, it is almost by definition the Psalms that are mentioned.[120] This is nothing new, as the following statement by Sorg, drawing on St. Basil, already shows: "While the whole of the Bible is inspired, yet it may truly be said that the subject-matter of the psalms excels in spirituality."[121] The question must be asked: why would this be so? Has, perhaps, liturgical tradition, often based on christological Psalm exposition, along with the relative brevity of the Psalm texts determined this? The rest of the Old Testament certainly offers much more than is, for a

---

[117] Cf. foundationally, Thiselton, *New Horizons in Hermeneutics*, and as a case study, F. E. Deist, *Ervaring, Rede en Metode in Skrifuitleg. 'n Wetenskapshistoriese Ondersoek na Skrifuitleg in die Ned. Geref. Kerk 1840–1990* (Pretoria: Raad vir Geesteswetenskaplike Navorsing, 1994).

[118] Cf. W. Dantine, "Phantasie zum Aufbruch aus dem Gewohnten. Spiritualität und geschichtliches Handeln," *Evangelische Kommentare* 9/10 (1976), 591–93; Claassen, "Christelike Spiritualiteit as Kommunikatiewe Handeling," 137–45.

[119] Cf. e.g. Claassen, "Christelike Spiritualiteit as Kommunikatiewe Handeling," 57–63, 115–27; Adam, *Hearing God's Words,* 19.

[120] Cf. J. S. Custer, *The Old Testament. A Byzantine Perspective* (Pittsburgh: God With Us Publications, 1994), 160; De Villiers, "The Psalms and Spirituality," 419–22; E. Sipkema and K. Lelyveld, "De Regel van de H. Benedictus en het Gebruik van de Psalmen. Een Spiritualiteit van de Psalmen," *Amsterdamse cahiers voor exegese van de Bijbel en zijn tradities* 18 (2000), 132,

[121] See Sorg, "The Spirituality of the Psalms," 535, cf. 537.

variety of reasons,[122] expected from it, even of the "driest" parts of the Old Testament library, such as the genealogies.[123]

---

[122] Cf. C. J. S. Lombaard, "The Old Testament in Christian Spirituality: Perspectives on the Undervaluation of the Old Testament in Christian Spirituality," *HTS Teologiese Studies/Theological Studies* 59, no. 2 (2003): 433–50.

[123] Cf. C. J. S. Lombaard, "Genealogies and Spiritualities in Genesis 4:17–22, 4:25–26, 5:1–32," in *The Spirit That Moves. Orientation and Issues in Spirituality* (ed. P. G. R. de Villiers, C. Kourie and C. J. S. Lombaard; *Acta Theologia* Supplementum 8; Bloemfontein: University of the Free State Press, 2006), 146–64.

BIBLIOGRAPHY

Adam, P. *Hearing God's Words. Exploring Biblical Spirituality*. New Studies in Biblical Theology 16. Downers Grove: InterVarsity, 2004.

Ballard, H. W. "Review of *Spirituality of the Psalms* by Walter Brueggemann." *Journal of Hebrew Scriptures* 4 (2002/2003). http://www.arts.ualberta.ca/JHS/reviews/review050.htm.

Bezuidenhout, L. C. "Perspektiewe uit die Psalms wat Lig Werp op die Wese van die Geloofsgemeenskap." *Hervormde Teologiese Studies* 51, no. 3 (1995): 712–19.

Brueggemann, W. *Spirituality of the Psalms*. Minneapolis: Fortress, 2002.

———. *Theology of the Old Testament: Testimony, Dispute, Advocacy*. Minneapolis: Fortress, 1997.

———. *The Psalms and the Life of Faith*. Minneapolis: Fortress, 1995.

———. *Abiding Astonishment: Psalms, Modernity and the Making of History*. Literary Currents in Biblical Interpretation. Louisville: Westminster John Knox, 1991.

———. *Israel's Praise. Doxology against Idolatry and Ideology*. Philadelphia: Fortress, 1988.

———. *The Message of the Psalms. A Theological Commentary*. Minneapolis: Augsburg, 1984.

———. *Genesis*. Interpretation: A Bible Commentary for Teaching and Preaching. Atlanta: John Knox, 1982.

———. *Praying the Psalms*. Winoa: St Mary's Press, 1982.

———. "Psalms and the Life of Faith: A Suggested Typology of Function." *Journal for the Study of the Old Testament* 17 (1980): 3–32.

Claassen, J. T. "Christelike Spiritualiteit as Kommunikatiewe Handeling." M.Th. verhandeling, Unisa, Pretoria, 2003.

Craghan, J. F. *Love and Thunder. A Spirituality of the Old Testament.* Collegeville, Minn.: The Order of St. Benedict, Inc., 1983.

Custer, J. S. *The Old Testament. A Byzantine Perspective.* Pittsburgh: God With Us Publications, 1994.

Dantine, W. "Phantasie zum Aufbruch aus dem Gewohnten. Spiritualität und geschichtliches Handeln." *Evangelische Kommentare* 9/10 (1976): 591–93.

Deist, F. E. *Ervaring, Rede en Metode in Skrifuitleg. 'n Wetenskapshistoriese Ondersoek na Skrifuitleg in die Ned. Geref. Kerk 1840–1990.* Pretoria: Raad vir Geesteswetenskaplike Navorsing, 1994.

———. *Witnesses to the Old Testament.* The Literature of the Old Testament, Vol. 5. Pretoria: NG Kerkboekhandel, 1988.

De Vaux, R. *Ancient Israel. Its Life and Institutions.* Translated by J. McHugh. London: Darton, Longman & Todd, 1961.

De Villiers, P. G. R. "The Psalms and Spirituality." *Old Testament Essays* 12, no. 3 (1999): 416–39.

Endres, J. C. "Psalms and Spirituality in the 21st Century." *Interpretation* 56 (2002): 143–54.

Firth, D. G. *Hear, o Lord. A Spirituality of the Psalms.* Cliff College Academic Series. Calver: Cliff College Publishing, 2005.

———. *Surrendering Retribution in the Psalms: Responses to Violence in the Individual Complaints.* Paternoster Biblical Monographs-PBM. Carlisle: Paternoster, 2005.

———. "Stages of Prayer through the Psalms." *South African Baptist Journal of Theology* 10 (2001): 1–9.

———. "Responses to Violence in Lament Psalms of the Individual." Ph.D. diss., University of Pretoria, 1996.

Gadamer, H.-G. *Wahrheit und Methode: Grundzuge einer philosophischen Hermeneutik.* Tubingen: Mohr, 1975.

Grimm, G. *Rezeptionsgeschichte. Grundlegung einer Theorie.* München: Wilhelm Fink, 1977.

Gunkel, G. *Die Psalmen*. Göttinger Handkommentar zum Alten Testament, II.2. Göttingen: Vandenhoeck & Ruprecht, 1926⁴.

——— and J. Begrich. *Einleitung in die Psalmen: Die Gattungen der religiosen Lyrik Israels*. Göttinger Handkommentar zum Alten Testament, 2. Göttingen: Vandenhoeck & Ruprecht, 1933.

Harper, J. S. "Old Testament Spirituality." Pages 311–26 in *Exploring Christian Spirituality. An Ecumenical Reader*. Edited by K. J. Collins. Grand Rapids: Baker, 2000.

Knierim, R. P. *The Task of Old Testament Theology. Substance, Method, and Cases*. Grand Rapids: Eerdmans, 1995.

Kourie, C. "What Is Christian Spirituality?" Pages 7–33 in *Christian Spirituality in South Africa*. Edited by C. Kourie and L. Kretzschmar. Pietermaritzburg: Cluster Publications, 2000.

Kuhn, T. S. *The Structure of Scientific Revolutions*. Second edition. Chicago: University of Chicago Press, 1970.

Küng, H. *Christ sein*. München: R. Piper, 1974.

Lombaard, C. J. S. "The Old Testament between Diachrony and Synchrony: Two Reasons for Favouring the Former." Pages 61–70 in *South African Perspectives on the Pentateuch between Synchrony and Diachrony*. Edited by J. H. le Roux and E. Otto. New York: T&T Clark, 2007.

———. "Genealogies and Spiritualities in Genesis 4:17–22, 4:25–26, 5:1–32." Pages 146–64 in *The Spirit That Moves. Orientation and Issues in Spirituality*. Edited by P. G. R. de Villiers, C. Kourie and C. S. J. Lombaard. *Acta Theologia* Supplementum 8. Bloemfontein: University of the Free State Press, 2006.

———. "South African Perspectives on the Communication of the Bible in Church and Society." Ph.D. diss., North-West University, Potchefstroom Campus, 2004.

———. "Four South Africans' Proposals for a Central Theme to 'Scriptural Spirituality.'" *Scriptura* 88, no. 1 (2005): 139–50.

———. "The Old Testament in Christian Spirituality: Perspectives on the Undervaluation of the Old Testament in Christian Spirituality." *HTS Teologiese Studies/Theological Studies* 59, no. 2 (2003): 433–50.

Mowinckel, S. *The Psalms in Israel's Worship*. Oxford: Blackwell, 1962.

———. *Psalmenstudien, I–VI.* Kristiania: J. Dybwad, 1922–1924.

Nowell, I. "Review of *The Spirituality of the Psalms* by Carrol Stuhlmueller." *Worship* 77, no. 5 (2003): 479–80.

Ollenburger, B. C., E. A. Martens and G. F. Hasel, eds. *The Flowering of Old Testament Theology. A Reader in Twentieth-Century Old Testament Theology, 1930–1990.* Surveys in Biblical and Theological Study 1. Winona Lake: Eisenbrauns, 1992.

Peale, N. V. *The Power of Positive Thinking*. New York: Simon & Schuster Adult Publishing, 1952.

Schneiders, S. M. "Scripture and Spirituality." Pages 1–20 in *Christian Spirituality: Origins to the Twelfth Century*. Edited by B. McGinn, J. Meyendorff and J. Leclerq. London: SCM, 1985.

Sipkema, E. and K. Lelyveld. "De Regel van de H. Benedictus en het Gebruik van de Psalmen. Een Spiritualiteit van de Psalmen." Pages 131–38 in *Amsterdamse cahiers voor exegese van de Bijbel en zijn traditie*s 18, 2000.

Snyman, S. D. "Spiritualiteit—'n Perspektief uit die Ou Testament." *In die Skriflig* 31, no. 4 (1997): 375–87.

Sorg, R. "The Spirituality of the Psalms." Pages 529–41 in *Orate Fratres* 22.12, 1948.

Stuhlmueller, C. *The Spirituality of the Psalms*. Collegeville, Minn.: Liturgical Press, 2002.

———. *Psalms 1 and 2*. Message of Biblical Theology series; Old Testament Message 21 and 22. Wilmington: Michael Glazier, 1983.

Thiselton, A. C. *New Horizons in Hermeneutics*. Grand Rapids: Zondervan, 1992.

Von Rad, G. *Theologie des Alten Testaments, Band 1: Die Theologie der geschichtlichen Überlieferungen Israels.* Fünfte, durchgesehen Auflage. München: Chr. Kaiser Verlag, 1962.

Waaijman, K. *Mystiek in de Psalmen.* Serie Mystieke Teksten en Thema's, 22. Baarn: Ten Have, 2004.

———. *Spiritualiteit: Vormen, Grondslagen, Methoden.* Gent: Carmelitana, 2000.

———. "The Soul as Spiritual Core Concept." *Spiritus* 6 (1996): 5–19.

———. *De Mystiek van Ik en Jij. Een Nieuwe Vertaling van "Ich und Du" van Martin Buber.* Kampen: Kok, 1990.

———. *Psalmen over de Schepping : Psalmen 8, 29, 33, 65, 74, 104, 136, 139, 147, 148.* Kampen: Kok, 1989.

———. *Psalmen over de Uittocht : Het Lied van Mirjam, het Lied van Mozes, Psalmen 66, 68, 77, 78, 80, 81, 95, 105, 106, 114, 135.* Kampen: Kok, 1983.

———. *Psalmen by Ziekte en Genezing.* Kampen: Kok, 1981.

———. *Psalmen over Recht en Onrecht : Psalmen 3, 4, 5, 7, 11, 17, 23, 26, 27, 57, 63.* Kampen: Kok, 1980.

Waaijman, C. J. *De Mystiek van Ik en Jij: Een Nieuwe Vertaling van "Ich und Du" van Martin Buber met Inleiding en Uitleg en een Doordenking van het Systeem dat Eraan ten Grondslag Ligt.* Proefschrift, Katholieke Universiteit Nijmegen; Utrecht: Bijleveld, 1976.

Westermann, C. *Genesis 1–11.* Biblischer Kommentar Altes Testament 1/1. Neukirchen-Vluyn: Neukirchener Verlag, 1983^3.

———. *Lob und Klage in den Psalmen.* 5., erw. Aufl. Göttingen: Vandenhoeck & Ruprecht, 1977.

Wölber, H.-O. "Der Königsweg der Spiritualität. Gedanken zur Frömmigkeit aus der Bibel." *Evangelische Kommentare* 9/12 (1976): 724–27.

Zenger, E. *Psalmen Auslegungen, I.* Freiburg: Herder, 2003.

Genealogies and Spiritualities in Genesis 4:17–22, 4:25–26, 5:1–32[*]

ABSTRACT
The three genealogies in Gen 4:17–22, 4:25–26 and 5:1–32 show different intentions: the first aims (amongst other purposes) to give an aetiology of the trades, the second wants to stress the importance of a new beginning, the third seeks to relate Adam to Noah. Each of these approaches to genealogy has a different intent; each aims to indicate a different aspect of God's care. Each thus evidences an own (though not unrelated) configuration of faith; that is, a different spirituality.

1. Of Faith in Old Testament Times, the Study of Spirituality, and Genealogy Scholarship

Recent Old Testament scholarship has increasingly become aware of the variety of configurations of faith within ancient Israel. This diversity does not involve simply a rather straightforward growth in the faith of Israel from one form of belief in God to, presumably, a more advanced form of belief in God. Such a *heilsgeschichtliche* approach—in the earlier sense of the term[1]— would be akin to "the concept of progressive revelation, a view which regarded Old Testament history as a process of divine education of the Israelite nation."[2]

---

[*] This essay was initially presented as a paper at the congress of the International Organization for the Study of the Old Testament, in August 2004, at the University of Leiden, The Netherlands.
[1] Cf. F. Mildenberger, "Heilsgeschichte," *RGG*⁴, Band 3 (Tübingen: Mohr Siebeck, 2000), 1585.
[2] J. Rogerson, "Can a Doctrine of Providence Be Based on the Old Testament?" in *Ascribe to the Lord: Biblical and Other Studies in Memory of Peter C. Craigie* (ed. P. C. Craigie, L. M. Eslinger and G. Taylor; JSOT Suppl. 67; Sheffield: JSOT Press, 1988), 537; cf. C. J. S. Lombaard, "The Old Testament in Christian Spirituality: Perspectives on the Undervaluation of the Old Testament

Rather, Old Testament scholarship has made us increasingly aware of different forms of faith within ancient Israel at different times, as well as such different expressions competing with one another at the same time. Particularly useful in this regard have been formulations such as those by Rainer Albertz and Philip Davies, the former referring to "Religionsinterner Pluralismus," the latter to "Judaisms."[3] The diversity of the expressions of faith in Yahweh in ancient Israel finds expression within the Old Testament to the extent that, once recognised, it cannot be ignored.

Another interesting development of late in theological scholarship in general, is the strong rise in interest in the discipline of Spirituality. This is demonstrated, for instance, by the founding of two new academic societies for the study of Spirituality during this past year (2003): in Africa, the Spirituality Association of South Africa, and in Europe, the European Association for the Study of Spirituality. In both cases, the Dutch scholar Kees Waaijman, who has been working in the field of Spirituality for some four decades,[4] has been instrumental in setting up these societies.

This growth in interest in Spirituality[5] may provide us with yet another avenue, alongside proposals such as those by Albertz and

---

in Christian Spirituality," *HTS Teologiese Studies/Theological Studies* 59, no. 2 (2003): 441.

[3] See R. Albertz, *Persönliche Frömmigkeit und offizielle Religion: Religionsinterner Pluralismus in Israel und Babylon* (Stuttgart: Calwer Verlag, 1978); and P. R. Davies, "Scenes from the Early History of Judaism," in *The Triumph of Elohim: From Yahwisms to Judaisms* (ed. D. V. Edelman; Grand Rapids: Eerdmans [American edition], 1996), 145–82. Neither of these is unique in the points they make: Albertz acknowledges as much in the opening paragraph of his Vorwort, and Davies takes his terminology from a number of authors he refers to in his footnotes.

[4] Cf. particularly K. Waaijman, *Spiritualiteit: Vormen, Grondslagen, Methoden* (Gent: Carmelitana, 2000).

[5] Spirituality may be described as, in essence, the ways in which faith finds expression in human thought and action. Spirituality and faith are thus not synonymous: pisteological orientation is, for these purposes, accepted as the

Davies, with which to analyse the faith of ancient Israel, as reflected in the Hebrew Bible. To be sure, the tone set by Albertz and Davies and others—despite differences in where they set the bar for accepting material as historically useful—should in my opinion be adhered to: that a fundamentally historical approach is the key to studying the spiritualities we encounter in the Bible. The concern that an approach which takes Spirituality as its express point of departure may gloss over exegetical and historical minutiae, is not unfounded.[6] However, I remain convinced[7] that working with precisely these minutiae will lead Old Testament scholarship to productive insights on the ways in which Israel related to Yahweh, and on how this faith was then related to later generations (be it orally, in writing, or through editing). After all,

---

given, with the subject matter of Spirituality being the cognitive, emotional, behavioural, and other results springing forth in certain particular ways, both conditioned and creative, from this existential orientation. For fuller descriptions of the concept of spirituality, cf. C. Kourie, "What Is Christian Spirituality?" in *Christian Spirituality in South Africa* (ed. C. Kourie and L. Kretzschmar; Pietermaritzburg: Cluster Publications, 2000), 9–33; J. W. Oostenbrink, "Gereformeerde Spiritualiteit as Korporatiewe Spiritualiteit," *In die Skriflig* 33, no. 3 (1999): 367–83; D. Marmion, *A Spirituality of Everyday Faith: A Theological Investigation of the Notion of Spirituality in Karl Rahner* (Louvain Theological and Pastoral Monographs 23; Louvain: Peeters Press, 1998), 3–40; M. Downey, *Understanding Christian Spirituality* (New York: Paulist Press, 1997), 5–29; K. Waaijman, "Toward a Phenomenological Definition of Spirituality," *Studies in Spirituality* 3 (1993): 5–57; D. J. Smit, "Kan Spiritualiteit Beskryf Word?" *Ned. Geref. Teologiese Tydskrif* 30, no. 1 (1989): 85–92.

[6] Cf. Lombaard, "The Old Testament in Christian Spirituality," 439–40; W. Brueggemann, *Spirituality of the Psalms* (Augsburg: Fortress, 2002), 59; J. L. Houlden, "Bible, Spirituality of the," in *Westminster Dictionary of Spirituality* (ed. G. S. Wakefield; Philadelphia: Westminster, 1983), 48. Albertz has for related reasons expressed similar reservations about Old Testament Theologies (see R. Albertz, *Religionsgeschichte Israels in alttestamentlicher Zeit* [Teil 1; Göttingen: Vandenhoeck & Ruprecht, 1992], 20–32).

[7] Cf. Lombaard, "The Old Testament in Christian Spirituality," 440

the faith of ancient Israel was nothing if not historical.[8] What is more, for scholars so inclined, such study of the faith we find reflected in the Old Testament may well prove valuable, by means of parallels and analogies, for considered use in modern contexts of faith.[9]

A third recent trend important for our purposes here, is a specific development in Old Testament genealogy research. Academic writings have tended to focus attention on historical (that is, referential and numerical)[10] and anthropological[11] issues.[12] Of late, though, and building forth on these publications, a greater exploration of the theological possibilities of Old Testament genealogies is found.[13] This explicit search for theology in

---

[8] Although, not, of course, in the modernist sense. Cf. G. von Rad, *Theologie des Alten Testaments, Band 1: Die Theologie der geschichtlichen Überlieferungen Israels* (Fünfte, durchgesehen Auflage; München: Chr. Kaiser Verlag, 1962), 118–25.

[9] See e.g. A. Nolan, *Biblical Spirituality* (Springs: The Order of Preachers [Southern Africa], 1982); cf. C. J. S. Lombaard, "Four South Africans' Proposals for a Central Theme to 'Scriptural Spirituality,'" *Scriptura* 88, no. 1 (2005): 139–50.

[10] See e.g. R. Heinzerling, "'Einweihung' durch Henoch? Die Bedeutung der Altersangaben in Genesis 5," *Zeitschrift für alttestamentlichen Wissenschaft* 110 (1998), 581–89; and D. V. Etz, "The Numbers of Genesis V 2–31: A Suggested Conversion and Its Implications," *Vetus Testamentum* XLIII, no. 2 (1993): 171–87.

[11] See e.g. T. J. Prewitt, "Kinship Structures and the Genesis Genealogies," *Journal of Near Eastern Studies* 40, no. 2 (1981): 87–98 and K. R. Andriolo, "A Structural Analysis of Genealogy and World View in the Old Testament," *American Anthropologist* 75 (1973): 1657–69.

[12] The latter is fraught with at least as many difficulties as the former—cf. M. D. Johnson, *The Purpose of the Biblical Genealogies, with Special Reference to the Setting of the Genealogies of Jesus* (2d ed.; Cambridge: Cambridge University Press, 1988), xiii–xiv.

[13] See e.g., K. F. Plum, "Genealogy as Theology," *Scandinavian Journal of the Old Testament* 1 (1989), 66–89; and J. Vermeylen, "La Descendance de Caïn et le Descendance d'Abel (Gen 4:17–26 + 5:28b–29)," *Zeitschrift für alttestamentlichen Wissenschaft* 103 (1991): 175–93. Based inter-culturally, see

genealogy to a greater extent opens up avenues for finding further meaning in these texts.

In this essay, I seek to bring together these three recent developments: the sensitivity to the multiple expressions of the faith we find reflected in the Old Testament, the increasing research interest in Spirituality, and the search for extended meaning in Old Testament genealogies. I have therefore chosen three Genesis genealogies—Gen 4:17–22, 4:25–26 and 5:1–32—to show how each has a different intent. Each aims to indicate a different aspect of God's care. Each of these genealogies thus evidences an own (though not unrelated) configuration of faith; that is, a different spirituality.

2. Some Remarks on Genealogies in General

Far from merely being lists of blood relations,[14] genealogies in cultures ancient and modern serve/d multiple purposes. These include matters of law, inheritance, politics and diplomacy, economics, ideology, administration, theology, identity, cultural criticism, historical and societal (re)presentation, association, power, status, aetiology, tradition, the military[15]—usually in one

---

R. De W. Oosthuizen, "African Experience of Time and Its Compatibility with the Old Testament View of Time as Suggested in the Genealogy of Genesis 5," *Old Testament Essays* 6 (1993): 190–204; and M. J. Paul, "Genesis 4:17–24: A Case-Study in Eisegesis," *Tyndale Bulletin* 47, no. 1 (1996): 143–62.

[14] British comedian Spike Milligan writes humorously of the "much begatting" one encounters in the Old Testament (see S. Milligan, *The Old Testament according to Spike Milligan* [London: Penguin, 1993]).

[15] If one wanted to choose between these options, as used to be the case in earlier research—and still is with e.g., K. Frankenfeld (*Genealogie der Bibel. Ein biblicher Stammbaum* [Frankfurt am Main: Haag und Herchen, 1997]) who is bent on pinpointing the exact biblical genealogy from Adam to Jesus—it would have to be done in respect of a specific genealogy, not genealogies in general, and—advancing on Wilson (see R. R. Wilson, "The Old Testament Genealogies in Recent Research," in *"I studied inscriptions from before the Flood": Ancient Near Eastern, Literary, and Linguistic Approaches to Genesis*

sense or another to provide legitimacy to some current state of affairs.[16] Genealogy, as Aufrecht observes,[17] is thus more than the patronymic phrase "X son of Y": once this phrase is multiplied, it becomes genealogy; once it is genealogy, it gains multiple denotations.

Despite Noth's distinction between genuine and secondary genealogies resting on the no longer accepted theory that names in genealogies are of necessity related to more extensive histories,[18] what remains important is his recognition that at least some genealogies serve narrative purposes.[19] The value of this insight is

---

1–11 [ed. R. S. Hess and D. T. Tsumura; Winona Lake: Eisenbrauns, 1994], 204)—even then, distinguishing between these possibilities would have to be done with circumspection. For brief overviews of research into Old Testament genealogies, cf. e.g., Wilson, "The Old Testament Genealogies in Recent Research," 200–201; Plum, "Genealogy as Theology," 68[3 & 4].

[16] Cf. M. Oeming, *Das wahre Israel: Die "genealogische Vorhalle" 1 Chronik 1–9* (Stuttgart: Kohlhammer, 1990), 9–36; Wilson, "The Old Testament Genealogies in Recent Research," 213–15; R. R. Wilson, "Between 'Azel' and 'Azel': Interpreting the Biblical Genealogies," *Biblical Archeologist* 42, no. 1 (1979): 19; W. E. Aufrecht, "Genealogy and History in Ancient Israel," in *Ascribe to the Lord: Biblical and Other Studies in Memory of Peter C. Craigie* (ed. P. C. Craigie, L. M. Eslinger and G. Taylor; JSOT Suppl. 67; Sheffield: JSOT Press, 1988), 208–9, 215–18, 223; Andriolo, "A Structural Analysis of Genealogy and World View in the Old Testament," 1659.

[17] See Aufrecht, "Genealogy and History in Ancient Israel," 206–7.

[18] See M. Noth, *Uberlieferungsgeschichte des Pentateuch* (2. Auflage; Stuttgart: Kohlhammer, 1948), 232–37; compare H. Gunkel (*Die Urgeschichte und die Patriarchen. Die Schriften des Alten Testaments 1/1* [Göttingen: Vandenhoeck & Ruprecht, 1911], 73) with G. von Rad (*Die Priesterschrift im Hexateuch* [Stuttgart: Kohlhammer. BWANT IV/13, 1934], 35) for, respectively, seeing this relationship as condensation or expansion; cf. also R. B. Robinson, "Literary Functions of the Genealogies in Genesis," *Catholic Biblical Quarterly* 48, no. 1 (1986): 603[15].

[19] See Wilson, "The Old Testament Genealogies in Recent Research," 202. This insight has seen further developments in structural analyses of genealogies in Genesis; cf. e.g., Johnson, *The Purpose of the Biblical Genealogies*, and N. Steinberg, "The Genealogical Framework of the Family Stories in Genesis," *Semeia* 45 (1989): 41–50.

that genealogies are now accorded interpretative value beyond what their significance in terms of historical accurateness may or may not be.[20] The historical setting in which genealogies were re/created (as reflected by the reconstructed textual history) have at least as much significance as the genealogical plot. Put differently: the history of the telling is central to the history of the told. Put differently again (in the language of Wilson[21]): the function of a genealogy is essential to understanding it.[22]

It remains interesting to note that in ancient Near Eastern societies priests were often the carriers of genealogies, probably because of the writing abilities, the social standing, and the political roles of priestly groups. This detail is open to assorted interpretations (cf. Ezra 2:62/Neh 7:64!). Suffice it for the moment to note that the multiplicity of denotations of Old Testament genealogies is perhaps a prime instance of its unmodernist fusion of religion and all other aspects of life.[23]

3. Initial Remarks on the Three Genealogies

In the brief descriptions of the three genealogies following below, I will not be pointing out all the detailed exegetical and interpretative intricacies on which I have based all my decisions. Rather, I will relate in a few words the contents of each genealogy,

---

[20] That is, Albright's historical reliability of genealogies (among other texts) versus Wellhausen's view that it is a social—or, in Laato's language, "ideological"—rather than a historical genre (see W. F. Albright, *From the Stone Age to Christianity* [2d ed.; New York: Doubleday Anchor Books, 1957], 72–76, cf. 239; J. Wellhausen, *Prolegomena zur Geschichte Israels* [6. Ausgabe; Berlin: De Gruyter, 1927], 206–7]; A. Laato, "The Levitical Genealogies in 1 Chronicles 5–6 and the Formation of Levitical Ideology in Post-Exilic Judah," *Journal for the Study of the Old Testament* 62 [June 1994]: 77–78). Cf. Wilson, "Between 'Azel' and 'Azel.'" 11–12, 21.
[21] Wilson, "The Old Testament Genealogies in Recent Research," 215, 222–23.
[22] Still Gunkel, after all these years…
[23] Cf. Plum, "Genealogy as Theology," 86.

en route to indicating the respective theologies and, from this, spiritualities we find reflected here. Where pertinent, though, I will briefly argue a point or refer to an interesting interpretation which occurs in the literature.

To start with precisely such a point: it seems clear to me that Gen 4:17–26 cannot be read as a single text. Thematically, the three sections of 4:17–22 (genealogy), 4:23–24 (the curse of Lamech), and 4:25–26 (genealogy) are quite diverse. Reading the three sections as one (as e.g. Bryan does),[24] joins together too many lines of genre, theme, and theology. The composite nature of this text is just too pronounced for such a treatment. Hence, I treat 4:17–22 and 4:25–26 independently.

3.1 Genesis 4:17–22 (Cainite genealogy; J)

Traditionally referred to as the Cainite genealogy, the "cultural genealogy" would probably be a better label in this instance. For here we have:

- In 4:17, Cain and his wife producing Enoch, and Cain[25] then going on to build a city, named for Enoch.[26]

---

[24] See D. T. Bryan, "A Re-evaluation of Gen 4 and 5 in light of Recent Studies in Genealogical Fluidity," *Zeitschrift für alttestamentlichen Wissenschaft* 99 (1987): 186–87.
[25] Despite objections (cf. e.g., R. R. Wilson, *Genealogy and History in the Biblical World* [Yale Near Eastern Researches 7; New Haven: Yale University Press, 1977], 157–58; and Wilson, "Between 'Azel' and 'Azel,'" 19, where the circularity of his argument renders it unpersuasive), the possibility that this genealogy may reflect Kenite tradition, and hence be an important consideration in the theory of the Kenite origins of Yahwism, remains intriguing; cf. Johnson, *The Purpose of the Biblical Genealogies*, 92.
[26] Wilson (in *Genealogy and History in the Biblical World*, 139–41) briefly weighs the problems of interpretation of 4:17, namely the possibility that the closing reference in 4:17 to Enoch is a gloss, thus opening up the etymologically satisfying possibility that the city referred to would be called Irad, which parallels Eridu, the first pre-Flood city in Mesopotamian narratives. Sasson favours a pun as the solution to the different but similar names in 4:17 and 5:15

- In 4:18, in the briefest possible manner, the birth of four new generations is named, from Enoch to Lamech. From Lamech, with his two wives Adah and Zillah (4:19),[27] spring the initiators of four other parts of culture:
    o in 4:20, Jabal (son of Adah), is the first of the tent-dwelling livestock farmers;
    o in 4:21, Jubal (son of Adah), is the first of the musicians (strings and pipes);
    o in 4:22, Tubal-Cain (son of Zillah), is the first metal smith; and
    o in 4:22, we also find the enigmatic three-word concluding phrase וַאֲחוֹת תּוּבַל־קַיִן נַעֲמָה: (thus, also daughter of Zillah).[28] This brief sentence has usually been ascribed to the persistence of a strand of tradition, awkwardly holding on for dear life

(see J. M. Sasson, "A Genealogical 'Convention' in Biblical Chronography?" *Zeitschrift für alttestamentlichen Wissenschaft* 90 (1978): 174). Genealogical fluidity (see below) would offer another possible solution.

[27] The atypical inclusion of the wives' names in 4:19 has been ascribed to the names being carried over from Lamech's song in 4:23 (see e.g. Wilson, *Genealogy and History in the Biblical World*, 141). The cohesive character of the narrative unit of 4:19–22, however, does not really warrant such a conjecture in this instance.

[28] Andersen's theory on genealogical indicators of importance falters here (among some other problems with his broad structural theory on Genesis), in that Naamah should be encountered more readily in Genesis, and not only here, based on his theory—cf. T. D. Andersen, "Genealogical Prominence and the Structure of Genesis," in *Biblical Hebrew and Discourse Linguistics* (ed. R. D. Bergen. Dallas: Summer Institute of Linguistics, 1994), 244.

A commonly held view, briefly referred to above, is that each of the names given in a genealogy would have been connected to a broader narrative, known to the Yahwist and his contemporaries. Wilson (in *Genealogy and History in the Biblical World*, 147[28], 163) seeks to refine this view by contending that only those genealogical notes which are accompanied by brief descriptions may be adduced to prior, broader narratives. However, Wilson's criticism that the common view is never supported by evidence is equally true of his proposal. Both alternatives thus remain possible.

here, or to the Yahwist's need for narratological/structural balance (i.e., a second child for Zillah too).[29] As it turns out, both possibilities may be correct (though not for the reasons they were proposed): continuing the pattern in 4:20–22 of a connection between name and profession, Naamah (= "Giver-of-pleasure"[30]) may well, according to Vermeylen,[31] be the initiator of prostitution.[32]

---

[29] Cf. Wilson, *Genealogy and History in the Biblical World*, 144.

[30] Brichto recognises the meaning, but not the professional implications raised here (see H. C. Brichto, *The Names of God: Poetic Readings in Biblical Beginnings* [New York: Oxford University Press, 1998], 305).

[31] See Vermeylen, "La Descendance de Caïn et le Descendance d'Abel," 176, 182. Vermeylen takes this interesting possibility from the 1973 edition of the Jerusalem Bible. The English edition (see *The New Jerusalem Bible* [London: Darton, Longman & Todd, 1985], 23i), preserves this interpretation, but does so through fine, nuanced formulation, without using the term prostitution—thus copying the style of the Yahwist here.

[32] This unforeseen interpretation renders earlier descriptions of these "originators" as "father of..." (e.g. Wilson, *Genealogy and History in the Biblical World*, 142) somewhat awkward. It also clears up other earlier problems: probably because Hess (see R. S. Hess, "The Genealogies of Genesis 1–11 and Comparative Literature," in *"I studied inscriptions from before the Flood": Ancient Near Eastern, Literary, and Linguistic Approaches to Genesis 1–11* [ed. R. S. Hess and D. T. Tsumura. Winona Lake: Eisenbrauns, 1994], 59) draws heavily on the distinction in Wilson (*Genealogy and History in the Biblical World*, 9–10, 18–37), who depends on Malamat (see A. Malamat, "King Lists of the Old Babylonian Period and Biblical Genealogies," in *"I studied inscriptions from before the Flood": Ancient Near Eastern, Literary, and Linguistic Approaches to Genesis 1–11* [ed R. S. Hess and D. T. Tsumura. Winona Lake: Eisenbrauns, 1994], 184–85), between segmented and linear genealogies, and ignores the distinction between narrative and list genealogies (see C. Westermann, *Genesis 1–11* [Biblischer Kommentar Altes Testament 1/1. Neukirchen-Vluyn: Neukirchener Verlag, 1974], 8–24, 438; and S. Tengström, *Die Toledotformel und die literarische Struktur der priesterlichen Erweiterungschicht im Pentateuch* [Uppsala: CWK Gleerup, 1981], 19–21). Hess seeks repetitive patterns, and finds little in Gen 4:17–22 and 4:25–26; only

When taken as a genealogy which has as its most important purpose the aetiology of certain facets of culture, the way in which the seven generations are referred to here seems less important to understanding these verses.[33] It remains true, of course, that only in the last generation, with Lamech's offspring, does the linear style change to a segmented style: recording different children and not only the main genealogical line.[34] However, the fact that a linear and segmented style are mixed, as are a list and a narrative style,[35] was not the prime concern of the Yahwist here.[36] These references—4:17, 4:20–22, and 4:26—are primarily what Golka would term aetiological notes: aetiologies without narratives, yet universal in scope (referring to events that touch the whole of humanity), affirming the present by extrapolating into the past,

---

4:18 evidences such a pattern (see Hess, "The Genealogies of Genesis 1–11 and Comparative Literature," 60). Vermeylen would now offer him one more pattern. In lighter vein: despite common wisdom, this interpretation also renders Naamah's profession only one of the oldest in the world.

[33] Cf. Hess, "The Genealogies of Genesis 1–11 and Comparative Literature," 64; Westermann, *Genesis 1–11*, 439; Sasson, "A Genealogical 'Convention' in Biblical Chronography?" 173.

[34] Wilson, *Genealogy and History in the Biblical World*, 138.

[35] Cf. Westermann, *Genesis 1–11*, 8–24, 438; and Tengström, *Die Toledotformel*, 19–21. Distinctions such as these, and those by Noth (in *Uberlieferungsgeschichte des Pentateuch*, 232–37), Malamat ("King Lists of the Old Babylonian Period and Biblical Genealogies," 184–185) and others, between kinds of genealogies, betray a clear scientific intention to refine this genre. Hence, declaring the whole of the Bible as "eigentlich selbst schon eine Genealogie" (see Frankenfeld, *Genealogie der Bibel*, 7) is unhelpful in this regard.

[36] These considerations do lend further credence to the Yahwist's role as editor, rather than as author.

ordering life rather than questioning it.[37] The past thus authorises the present.[38]

The purpose of this genealogy is thus, on the one hand, to pinpoint the origins of key parts of ancient Near Eastern society: urban and rural settlement, music,[39] metal work and sex work (and, in 4:26b, religion). The implication this would have for the Yahwist's intended audience is to indicate these activities as ancient and, therefore, legitimate. This stands in distinction to other ancient Near Eastern narratives on the origins of components of civilisation, which tend to be mythological in nature.[40] J, however, posts these developments *in* history, related to human figures. This is an important theological and anthropological point, demythologising society's activities.[41]

Because this pericope follows directly on the Cain-Abel fratricide narrative, its interpretational history has tended to see these cultural/technological developments as negative.[42] The text itself gives no indication of this, though. Yet, this text, together with 4:25–26, leads Paul[43] to the following insightful remarks:

> The manner in which the story is told indicates a correlation between man's rejection of serving God and the introduction of technology… Cain's descendents are dedicated to

---

[37] See F. W. Golka, "The Aetiologies in the Old Testament, Part 2," *Vetus Testamentum* 27, no. 1 (1977), 44; read with F. W. Golka, "The Aetiologies in the Old Testament, Part 1," *Vetus Testamentum* 26, no. 4 (1976): 411.

[38] Golka, "The Aetiologies in the Old Testament, Part 2," 46–47.

[39] Music as a profession, rather than as a phenomenon; hence: "entertainment"— see Sasson, "A Genealogical 'Convention' in Biblical Chronography?" 173.

[40] Cf. Wilson, *Genealogy and History in the Biblical World,* 149–55 and Wilson, "Between 'Azel' and 'Azel,'" 13–18 for an overview.

[41] Could it be that we have here also a sociological point, namely the endorsement of diversity within society, that lies as (another) motivation behind this text?

[42] Cf. Paul, "Genesis 4:17–24: A Case-Study in Eisegesis," 144–60.

[43] Ibid., 161–62; cf. Westermann, *Genesis 1–11,* 453.

technological progress yet reject God, but Seth's descendents call upon the name of the Lord... that is of enormous significance for our own involvement in science and in society.

Naturally, the suggestion by Vermeylen[44] that Naamah is the mother of prostitution, would make such theologising for modern times more difficult, given moral sensitivities to such practice. Such objections could read into the comparatively understated formulation of 4:22b that the Genesis text itself gives a hint of dissatisfaction. However, whether that is the case remains a matter for further investigation.

3.2 Genesis 4:25–26 (Sethite genealogy; J/D?)

This, the shortest of the Genesis genealogies, filled with narrative,[45] relates four matters: first, that Adam and his wife bore another son, Seth; second, that by the grace of Elohim Seth replaces the murdered Abel;[46] third, that Seth has a son, Enosh; and fourth, that prayer to Yahweh then began.[47]

Clearly, the theme of this genealogy has to do with new beginnings. This may even be reflected in the word play of Enosh

---

[44] See Vermeylen, "La Descendance de Caïn et le Descendance d'Abel," 176, 182.

[45] Cf. Hess, "The Genealogies of Genesis 1–11 and Comparative Literature," 60.

[46] Seth's name indication is followed by the explanatory note that Seth replaces Abel—a contradiction with Gen 5:3 where Seth is the first son; cf. Wilson, *Genealogy and History in the Biblical World,* 145.

[47] The beginnings of Yahwist faith described here does not accord with either Gen 4:4–5 or Exod 6:1–7 (cf. e.g. Wilson, *Genealogy and History in the Biblical World,* 145). Proposals, such as, that we have here only the first *public* worship or, that worship is now renewed, do not take seriously the literary independence of the traditions reflected in these texts. Cf. further Westermann, *Genesis 1–11,* 461–66.

("man") on Adam ("man"),[48] and is indicated by the initiation of the cult, which indicates a positive human-divine relationship. On a grander scale, Von Rad's famous theological construct[49] of Genesis as a history of the growth of sin[50] offers us another perspective for interpreting this genealogy. For here we have an instance of a new beginning (a concept which is, of course, of central importance within the Old Testament and, broader, to Christian theology). With Seth no victim of the curse of Cain (Gen 4:11–12), with prayer to Yahweh originating in the very next generation after Seth,[51] and because there is further offspring (= blessing), the overriding theme characterising this genealogy may be formulated as: "harmony restored," or more theologically formulated: "grace."

Although this genealogy is usually ascribed to J, Vermeylen makes an interesting case for a deuteronomistic—that is, in essence, a theological—redaction of 4:17–24 and 4:25–26 + 5:28b–29 (thus, the latter two taken together, with 5:28b–29 relocated from its present position to follow on 4:24–26 directly).[52] This redaction stresses God's justice in rejecting exilic Israel for their Cain-like deeds, yet includes beginning anew via Seth.[53]

---

[48] See Sasson, "A Genealogical 'Convention' in Biblical Chronography?" 175; Vermeylen, "La Descendance de Caïn et le Descendance d'Abel," 187.

[49] Cf. also, with some differences, D. J. A. Clines, *The Theme of the Pentateuch* (JSOT Suppl. 10. Sheffield: JSOT Press, 1978).

[50] Referred to also by Wilson, Genealogy and History in the Biblical World, 155; and N. A. Bailey, "Some Literary and Grammatical Aspects of Genealogies," in *Biblical Hebrew and Discourse Linguistics* (ed. R. D. Bergen; Dallas: Summer Institute of Linguistics, 1994), 269.

[51] Wilson, *Genealogy and History in the Biblical World,* 155–56.

[52] See Vermeylen, "La Descendance de Caïn et le Descendance d'Abel," 188–91.

[53] This attractive possibility (see below) would call for greater nuance in remarks such as those by Johnson (in *The Purpose of the Biblical Genealogies,* 3) on D and genealogy.

3.3 Genesis 5:1–32 (P)

This independent,[54] narrative[55] genealogy starts "beyond the realm of actual history,"[56] by referring back to the Priestly creation narrative of Gen 1:1–2:4a.[57]

Starting with Adam, and concluding with the three sons of Noah, Gen 5 offers a highly structured account of twelve generations. The usual structure of this writing is:

- Name and age of X when he fathers Y (and Y is X's oldest son);
- After the birth of Y, X lived a certain number of years longer, fathered more children (unnamed and uncounted, but of both genders);
- The total age of X is then given, and his death indicated.[58]

Apart from 1), the introductory verses (5:1–3) linking this genealogy with Gen 1, two brief narratives break the structural monotony of Gen 5, namely 2), 5:24 (Enoch being taken away by Elohim) and 3), 5:29 (indicating the approaching role of Noah)—often ascribed to P preserving J-elements in his genealogical editing.[59] Furthermore, 4), an atypical presentation is given of the next generation in the closing verse of Gen 5 (in that three sons are

---

[54] Westermann, *Genesis 1–11*, 458.
[55] Tengström, *Die Toledotformel*, 19–21. Narrative, in the sense that, except for "Noah and his three sons, all the names in the genealogy also appear in some form in the Yahwist's genealogical narrative" (see Wilson, *Genealogy and History in the Biblical World*, 163).
[56] Malamat, "King Lists of the Old Babylonian Period and Biblical Genealogies," 187.
[57] Cf. Robinson, "Literary Functions of the Genealogies in Genesis," 599–600.
[58] Cf. Hess, "The Genealogies of Genesis 1–11 and Comparative Literature," 61; Oeming, *Das wahre Israel*, 73; Tengström, *Die Toledotformel*, 21; Wilson, *Genealogy and History in the Biblical World*, 159–60; Westermann, *Genesis 1–11*, 470.
[59] See e.g. Wilson, *Genealogy and History in the Biblical World*, 160.

98   *The Old Testament and Christian Spirituality*

introduced to the reader, rather than the main genealogical line only).

A note on each of these four narrative interpolations to this otherwise tightly structured genealogy, is in order:

1   P, here as in Gen 1, offers a reinterpretation of J's creation narrative, in this case emphasising God's blessing of the generations, which includes, implicitly, the multiplication itself (Gen 5:2) and, explicitly, the indication that creation in God's image (cf. Gen 1:26–27) is continued into the next generation/s (Gen 5:3). This, Wilson argues, is a decidedly more positive view than J's switch between sin and grace.[60]

2   It does not seem necessary to attribute 5:24 to a non-P hand because of stylistic reasons, that is, because of its narrative nature: the usual structure of the Gen 5 genealogical notes remains intact here; the וַיָּמֹת-note is merely replaced by what the tradition regarding Enoch had to offer in its place. Neither does the theological stand indicate a hand other than P. Enoch's being taken by God without dying differs from Sumerian and Akkadian parallels in the theologically important respect that it is God who is the subject of the action here.[61] This accords well with a broader theme in P, of God providing certain pious men. This theme has as its purpose the encouragement of the exilic community to whom P is addressed.[62]

3   Vermeylen proposes that 5:28b–29 should be read in direct continuation of 4:26.[63] The content of 5:28b–29 certainly

---

[60] Wilson, *Genealogy and History in the Biblical World*, 163–64.
[61] See A. Schmit, "Zum Thema 'Entruckung' im Alten Testament," *Biblische Zeitschrift* 26 (1982): 41.
[62] Ibid., 43–44.
[63] Vermeylen, "La Descendance de Caïn et le Descendance d'Abel," 177–78. If this attractive proposal is generally accepted, it would force the re-examination of a great many analyses of the depth ("how many generations?") and number

would not argue against such an interpretation: this text alludes to Gen 3:17–19, which is J. Furthermore, unlike the case with 5:24, 5:29 constitutes a definite break in the usual Gen 5 genealogical style. From both these arguments, it follows that this is not inherently Priestly material. In addition, the styles of 4:25–26 and 5:28b–29 are compatible. The case could therefore be made strongly that 4:25–26 + 5:28b–29 is a deuteronomistic redaction of, respectively, J and P.[64] The purpose of this redaction, as indicated above, would be to underscore the theological theme of new beginnings.[65]

4 The brief narrative in Gen 5:32, constituting only the opening line of the usual Gen 5 genealogical pattern ("Name and age of X when he fathers Y"), and indicating the *three* sons of Noah, clearly has to do with the nature of this verse as introduction to the subsequent Noah story (Gen 6 ff.).

A last issue remains here: the similarities between the names in the Gen 4 and 5 genealogies are usually attributed to either— source critically—varying interpretations/applications of a basis genealogy, or—culturally—to genealogical fluidity.[66] The latter

---

("how many members mentioned in the genealogy?"; cf. Bryan, "A Re-evaluation of Gen 4 and 5," 185) of the Gen 4 and 5 genealogies.

[64] Vermeylen, "La Descendance de Caïn et le Descendance d'Abel," 188–91.

[65] Not to beg the question as to why the combined text would then later be divided into two, with 5:28b–29 placed in its current position: the most obvious possibility is that the reference to Noah in 5:30 tempted a later editor to commit the modification.

[66] Genealogical fluidity refers to the process by which a genealogy is edited (i.e., substitution, removal, addition; altering the spelling, order and relationship of names, etc.) in order to reflect new social or political circumstances. Whereas our modern sensibilities on authorship and copyright might shudder at such practices, this fluidity occurs quite naturally in an oral or written culture where genealogy serves to indicate/stabilise current social and other relationships, rather than to retain the past with historical accuracy. As Wilson continually pointed out in his publications on this matter, the *function* of a genealogy influences its form. Cf. Bryan, "A Re-evaluation of Gen 4 and 5," 180; Wilson,

generally offers a more satisfying explanation of variance. It also leaves us free to interpret the intentions of Gen 5 (*sans* verses 28b–29, as argued above) as a genealogy.

Apart from God's continued blessing and the explicit continuation in this genealogy of the concept of the image of God, mentioned above, a third and related theological thread here is the uniqueness of Israel. This genealogy (similar to 1 Chr 1–9, and different to Gen 10)[67] does not intend to indicate the unity of humanity. The current identity of Israel, during or after the exile, is related through the continued blessing of descendants to their ancient ancestry.[68] P seeks security for the present in the continuation with past generations.

4. Three Configurations of Faith

We have now taken a closer look at our three genealogies, indicating in each instance some theological dimensions inherent to the genealogy as well. It is quite clear that we have here three very different intentions expressed by means of the same genre. In a sense, genealogies could be described as a form of ancient Near Eastern wisdom: the world as known at present is summarised and

---

Genealogy and History in the Biblical World, 161–63; Hess, "The Genealogies of Genesis 1–11 and Comparative Literature," 64–65.

[67] In genealogies referring to other nations too, it is possible that the understanding of their shared heritage with Israel may reflect their understanding as well (Malamat, "King Lists of the Old Babylonian Period and Biblical Genealogies," 185).

[68] Cf. Oeming, *Das wahre Israel,* 108–209; cf. also Brodie who sees as part of a deliberately unifying pattern in Genesis a parallel between Gen 4:17–26 (taken as a single unit) and Gen 5 (see T. L. Brodie, "Genesis as Dialogue: Genesis' Twenty-Six Diptychs as a Key to Narrative Unity and Meaning," in *Studies in the Book of Genesis: Literature, Redaction and History* [ed. A. Wénin; Louvain: Leuven University Press; Uitgeverij Peeters; Bibliotheca Ephemeridum Theologicarum Lovaniensium CLV, 2001], 301. These parallel genealogies would both illustrate a turnaround from disharmony to restoration, a view that calls for some rather circuitous argumentation.

ordered.[69] However, as is the case with the varied intentions of different wisdom writings, what is unique to each genealogy should not be subsumed to the traits it shares with other expressions of the genre. Cognisance must be taken of both the general and the specific aspects of genealogies.

Old Testament genealogies may share certain form and function coordinates with genealogical lists in the greater ancient Near East. However, taken together, they also differ. For instance, whereas Sumerian, Assyrian and Babylonian royal genealogies place the rulers as direct descendants of the gods,[70] Canaanite genealogies tend not to do so.[71] Within this context, genealogy in Israel too was a demythologised enterprise.[72] The distinction between the world of God/the gods and the human world is maintained, though not with the interrelation between these worlds denied. This feature makes a relationship between the human and divine possible.[73]

---

[69] Oeming, *Das wahre Israel*, 208.
[70] See Wilson, *Genealogy and History in the Biblical World*, 56–119; cf. Oeming, *Das wahre Israel*, 23
[71] Wilson, *Genealogy and History in the Biblical World*, 119–25; Oeming, *Das wahre Israel*, 23; Westermann, *Genesis 1–11*, 11–12, 472.
[72] Oeming, *Das wahre Israel*, 35.
[73] It has become common to add two more general features: (1) whereas ancient Near Eastern genealogies in general relate to the political and religious elite only, the Genesis genealogies tend not to do so (see Hess, "The Genealogies of Genesis 1–11 and Comparative Literature," 65); and (2) the purpose of the Genesis genealogies is not to idealise the earlier/earliest generations (see Hess, "The Genealogies of Genesis 1–11 and Comparative Literature," 68). However, both these matters require further scrutiny. The detail that the genealogies were the work of priestly groups who had elite political and other aspirations draws into question the former assertion. In addition: though perhaps not idealised (because negative aspects may also be included in a genealogy), the earlier generations were important for the genealogists and their audience in that they (in)formed the identity of the later generations in various ways. Here is room for further refinement.

The question now is, how is this general relationship concretised in our three specific genealogies?

The Cainite genealogy (Gen 4:17–22), we have seen, is a cultural genealogy. Aetiological in nature, this genealogy affords current cultural practices legitimacy. Not explicitly related to God, but implicitly only, this reflects an earthy kind of atmosphere (the kind of description often related to J's Gen 2 creation narrative!). This is a "spirituality of the road"[74]—involved directly with the usual patterns of practices in the lives of ordinary people. These normal, daily habits are authentic: they come from ancient times, almost from the beginning of time. These practices are not religious *per se*: they do not come from gods, nor are the practices related to gods. These cultural artefacts stem from people, and have continued through the ages, by the grace of God, blessing each generation with a subsequent generation. In this "vague" sense (again, similar to aspects of Old Testament wisdom), God is involved in human enterprise. Here, God is not directly present, as with cultic exercises, or steering human actions directly, as through law, but—a standard view expressed in scholarly literature on Old Testament wisdom—God is present "behind the scenes," as it were. This approaches, in some respects, lay spirituality.[75]

Thinking through theologically the relationship between science and faith, as was indicated above, is a second strand of thought from this genealogy that can inform our spirituality. In societies where technological advance and decline in religious interest have coincided, in the presently popular academic debate between natural science and theology, in the recently rising intersection between business and ethics, and in the current

---

[74] Cf. D. J. Bosch, *A Spirituality of the Road* (Pretoria: Institute for Missiological and Ecumenical Research, 1994).

[75] Cf. K. Waaijman, *Spiritualiteit: Vormen, Grondslagen, Methoden* (Gent: Carmelitana, 2000), 23–116. Interestingly, Waaijman refers on the first page of this section to Albertz, *Persönliche Frömmigkeit und offizielle Religion: Religionsinterner Pluralismus in Israel und Babylon*.

resurgence of interest in "spirituality" (here meant as "anything vaguely but not specifically religious") and the media, including the internet, Gen 4:17–22, and also with 4:25–26 + 5:28b–29, offers us interesting points of reference. Faith and culture, an ancient concern, remains "in the air."

The theme of the Gen 4:25–26 + 5:28b–29 genealogy has already been indicated a few times as "new beginnings." What murder destroyed, the continued blessing of fertility restores; worship starts; Noah's birth holds promise of lifting the curse of Gen 3:17. This would generally have been contextualised within the broader Yahwist theology of sin and redemption. The deuteronomistic theology, not unrelated in this respect to J's thinking and, it seems, a more accurate context for these verses, would emphasise a new start, post the 586 B.C.E. exile event. God's grace has offered new hope in the past, and will do so in future. This is the spirituality of hope, with substantive pastoral, political, and ecclesial application possibilities in our time.

In the Gen 5 genealogy, three (related) theological lines have been identified above: God's continued blessing through each next generation, the maintenance of the image of God in each successive generation, and the distinctiveness of Israel. The post 586 identity of Israel is fed, in this genealogy, by a text that uses the continuity of past generations to give security in the present. Particularly with the open-endedness of the closing verse, the implication for P's audience is that hope remains: the stability of succeeding generations will continue. Within this re-generation, the likeness of Elohim continues. The unique group of Israel will thus continue.

Though this message of hope seems at first to offer possibilities for greater application, this is tempered by the exclusivist tone (similar to the problem one encounters with Ezra-Nehemiah). This is not a universalising spirituality. The theological lines of continued blessing by means of each new generation and the concept of the image of God may offer some possibilities. The former possibility, though, is difficult in cultures (such as Western/ised cultures) where God's blessing and fertility may not be equated as strongly. Perhaps by placing this genealogy within the broader context of the *Toledot*-books within P, further possibilities will develop. As to the image of God concept, it remains such a widely used concept, called in support of almost any cause (e.g., political freedom, social and economic justice, the abortion debate, the legalisation of marijuana, etc.), that it can hardly be used within narrower exegetical delineations.

Nevertheless, this has brought us to a point where we may acknowledge that the intersection between the diversity of the faith we find reflected in the Old Testament offers us some avenues for intersecting with the diversity of faith we find reflected in the modern world. Spiritualities may in/form spiritualities. Even with genealogies, a genre not very attractive to Western/ised audiences, such possibilities exist.

BIBLIOGRAPHY

Albertz, R. *Religionsgeschichte Israels in alttestamentlicher Zeit.* Teil 1. Grundrisse zum Alten Testament, Ergänzungsreihen, ATD Band 8/1. Göttingen: Vandenhoeck & Ruprecht, 1992.

———. *Persönliche Frömmigkeit und offizielle Religion: Religionsinterner Pluralismus in Israel und Babylon.* Stuttgart: Calwer Verlag, 1978.

Albright, W. F. *From the Stone Age to Christianity.* Second edition. New York: Doubleday Anchor Books, 1957.

Andersen, T. D. "Genealogical Prominence and the Structure of Genesis." Pages 242–66 in *Biblical Hebrew and Discourse Linguistics.* Edited by R. D. Bergen. Dallas: Summer Institute of Linguistics, 1994.

Andriolo, K. R. "A Structural Analysis of Genealogy and World View in the Old Testament." *American Anthropologist* 75 (1973): 1657–69.

Aufrecht, W. E. "Genealogy and History in Ancient Israel." Pages 205–35 in *Ascribe to the Lord: Biblical and Other Studies in Memory of Peter C. Craigie.* Edited by P. C. Craigie, L. M. Eslinger and G. Taylor. JSOT Suppl. 67. Sheffield: JSOT Press, 1988.

Bailey, N. A. "Some Literary and Grammatical Aspects of Genealogies." Pages 267–82 in *Biblical Hebrew and Discourse Linguistics.* Edited by R. D. Bergen. Dallas: Summer Institute of Linguistics, 1994.

Bosch, D. J. *A Spirituality of the Road.* Pretoria: Institute for Missiological and Ecumenical Research, 1994.

Brichto, H. C. *The Names of God. Poetic Readings in Biblical Beginnings.* New York: Oxford University Press, 1998.

Brodie, T. L. "Genesis as Dialogue: Genesis' Twenty-Six Diptychs as a Key to Narrative Unity and Meaning." Pages 297–314 in *Studies in the Book of Genesis: Literature, Redaction and History.* Edited by A. Wénin. Louvain: Leuven University Press; Uitgeverij Peeters; Bibliotheca Ephemeridum Theologicarum Lovaniensium CLV, 2001

Brueggemann, W. *Spirituality of the Psalms.* Augsburg: Fortress, 2002.

Bryan, D. T. "A Reevaluation of Gen 4 and 5 in light of Recent Studies in Genealogical Fluidity." *Zeitschrift für alttestamentlichen Wissenschaft* 99 (1987): 180–88.

Clines, D. J. A. *The Theme of the Pentateuch.* JSOT Suppl. 10. Sheffield: JSOT Press, 1978.

Davies, P. R. "Scenes from the Early History of Judaism." Pages 145–82 in *The Triumph of Elohim: From Yahwisms to Judaisms.* Edited by D.V. Edelman. Grand Rapids: Eerdmans (American edition), 1996.

Downey, M. *Understanding Christian Spirituality.* New York: Paulist Press, 1997.

Etz, D. V. "The Numbers of Genesis V 2–31: A Suggested Conversion and Its Implications." *Vetus Testamentum* XLIII, no. 2 (1993): 171–87.

Frankenfeld, K. *Genealogie der Bibel. Ein biblicher Stammbaum.* Frankfurt am Main: Haag und Herchen, 1997.

Golka, F. W. "The Aetiologies in the Old Testament, Part 1." *Vetus Testamentum* 26, no. 4 (1976): 410–28.

———. "The Aetiologies in the Old Testament, Part 2." *Vetus Testamentum* 27, no. 1 (1977): 36–47.

Gunkel, H. *Die Urgeschichte und die Patriarchen. Die Schriften des Alten Testaments 1/1.* Göttingen: Vandenhoeck & Ruprecht, 1911.

Johnson, M. D. *The Purpose of the Biblical Genealogies, with Special Reference to the Setting of the Genealogies of Jesus.* Second edition. Cambridge: Cambridge University Press, 1988.

Heinzerling, R. "'Einweihung' durch Henoch? Die Bedeutung der Altersangaben in Genesis 5." *Zeitschrift für alttestamentlichen Wissenschaft* 110 (1998): 581–89.

Hess, R. S. "The Genealogies of Genesis 1–11 and Comparative Literature." Pages 58–72 in *"I studied inscriptions from before the Flood": Ancient Near Eastern, Literary, and Linguistic Approaches to Genesis 1–11*. Edited by R. S. Hess and D. T. Tsumura. Winona Lake: Eisenbrauns, 1994 = *Biblica* 70 (1989): 241–54.

Houlden, J. L. "Bible, Spirituality of the." Pages 48–51 in *Westminster Dictionary of Spirituality*. Edited by G. S. Wakefield. Philadelphia: Westminster, 1983.

Kourie, C. "What Is Christian Spirituality?" Pages 7–33 in *Christian Spirituality in South Africa*. Edited by C. Kourie and L. Kretzschmar. Pietermaritzburg: Cluster Publications, 2000.

Laato, A. "The Levitical Genealogies in 1 Chronicles 5–6 and the Formation of Levitical Ideology in Post-Exilic Judah." *Journal for the Study of the Old Testament* 62 (June 1994): 77–99.

Lombaard, C. J. S. "Four South Africans' Proposals for a Central Theme to 'Scriptural Spirituality.'" *Scriptura* 88, no. 1 (2005): 139–50.

———. "The Old Testament in Christian Spirituality: Perspectives on the Undervaluation of the Old Testament in Christian Spirituality." *HTS Teologiese Studies/Theological Studies* 59, no. 2 (2003): 433–50.

Malamat, A. "King Lists of the Old Babylonian Period and Biblical Genealogies." Pages 183–99 in *"I studied inscriptions from before the Flood": Ancient Near Eastern, Literary, and Linguistic Approaches to Genesis 1–11*. Edited by R. S. Hess and D. T. Tsumura. Winona Lake: Eisenbrauns, 1994 = *Journal of the American Oriental Society* 88 (1968): 163–73.

Marmion, D. *A Spirituality of Everyday Faith: A Theological Investigation of the Notion of Spirituality in Karl Rahner.* Louvain Theological and Pastoral Monographs 23. Louvain: Peeters Press, 1998.

Mildenberger, F. "Heilsgeschichte." *RGG*⁴, Band 3, 1584–86. Tübingen: Mohr Siebeck, 2000.

Milligan, S. *The Old Testament according to Spike Milligan.* London: Penguin, 1993.

Nolan, A. *Biblical Spirituality.* Springs: The Order of Preachers (Southern Africa), 1982.

Noth, M. *Uberlieferungsgeschichte des Pentateuch.* 2. Auflage. Stuttgart: Kohlhammer, 1948.

Oeming, M. *Das wahre Israel: Die "genealogische Vorhalle" 1 Chronik 1–9.* Stuttgart: Kohlhammer, 1990.

Oostenbrink, J. W. "Gereformeerde Spiritualiteit as Korporatiewe Spiritualiteit." *In die Skriflig* 33, no. 3 (1999): 367–83.

Oosthuizen, R. De W. "African Experience of Time and Its Compatibility with the Old Testament View of Time as Suggested in the Genealogy of Genesis 5." *Old Testament Essays* 6 (1993): 190–204.

Paul, M. J. "Genesis 4:17–24: A Case-Study in Eisegesis." *Tyndale Bulletin* 47, no. 1 (1996): 143–62.

Plum, K. F. "Genealogy as Theology." *Scandinavian Journal of the Old Testament* 1 (1989): 66–89.

Prewitt, T. J. "Kinship Structures and the Genesis Genealogies." *Journal of Near Eastern Studies* 40, no. 2 (1981): 87–98.

Robinson, R. B. "Literary Functions of the Genealogies in Genesis." *Catholic Biblical Quarterly* 48, no. 1 (1986): 595–608.

Rogerson, J. "Can a Doctrine of Providence Be Based on the Old Testament?" Pages 529–43 in *Ascribe to the Lord: Biblical and Other Studies in Memory of Peter C. Craigie.* Edited by P. C. Craigie, L. M. Eslinger and G. Taylor. JSOT Suppl. 67. Sheffield: JSOT Press, 1988.

Sasson, J. M. "A Genealogical 'Convention' in Biblical Chronography?" *Zeitschrift für alttestamentlichen Wissenschaft* 90 (1978): 171–85.
Schmit, A. "Zum Thema 'Entruckung' im Alten Testament." *Biblische Zeitschrift* 26 (1982): 34–49.
Smit, D. J. "Kan Spiritualiteit Beskryf Word?" *Ned. Geref. Teologiese Tydskrif* 30, no. 1 (1989): 83–94.
Steinberg, N. "The Genealogical Framework of the Family Stories in Genesis." *Semeia* 45 (1989): 41–50.
Tengström, S. *Die Toledotformel und die literarische Struktur der priesterlichen Erweiterungschicht im Pentateuch*. Uppsala: CWK Gleerup, 1981.
The New Jerusalem Bible. London: Darton, Longman & Todd, 1985.
Vermeylen, J. "La Descendance de Caïn et le Descendance d'Abel (Gen 4:17–26 + 5:28b–29)." *Zeitschrift für alttestamentlichen Wissenschaft* 103 (1991): 175–93.
Von Rad, G. *Theologie des Alten Testaments, Band 1: Die Theologie der geschichtlichen Überlieferungen Israels*. Fünfte, durchgesehen Auflage. München: Chr. Kaiser Verlag, 1962.
———. *Die Priesterschrift im Hexateuch*. Stuttgart: Kohlhammer. BWANT IV/13, 1934.
Waaijman, K. *Spiritualiteit: Vormen, Grondslagen, Methoden*. Gent: Carmelitana, 2000.
———. "Toward a Phenomenological Definition of Spirituality." *Studies in Spirituality* 3 (1993): 5–57.
Wellhausen, J. *Prolegomena zur Geschichte Israels*. 6. Ausgabe. Berlin: De Gruyter, 1927.
Westermann, C. *Genesis 1–11*. Biblischer Kommentar Altes Testament 1/1. Neukirchen-Vluyn: Neukirchener Verlag, 1974.

Wilson, R. R. "The Old Testament Genealogies in Recent Research." Pages 200–223 in *"I studied inscriptions from before the Flood": Ancient Near Eastern, Literary, and Linguistic Approaches to Genesis 1–11*. Edited by R. S. Hess and D. T. Tsumura. Winona Lake: Eisenbrauns, 1994 = *Journal of Biblical Literature* 94 (1975): 169–89.

———. "Between 'Azel' and 'Azel': Interpreting the Biblical Genealogies." *Biblical Archeologist* 42, no. 1 (1979): 11–22.

———. *Genealogy and History in the Biblical World*. Yale Near Eastern Researches 7. New Haven: Yale University Press, 1977.

What Is Biblical Spirituality? Perspectives from a Minor Genre of Old Testament Scholarship[*]

ABSTRACT
The field of Biblical Spirituality as a sub-discipline within the overlapping subject areas of Spirituality and Biblical Studies (alternatively, Old and New Testament Studies) is still in its infancy. In this essay, an overview of some of what has been written on this sub-discipline is provided, *en route* to proposing in brief a model for the working field of Biblical Spirituality.

1. Background to This Study

Although the phrase "biblical spirituality" has been in use for some time now, the discipline of Biblical Spirituality[1] is rather recent. What has been written about Biblical Spirituality has more often than not been theoretical, discerning possible boundaries to and contents of the field. Yet, on the other hand, much of what has been written about faith in the Bible and faith from the Bible—put in more traditional terms: exegesis and hermeneutics—may well be classified as Biblical Spirituality. Drawing from these streams, and building forth on a series of earlier publications,[2] I begin to

---

[*] This essay was initially presented as a paper at a Biblical Spirituality seminar at the Titus Brandsma Institute, Radboud University, in June 2007, in Nijmegen, The Netherlands.
[1] When capitalised, I use "Biblical Spirituality" to refer to the academic discipline; without capitals, the phrase refers to the practice of a spirituality which relates itself specifically to the Bible.
[2] See C. J. S. Lombaard, "The Old Testament in Christian Spirituality: Perspectives on the Undervaluation of the Old Testament in Christian Spirituality," *HTS Teologiese Studies/Theological Studies* 59, no. 2 (2003), 433–50; C. J. S. Lombaard, "Four South Africans' Proposals for a Central Theme to 'Scriptural Spirituality,'" *Scriptura* 88, no. 1 (2005): 139–50; C. J. S. Lombaard, "Genealogies and Spiritualities in Genesis 4:17–22, 4:25–26, 5:1–32," in *The Spirit That Moves. Orientation and Issues in Spirituality* (ed. P. G. R. de Villiers, C. Kourie and C. J. S. Lombaard; *Acta Theologia* Supplementum 8;

negotiate in the following pages a route to what I propose may be a future working model for the discipline we have come to call Biblical Spirituality. This is done below in conversation with four publication projects, spread over five decades, on Old Testament Spirituality and, in one case, on Biblical Spirituality.

2. Still History, after All These Years

Despite claims to the contrary, the historical-critical paradigm of exegesis still dominates the scholarly reading of the Bible. Often, reaction against historical-critical exegesis still presupposes an underlying positivism that was present in the early, modernistic stage of the development of the historically oriented methods,[3] but which is now largely absent. The reason behind such reactions is usually quite clear: the plea is for faith, rather than history alone.

Bloemfontein: University of the Free State Press, 2006), 146–64; C. J. S. Lombaard, "Four Recent Books on Spirituality and the Psalms: Some Contextualising, Analytical and Evaluative Remarks," *Verbum et Ecclesia* 27, no. 3 (2006): 909–29; C. J. S. Lombaard, "Teks en Mens. J. H. le Roux se Lees van die Bybel binne die Konteks van Hoofstroom-Eksegese in Suid-Afrika," *Old Testament Essays* 19, no. 3 (2006 [special ed.]), 912–25; C. J. S. Lombaard, "The Relevance of Old Testament Science in/for Africa: Two False Pieties and Focussed Scholarship," *Old Testament Essays* 19, no. 1 (2006): 144–55; C. J. S. Lombaard, "The Old Testament between Diachrony and Synchrony: Two Reasons for Favouring the Former," *Journal for Semitics/Tyskrif vir Semitistiek* 15, no. 1 (2006): 18–31.

[3] Fee identifies aspects of historical exegesis as including *questions of context*—which refer to the genre of the biblical literature at hand, the historical context, and the literary context—and *questions of content*, which relates to an original text (where possible), word meaning, grammar, and historical background (see G. Fee, "History as Context for Interpretation," in *The Act of Bible Reading. A Multi-Disciplinary Approach to Bible Interpretation* [ed. E. Dyck. Downer's Grove: InterVarsity, 1996], 15–32; cf. F. E. Deist, *Witnesses to the Old Testament* [The Literature of the Old Testament, vol. 5; Pretoria: NG Kerkboekhandel, 1988], 41–71).

Not only what a text meant in the past, that is, in its textually reconstructable contexts, but also what it may mean for the reader of today, is sought. The problem of what to do with history lies central here.

A recent case in point again is the argument by Le Marquand:[4] that in the model of Bible scholarship developed in the notional West,[5] "[l]ess attention is given to the more 'theological' task of clarifying 'the meaning of the word of God in scripture' or to the 'pastoral' task of encouraging the faithful,"[6] than to historically-oriented exegesis:

> In effect, the biblical guild edited out how other interests could be involved in the task of interpreting the Bible. Its view of history necessarily became narrowed. Historical study came to mean only the history of the text in its ancient setting as this was understood according to the canons of modern critical research. The scholarly task became confined to uncovering the past. It became enough for scholars to attempt to describe the meaning of the text to its assumed original authors and readers. Historical research came to be considered an objective description of past events and ideas.[7]

The problem, after all these years, is still history.

The search for which Le Marquand argues, like many others before him, namely for meaning—personal, faith-oriented and existential—from the Bible for today, is of course valid. It is a

---

[4] G. le Marquand, "Siblings or Antagonists? The Ethos of Biblical Scholarship from the North Atlantic and African Worlds," in *Biblical Interpretation in African Perspective* (ed. D. Adamo; Lanham, Md.: University Press of America, 2006), 61–85.
[5] Usually when Western exegesis is called to account in this manner, the "West" referred to is more or less limited to Germany, The Netherlands, France, the United Kingdom and the North American continent.
[6] Le Marquand, "Siblings or Antagonists?" 62.
[7] Ibid., 63

search to which Bible scholars have not been blind, with numerous attempts being offered. Within Old Testament scholarship a significant genre of such writing has developed, which has come to be known as Old Testament Theology.[8] However, a much smaller genre, that of Old Testament Spirituality, has also come into being. Keeping to the latter, four such attempts are taken into review in the following section. Three of these publication projects are explicitly titled or sub-titled "Old Testament Spirituality"; the newest of the four projects is titled "Biblical Spirituality." Since the latter is a recent publication whose assumptions hold equally true for the Semitic and Hellenistic sections of the Bible, it is included here.

Interestingly, the problem of history, that is, how to relate a text from the past to lives in the present, lies at the heart of the respective publications. All four projects attempt to cross the bridge of history differently. We look at these publications in chronological order.

3. An Old Testament Spirituality by De la Croix?

From 1961 to 1963 a triple-volume work by De la Croix, with the promising title *Old Testament Spirituality*, was published.[9] Closer investigation shows, however, that this is not a work in the nascent tradition of Biblical Spirituality; rather, it stands closer to the Old Testament Theology genre. This inclination is explained by the

---

[8] The standard overview is B. Ollenburger, *Old Testament Theology: Flowering and Future* (revised ed.; Winona Lake: Eisenbrauns, 2004). For reservations on whether the genre of Old Testament Theology is theological enough, precisely because it is not historical enough, cf. R. Albertz, *Religionsgeschichte Israels in alttestamentlicher Zeit* (vols. 1 and 2; Göttingen: Vandenhoeck & Ruprecht, 1992), 17–38.

[9] See P. M. de la Croix, *God and the Soul* (Spirituality of the Old Testament, vol. 1; St. Louis: Herder, 1961); P. M. de la Croix, *Divine Love* (Spirituality of the Old Testament, vol. 2; St. Louis: Herder, 1962). P. M. de la Croix, *Divine Pathways* (Spirituality of the Old Testament, vol. 3; St. Louis: Herder, 1963).

fact that these volumes are translations (by Elizabeth McCabe) from a French original, *L'Ancien Testament, source de vie spirituelle* (1952), in which context "spirituelle" carries connotations of faith truths rather than living in relation to the Scriptures. Based on an idea of progressive revelation by God in the Bible,[10] from Genesis 1 onwards, the Old Testament is primarily concerned in this view with "theological and moral doctrine, [... which] teaches man how he is loved by God."[11] This approach is clearly pre-*Vaticanum II*, reflecting nothing of the classical 1787 distinction by Gabler between the dogmatic and historical approaches to writing an Old Testament Theology. Therefore, De la Croix's contribution is in line with an earlier, now discarded, tradition within Old Testament Theologies of applying categories from systematic theology to the analysis of the Hebrew Bible texts, rather than abstracting categories from the texts themselves and/or from the scholarly exegetical literature. Not what the texts in their socio-historical and literary contexts may have said, and from this, what they can be said to say today, but dogmatological pronouncements from the texts are presented as if of the texts.

No hermeneutical processes through which the deductions are funnelled, are acknowledged. Verses from different sections of the Bible, all taken literally and a-contextually, are copiously cross-referenced, at times amplified with references to *doctores* of the church; not once, though, is acknowledgement given to an academic work. In the footnotes, the slightest of hints to ancient Near Eastern socio-religious backgrounds and authorship questions may be detected, though very infrequently. For the most part, the strong impression is given that pure, holy, Christian words are found in the Old Testament. The category of revelation is prime; history is read naïvely, from Adam as a historical person onwards.

---

[10] Cf. De la Croix, *God and the Soul*, viii–x.
[11] Ibid., ix

Therefore, the impression the book as a whole gives, is of a work intended for use in catechesis of a certain kind. Nothing about the Bible is presented as problematical; neither are hermeneutics and history ever problems. Issues are not argued from different sides, but Bible verses are stacked together in order to present cogent pictures on, for instance, the nature of God or human purification. Here, a certain view of Christian truth supersedes all historical conditioning.

4. Craghan's Old Testament Spirituality

Another Catholic writer's Old Testament Spirituality, though of a wholly different order than that of De la Croix's, is the 1983 volume by Craghan.[12] Craghan's approach to writing a Spirituality of the Old Testament seems at first dialectical: its title suggests that *within* "love" and "thunder," and also *between* "love" and "thunder," God can be found. However, this creative tension is left largely unexplored in the book. The most important way in which creative tension is explored by Craghan, is by what may be called a mix of times: "Spirituality thus becomes a present reflection of a past record in view of future needs." [13] For this, hermeneutics is considered to be an indispensable mediator:

> These musty, dusty accounts from the ancient Near East are not simply our heirlooms. They are our identity papers. ... Our concern[14] is not to determine the intention of the original author for the purposes of historical analysis, although such a quest is invaluable. Instead, our quest is hermeneutical—we are

---

[12] See J. F. Craghan, *Love and Thunder. A Spirituality of the Old Testament* (Collegeville, Minn.: The Order of St. Benedict, Inc., 1983).

[13] Craghan, *Love and Thunder,* 2. The reference of the "past record" here is to the biblical text.

[14] With "concern" and "quest" here is denoted the ultimate purpose of biblical exegesis.

anxious to learn how the story or stories concern us... [B]y releasing God [i.e., through the act of interpreting the biblical stories], we are able to find ourselves.[15]

Interestingly, the givenness of the canon is to our good, precisely because of the contradictions it contains, which militates against singular or dictatorial spiritualities in any time and place.[16] It is the *diversity* of Old Testament presentations of God—as male and female, for instance[17]—that feeds us. Covenant features as a metaphor for the relationship between God and humans, with the latter standing in fundamental relationships with other humans and with nature too.[18] These and other themes—some of which relate closely to traditional topics in spiritual writings: the image of God; freedom; wisdom—are presented as invitations. In this way, most of the literary genres in the Old Testament are covered, even though some do lend themselves better than others to a presentation as invitation.

As a general approach, Craghan chooses a theme for each chapter of the book that is discussed in an applicatory introduction and conclusion, which together sandwich an expository section. The latter comprises mature exegetical-theological analyses of the theme from different sections of the Old Testament primarily, but often with brief references to New Testament passages, too. These analyses draw unapologetically and, frankly, piously (though never pietistically), on historical-critical studies, with the implicit assumption that the reader is aware of the basic aspects of historical methodology. The J and P sources of the Pentateuch, as they were understood in the 1970s and 1980s, feature prominently

---

[15] Craghan, *Love and Thunder*, 75
[16] Ibid., 4–5.
[17] Ibid., 7–15; cf. ix, 195–211. Here Craghan draws strongly on the works of Phyllis Trible.
[18] Ibid., 29–39, 17–27, *passim*.

118   *The Old Testament and Christian Spirituality*

in Craghan's writing. Craghan also draws on the ancient Near Eastern cultural and textual backgrounds.

With this approach, Craghan seeks to merge histories: the past histories we find reflected in the holy texts, with the present histories of people living their lives in discussion with these texts. In so doing, Craghan draws heavily on the works of Gerhard von Rad[19] and Walter Brueggemann,[20] both of whom share with Craghan a strong inclination of bringing ancient texts and modern concerns into critical dialogue—with neither ever in a historically decontextualised setting. Here, history meets history, with both the uncertainties and the concreteness this implies intact.

5. Sheriffs's Old Testament Spirituality

Taking his cue from Ps 25, Sheriffs's Old Testament spirituality is arranged around the theme of the friendship of the Lord.[21] This choice is not entirely secure, since it is only the *New Revised Standard Version* translation of 1989 that renders סוֹד יְהוָה in Ps 25:14 as "friendship of the Lord," and rarely are any of the other six occurrences of סוֹד interpreted as "friendship." However, this theme is not put forward in such a forceful way that it runs into the same reductionist difficulties as have many Old Testament Theologies,[22] even though Sheriffs is more consistent than Craghan in employing his chosen central theme.

Acknowledging the importance of the historical contexts of the Old Testament texts, the role of hermeneutics, and the fact that the

---

[19] Cf. e.g. G. von Rad, *The Problem of the Hexateuch and Other Essays* (Edinburgh: Oliver & Boyd, 1966).
[20] Cf. e.g. W. Brueggemann, *In Man We Trust. The Neglected Side of Biblical Faith* (Richmond: John Knox, 1972).
[21] See D. Sheriffs, *The Friendship of the Lord. An Old Testament Spirituality* (Repr., Eugene, Ore.: Wipf & Stock, 2004).
[22] Cf. H. D. Preuß, *Theologie des Alten Testaments, Band 1: JHWHs erwählendes und verpflichtendes Handeln* (Stuttgart: Kohlhammer, 1991), 1–27.

modern interpreter should be interpreted too,[23] Sheriffs offers exegetical observations on his selected texts, traces certain ideas from the Old Testament to the New, and frequently offers commentary related to the ancient and modern contexts as, respectively, explanation and application. The latter he regards as particularly important. Yet, interestingly, and drawing on his academic background,[24] much information of the ancient Near Eastern religio-cultural environment to the Old Testament is included. Particular emphasis is placed on the topics of covenant and treaty, reflecting in these respects the leanings of his doctoral supervisor Fensham[25] and *via* him, Albright[26] though with greater hermeneutic caution.[27]

At times, the book reads like an introductory course on the Old Testament, with many basic elements being explained; at other times, the indications of present relevance seem almost sermon-like, even forced. With repeating themes such as friendship, journey, and covenant, and with much made of the rhythms of time towards the end of the book, this volume gives valuable pointers on how we may attempt to bring the ancient biblical texts into lively discussion with important themes from the history of spirituality and with modern-day issues. That the ancient contexts must be brought to bear on Biblical Spirituality is correctly emphasised by this contribution, although the way in which this is

---

[23] Sheriffs, *The Friendship of the Lord,* xi, 1–2.
[24] See D. Sheriffs, "Empire and the Gods: Mesopotamian Treaty Theology and the Sword in the First Millennium B.C." (D.Litt. diss., University of Stellenbosch, 1976).
[25] Cf. e.g. C. Fensham, "The Treaty between Israel and the Gibeonites," *The Biblical Archaeologist Reader* 3 (1970): 121–26.
[26] Cf. e.g. W. F. Albright, *Archaeology and the Religion of Israel: The Ayer Lectures of the Colgate-Rochester Divinity School* (3rd ed.; Baltimore: Johns Hopkins University Press, 1953).
[27] J. H. le Roux, "A Story of Two Ways. Thirty Years of Old Testament Scholarship in South Africa" (*Old Testament Essays* Supplement Number 2; Pretoria: Verba Vitae, 1993), 114–40

done may well be improved by including more recent approaches (e.g. the religion-historical approach of Albertz[28]), and by being less introductory in presentation.

6. "Biblical Spirituality" in *The Southern Baptist Journal of Theology*

The winter 2006 edition of *The Southern Baptist Journal of Theology* is dedicated to the theme of "Biblical Spirituality." From the series of six articles, an Introduction and a Forum,[29] a picture of Biblical Spirituality different from those mentioned above emerges.

Starkly absent from the whole are two dimensions, the first of which is a historical consciousness. Directly related to this is the lack of a fundamental sense of self-awareness. The security of faith one finds here would have been admirable, had it not been so insular, that is, biblical spirituality seems to be understood here as identical to the way the authors view matters; all else is unbiblical and hence unacceptable.[30] There *is* something like "a *true* and

---

[28] See R. Albertz, *Religionsgeschichte Israels*.
[29] See S. Wellum, "Editorial: 'Spirituality'—*Caveat Emptor*," *The Southern Baptist Journal of Theology* 10, no. 4 (2006): 2–3; R. Plummer, "Are the Spiritual Disciplines of 'Silence and Solitude' Really Biblical?" *SBJT* 10, no. 4 (2006): 4–12; G. Goldsworthy, "A Biblical-Theological Perspective on Prayer," *SBJT* 10, no. 4 (2006): 14–25; P. Adam, "God's Powerful Words: Five Principles of Biblical Spirituality in Isaiah 55," *SBJT* 10, no. 4 (2006): 28–37; S. Wright, "The Reformation Piety of Theodore Beza," *SBJT* 10, no. 4 (2006), 38–53; M. Haykin, "'Draw Nigh unto my Soul': English Baptist Piety and the Means of Grace in the Seventeenth and Eighteenth Centuries," *SBJT* 10, no. 4 (2006): 54–73; P. Johnson, "What's New with the New Age? Why Christians Need to Remain on Guard against the Threat of New Age Spirituality," *SBJT* 10, no. 4 (2006): 74–83; "The *SBJT* Forum: Thinking about True Spirituality (including interviews with D. A. Carson, Mark Coppenger, Joel Beeke and Pierre Constant)," *SBJT* 10, no. 4 (2006): 84–96.
[30] The order of the two "un"-words may equally be inversed here: these writers seem to accept that such and such *is* the biblical way, and therefore it must be

biblical spirituality,"[31] with the strong implication that what Southern Baptists do constitutes that biblical spirituality. Even the contributions which seem not to have any direct bearing on the Bible[32] reflect for them biblical spirituality, because the way this group believes is *the* biblical path.

No serious attention is given in the article series to the vast gap that exists between the views expressed in the Bible and the way these modern authors see things; "der garstig breite Graben" of Lessing[33] between the then and now, and the intense philosophical-hermeneutical scholarship this awareness has elicited,[34] finds no reflection here. The link between ancient text and modern faith is understood to be both simple and direct; such a straightforward "hearing words from the mouth of God"[35] is biblical spirituality. The bridge of history is easily passed over. Moreover, no room is left for different or even opposing views both *in* and *from* the

---

followed. There is little or no sense here of the hermeneutical circle, in which meaning is as much imposed as it is taken. Cf. e.g. Wright, "The Reformation Piety of Theodore Beza," 43; "The *SBJT* Forum," 86–88, 90, 91.

[31] Wellum, "Editorial: 'Spirituality,'" 3, following F. Schaeffer, *True Spirituality* (Wheaton: Tyndale House, 1971); cf. "The SBJT Forum," 95.

[32] Cf. Wright, "The Reformation Piety of Theodore Beza," 38–53; Haykin, "'Draw Nigh unto my Soul,'" 54–73; Johnson, "What's New with the New Age?" 74–83.

[33] See G. E. Lessing, "Über den Beweis des Geistes und der Kraft," In *Werke, 8. Bd.: Theologiekritische Schriften III, Philosophische Schriften* (ed. H. Göpfert; München, 1777), 13.

[34] Cf. e.g., E. Troeltsch, Über historische und dogmatische Methode in der Theologie (Gesammelte Schriften, II; Tübingen: JCB Mohr, 1922); F. Schleiermacher, *Hermeneutik und Kritik. Mit einem Anhang sprachphilosophischer Texte Schleiermachers* (hrsg. Manfred Frank; Frankfurt am Main: Suhrkamp Verlag, 1977); H.-G. Gadamer, *Wahrheit und Methode. Grundzuge einer philosophischen Hermeneutik* (Tübingen: Mohr, 1975); J. Derrida, Of Grammatology (Baltimore: Johns Hopkins University Press, 1976); J. Habermas, *Theorie des kommunikativen Handelns* (Bd.1: *Handlungs-rationalität und gesellschaftliche Rationalisierung*, Bd. 2: *Zur Kritik der funktionalistischen Vernunft*; Frankfurt am Main: Suhrkamp Verlag, 1981).

[35] Adam, "God's Powerful Words," 28; cf. 32–35.

122   *The Old Testament and Christian Spirituality*

Bible, nor for positive a-biblical socio-cultural influence.[36] This cannot but create the impression of a Scripture domesticated to serve what has already been established;[37] a critical attitude, even though it exists,[38] is limited to the refinement of received views. The Bible is not so different from the "us" here; the Bible is "our" book. History is no problem.

7. Old Testament/Biblical Spirituality in Overview

The four publication projects reviewed above indicate various ways of treating the Bible and its relationship to modern readers; that is, the historical bridge between the texts from the past and the lives in the present is crossed differently. The first and last projects reviewed altogether disregard the existence of a rupture in need of bridging. In the De la Croix volumes, the Bible texts are systematised in order to reflect timeless theological truths; in *The*

---

[36] Paradoxically, underlying such strands of Christianity is a clearly non-biblical, namely ancient Greek-philosophical view of the nature of truth, which then is made to determine the whole identity of this Christian conception—cf. Lombaard, "Teks en Mens. J. H. le Roux se Lees van die Bybel," 914³.

[37] Cf. C. J. S. Lombaard, "The Bible in the Apartheid Debate," in *1948 + 50 Years. Theology, Apartheid and Church: Past, Present and Future* (ed. J. W. Hofmeyr, C. J. S. Lombaard and P. J. Maritz; Perspectives on the Church/Perspektiewe op die Kerk, Series 5: Vol. 1; Pretoria: IMER [Institute for Missiological and Ecumenical Research], University of Pretoria, 2001), 84–86, following Maimela (see Maimela, S. *Proclaim Freedom to My People. Essays on Religion and Politics* [Braamfontein: Skotaville Publishers, 1987], 36) and Deist (see F. E. Deist, "Using the Bible: The Hermeneutics of the Kairos Document," in *Perspektiewe op Kairos/Perspectives on Kairos* [ed. J. W. Hofmeyr, J. H. H. du Toit and C. J. J. Froneman; Kaapstad: Lux Verbi, 1987], 128–29).

[38] See F. W. Graf, "Protestantischer Fundamentalismus und liberaler Rechtsstaat," in *Köktendincilik ve Çogulculuk. Fundamentalismus und Pluralismus* (ed. C. San; Schriftenreihe des türkisch-deutschen Kulturbeirats, 10; Ankara, 1996), 5–26.

Southern Baptist Journal of Theology's articles, the way the writers believe and do are understood to be direct expressions of prescribed ways in the Bible. In neither case does history present a problem. Though the two projects differ in the sense that the older one is more essentialist in nature and the newer one more pragmatically oriented, they agree to the extent that a false simplicity is accepted. The Bible is presented as a seamless book; the way it is read is unproblematic; the historical context of both the then and the now is subordinated to such an extent to the supernatural worth of the Bible that their importance shows through nowhere. We are told, simply and directly, *in* the Bible (De la Croix) and *by* the Bible (*The Southern Baptist Journal of Theology*) how matters are.

With Craghan and Sheriffs, how matters are is much more complex. The Bible texts are born within ancient Near Eastern contexts; the texts themselves developed and dialogued internally; a centuries-long interpretational history stands between the then and the now; the cultural and historical breaches between texts and readers are of fundamental importance, hence the significance of hermeneutics; yet, the Bible must be brought to speech in our time, since it remains, not despite, but precisely because of its socio-historical placement, the Word of God that addresses us, *and* in both supporting and critical modes. Whereas Sheriffs's contribution may be somewhat too self-conscious, even forced, suggesting perhaps a lingering sense of difficulty in bringing together all these strands of complexity, Craghan's publication is more thoroughly reflective, showing a certain restful ripeness amid these intricacies. In both these cases, though, the fact that the historical givenness of the biblical texts and the modern readers is taken seriously renders them intellectually, existentially, and theologically more satisfying than the other two attempts. The fundamentally historical nature of the Christian faith has to be accepted lest Christianity finds itself in the category of esoteric philosophy; more importantly, it has to be accepted so as to give recognition to the concreteness of God's intervention in this world.

8. Towards a Working Model for Biblical Spirituality

The at once individual-yet-communal nature of spirituality[39] precludes the possibility of prescribing to all interested any single model of practicing the subject of Biblical Spirituality. What follows, then, are the outlines of one proposal only, drawing on the analysis above as well as on my previous studies indicated above.[40] These outlines are presented only briefly here, to be developed more fully later, and consist of four delineations.

8.1 The Bible itself is a focal point of spirituality

Already during the time of the post-exilic reconstruction of the Israelite community, the reading of the biblical texts had become part of the practice of faith—that is, the spirituality—of ancient Israel. In Neh 7:72b–8:18 we see the beginnings of an expression of faith in which the reading of Scripture and its exposition is at once transposed back to a mythologically idealised time of Moses *and* instituted as part of the festival culture of Israel, to be maintained in perpetuity. In the Torah, past and present, text

---

[39] Cf. C. J. S. Lombaard, "Four South Africans' Proposals," 148, on the "I" and "us" of faith; more broadly, C. J. S. Lombaard, "Spirituality: Sense and Gist. On Meaning, God and Being," in *The Spirit That Empowers: Perspectives on Spirituality* (ed. P. G. R. de Villiers, C. Kourie and C. J. S. Lombaard; *Acta Theologica* Supplementum 11; Bloemfontein: University of the Free State Press, 2008), 94–107.

[40] Cf. also J. Donahue, "The Quest for Biblical Spirituality," in *Exploring Christian Spirituality. Essays in Honor of Sandra M. Schneiders, IHM* (ed. B. Lescher and E. Liebert; Mahwah: Paulist Press, 2006), 73–97; B. E. Bowe, *Biblical Foundations of Spirituality: Touching a Finger to the Flame* (Lanham, Md.: Rowman & Littlefield Publishers, 2003).

explication and sense application are combined, in order to bestow on the faithful their (re)new(ed) religious identity.

Though the nature of the Bible, the identity of the faith concerned, the manner of reading, and a host of other factors have changed much over the intervening two and a half millennia, the essence of this spirituality has remained. It is in the Bible that we find our being interpreted.[41] This is clearly an implicit foundation inherent to the discipline of Biblical Spirituality.

However, we should not be led to think that from the Second Temple period onwards only one spirituality existed. The competing conceptions of faith we find reflected in the scriptural and cultural deposits from ancient Israel indicate that devotion had never been singular: rival strands of the same religion competed then,[42] have done so through the centuries, and certainly do so today. It would be misguided to think of any strand of faith giving full(est) expression to the Christian tradition; equally, it would be committing hubris to think of Biblical Spirituality as somehow superior within the broader disciplines of Spirituality to which it relates.

8.2 The relationship of history and faith

Christianity remains an inherently historical faith: what God has done in the history of Israel, and what Christ has done in the history of the church remains of central import. However, history is no simple matter:[43] reducing historiography to simply "telling it

---

[41] Cf. H. W. Rossouw, *Klaarheid en Interpretasie. Enkele Probleemhistoriese Gesigspunte in verband met die Leer van die Duidelikheid van die Heilige Skrif* (D.Th. proefskrif, Vrije Universiteit; Amsterdam: Drukkerij en uitgeverij Jacob van Campen N.V., 1963).

[42] See Albertz, *Religionsgeschichte Israels*.

[43] Cf. C. J. S. Lombaard, "Geloof en Geskiedenis," *Vox Voetianorum* 26, no. 1 (2002): 43–45. Recent discussion on the nature of historiography has taken seriously the narrative implications of writing history, that is, that the art of historiography and the art of fiction writing are not that far apart. Between the

how it was" is naïve—both in terms of modern history writing and the ways in which the past is rendered in biblical texts.[44] One must draw insights from the philosophy of history[45] and of science[46] in order to come to terms with the inherently narratological nature of

---

two resulting extremes of a positivistic view of historiography and an extreme post-modernistic one, the view that history has a truth claim whereas pure narrative does not, has been offered—cf. H. Barstad, "'Fact' versus 'Fiction' and Other Issues in the History Debate, and Their Relevance for the Study of the Old Testament," in *Vergegenwärtigung des Alten Testaments. Beiträge zur biblischen Hermeneutik* (Festschrift für Rudolf Smend zum 70. Geburtstag; ed. Christoph Bultmann, W. Dietrich and C. Levin; Göttingen: Vandenhoeck & Ruprecht, 2002), 439–43. However, this too is too simplistic for a fully nuanced view of Old Testament texts, even when restricted to the more historically oriented texts in the Hebrew Bible, for the texts of the Old Testament, such as the Deuteronomistic History versus the Chronicler's history, present history not as a truth claim about what happened, but as a truth claim about the meaning of the past. This current truth claim of the text, its kerugmatic historiography, is much more important for Old Testament texts than "what actually happened," to the point that ancient stories may be completely retold, expanded or even invented, for the sake of conveying an intended message. This way of working with the past is closer to the uncertainties offered us by post-modernist approaches to historiography than to the securities of modernism (cf. Barstad, "'Fact' versus 'Fiction,'" 443–46). Greater certainties can, however, be gained if historical-exegetical research focuses not only on the "narrated time," but also on the "time of narration," that is, the context and purposes to which a history is (re)told. The more editorial work on the text one can detect (whether smaller emendations or the larger work of placing existing texts within newer textual contexts), the greater the amount of material that renders us to trace a history of interpretation, already within the particular biblical texts, rendering us certain trajectories of meaning, upon which we may then expand.

[44] Cf. C. J. S. Lombaard, "Wat Dateer Ons? Enkele Opmerkings rondom die Datering van Bybelse Tekste," *HTS Teologiese Studies/Theological Studies* 58, no. 4 (2002), 1859–63.

[45] See e.g., R. G. Collingwood, *The Idea of History* (Oxford: Clarendon, 1994); J. H. le Roux, "The Nature of Historical Understanding" (or: "Hermeneutics and History"), *Studia Historiae Ecclesiasticae* XIX, no. 1 (1993): 35–63

[46] See e.g., T. S. Kuhn, *The Structure of Scientific Revolutions* (Chicago: University of Chicago Press, 1962); K. Popper, *Conjectures and Refutations: The Growth of Scientific Knowledge* (London: Routledge, 1989).

all history writing. It is this relationship between history and faith that has for three centuries of critical Bible scholarship been the (often unacknowledged) main cause of tension, at times to breaking point, between exegesis and confession, academia and church, text and faith. The relationship of history to faith must thus remain an important feature on the agenda of Biblical Spirituality.

Any attempt to circumvent a historical reading would be fatally flawed. The point is not, as is often stated in criticisms of such exegetical approaches, that historical criticism goes too far. Rather, the case is that historical criticism has tended not to have gone far enough! Partly because of the problem of specialisation, partly because of the initially inimical relationship between historical exegesis and church theology (the negative character of which may be laid before both parties concerned here[47]), historical exegesis has often halted at the point of coming to an understanding of a given text in its ancient contexts. For Biblical Spirituality, this is certainly not bad, but it is also definitely, and definitively, not enough. The hazardous process of crossing the centuries to speak theologically and faithfully to the people and issues of our time is part of the core tasks of this discipline.

8.3 The spiritualities we find reflected in the Bible

The popular expectation of the Bible remains one akin to an oracle: a single answer to a certain question would be given in these texts, and in clear terms. Interestingly, this is an expectation shared by religiously fundamentalist readers of the Bible and by fundamentally a- or anti-religious commentators on the Bible. For

---

[47] Houston relates the problematic role of the Bible to faith as consisting of certain dimensions, which may be reduced to two trends: that scholarship tends not to exceed its boundaries, and that Bible readers tend not to exceed theirs (see J. Houston, "Toward a Biblical Spirituality," in *The Act of Bible Reading. A Multi-Disciplinary Approach to Bible Interpretation* [ed. E. Dyck. Downer's Grove: InterVarsity, 1996], 167–73).

opposing reasons, certainly, and therefore with different emphases (respectively smoothing over repetitions and contradictions or stressing them), a shared view of how a Holy Scripture should be can be detected here. To inform these warped expectations of the Bible, in the hope of changing them towards more realistic views of these texts, should be a part of the programme of Biblical Spirituality.

Clearly, accepting the internally dialogical nature of the biblical texts themselves and of the competing expressions of faith that underlie these texts is fundamental to understanding their communicative intent.[48] It is therefore impossible to speak of *the* message of the Bible, or of a golden thread running through the texts, or of a central thrust to the biblical confessions. The diversity, complexity and concurrent nature of the messages we find in the Bible must be acknowledged, if we are to remain true to the nature of the Bible. What is more, it has now become clear that these identified differences are not simply modern analytical techniques forced onto the Scriptures. The biblical writers themselves purposely intended to indicate to their readers these internal editorial, and therefore, debating activities.[49] These are indeed deliberately "writerly" texts[50] that both exhort and inform later, including modern, dialogue. The educational value of such insights can hardly be overestimated. The Bible contains different, overtly competing spiritualities. No secret should be made of this, for the sake of countering the fundamentalisms (both religious and anti-religious) of our time.

---

[48] Cf. Albertz, *Religionsgeschichte Israels*.

[49] E. Otto, "A Hidden Truth behind the Text or the Truth of the Text: At a Turning Point of Biblical Scholarship Two Hundred Years after De Wette's *Dissertatio Critico-Exegetica*," in *South African Perspectives on the Pentateuch between Synchrony and Diachrony* (ed. J. H. le Roux and E. Otto; New York: T&T Clark, 2007), 19–28.

[50] A. C. Thiselton, *New Horizons in Hermeneutics* (Grand Rapids: Zondervan, 1992), 98.

8.4 The way in which latter-day spiritualities draw on the Bible

One of the greater concerns in our time is that the faith put in/related to the Bible leads to the Scriptures becoming a fetish of power, either in its US Bible Belt form or in its cultural, for example, African fundamentalist,[51] varieties. Though these are certainly forms of spirituality that draw in very specific ways on the Bible, namely directly and uncritically, the exegetical, hermeneutical and theological difficulties such approaches elicit must be pointed out. The historical situatedness of all spiritualities must be acknowledged fully, in order for the different strands of Christianity, of other religions, and of non-faiths, to understand themselves and others. We cannot claim, for instance, that our matrix of beliefs-and-actions comes from the Bible alone:[52]

> In sincerity we have to acknowledge to ourselves that our faith and practices are born "neither from the whole of the Bible, nor from the Bible alone."[53] Our faith is rather (in)formed by (expanding here on Wogaman[54]) Scripture, Christian history and tradition, experience, our thoughts and actions and those of others, the church, philosophy, societal norms and practices—all these and more, in different and ever changing measures.

---

[51] The latter is demonstrated, for instance, by the song quoted in T. Maluleke, "The Bible among African Christians: A Missiological Perspective," in *To Cast Fire upon the Earth. Bible and Mission Collaborating in Today's Multicultural Global Context* (ed. T. Okure; Pietermaritzburg: Cluster Publications, 2000), 97:
  Aka na mandla uSathane (Satan has no power)
  S'omshaya nge vhesi (We will clobber him with a [biblical] verse).
[52] Quote from Lombaard, "The Bible in the Apartheid Debate," 86.
[53] See F. E. Deist, "The Bible—the Word of God, or: Searching for the Pearl in the Oyster," in *Scripture and the Use of Scripture* (ed. W. S. Vorster. Pretoria: Unisa, 1978), 58.
[54] See J. P. Wogaman, *Christian Ethics. A Historical Introduction* (Louisville: John Knox, 1993), 1–22.

There is no simple correlation between faith in the Bible and modern faith, nor even a one-to-one match between some of the diversity of spiritualities we encounter in the Bible and some of the diversity of spiritualities we encounter among believers. The complexity and historical situatedness of all these expressions of faith preclude the drawing of simplistic connections. It is for precisely these reasons that the ways in which post-biblical (i.e, after the time of the Bible, including our time) spiritualities employ the Bible forms a legitimate and important study field within Biblical Spirituality, most probably drawing heavily also on social sciences such as Sociology, Anthropology, and Communication Studies. Christian faith lived is the Bible interpreted. How this interpretation is effected affects Biblical Spirituality.

9. The Last(ing) Word

"[S]pirituality is not a method of literary analysis but of appropriation,"[55] that is, a "response to the Word of God."[56] However, this דָּבָר includes not only the oral word, but also actions and occurrences through which God "speaks." In the preceding pages, four attempts at describing this process have been discussed. This has led me to identify four aspects as the tentative outlines of a possible working model for the discipline of Biblical Spirituality:
- The Bible itself is a focal point of spirituality;
- The relationship of history and faith;
- The spiritualities we find reflected in the Bible; and
- The way in which latter-day spiritualities draw on the Bible.

---

[55] Sheriffs, *The Friendship of the Lord*, 4.
[56] Craghan, *Love and Thunder*, 1.

Within the context of our time, and the ways in which the Bible is viewed and treated within our time, the recurring theme in this essay remains the central concern: the problem of history. It is on this terrain that the debate will be waged between orthodoxy, liberalism, fundamentalism, and secularism during the coming decades. History remains contested, in more than one way.

As far as Biblical Spirituality is concerned, faith happens where histories meet, that is, where there is overlap between the texts of Scripture and the substance of peoples' lives. "A biblical spirituality of the Old Testament is thus bound up with a real God interacting with real people in real situations."[57] This is no simplistic matter; the matrix of overlap is perhaps indiscernibly intricate. The word "mystery" would therefore not be out of place here. Yet mystery, precisely, calls forth spirituality....

---

[57] Ibid., 2.

BIBLIOGRAPHY

Adam, P. "God's Powerful Words: Five Principles of Biblical Spirituality in Isaiah 55." *The Southern Baptist Journal of Theology* 10, no. 4 (2006): 28–37.

Albertz, R. *Religionsgeschichte Israels in alttestamentlicher Zeit.* Vol. 1 and 2. Göttingen: Vandenhoeck & Ruprecht, 1992.

Albright, W. F. *Archaeology and the Religion of Israel: The Ayer Lectures of the Colgate-Rochester Divinity School.* Third edition. Baltimore: Johns Hopkins University Press, 1953.

Barstad, H. "'Fact' versus 'Fiction' and Other Issues in the History Debate, and Their Relevance for the Study of the Old Testament." Pages 439–43 in *Vergegenwärtigung des Alten Testaments. Beiträge zur biblischen Hermeneutik.* Festschrift für Rudolf Smend zum 70. Geburtstag. Edited by Christoph Bultmann, W. Dietrich and C. Levin. Göttingen: Vandenhoeck & Ruprecht, 2002.

Bowe, B. E. *Biblical Foundations of Spirituality: Touching a Finger to the Flame.* Lanham, Md.: Rowman & Littlefield Publishers, 2003.

Brueggemann, W. *In Man We Trust. The Neglected Side of Biblical Faith.* Richmond: John Knox, 1972.

Collingwood, R. G. *The Idea of History.* Oxford: Clarendon, 1994.

Craghan, J. F. *Love and Thunder. A Spirituality of the Old Testament.* Collegeville, Minn.: The Order of St. Benedict, Inc., 1983.

Deist, F. E. *Witnesses to the Old Testament.* The Literature of the Old Testament. Volume 5. Pretoria: NG Kerkboekhandel, 1988.

———. "Using the Bible: The Hermeneutics of the Kairos Document." In *Perspektiewe op Kairos/Perspectives on Kairos.* Edited by J. W. Hofmeyr, J. H. H. du Toit and C. J. J. Froneman. Kaapstad: Lux Verbi, 1987.

———. "The Bible—the Word of God, or: Searching for the Pearl in the Oyster." Pages 41–71 in *Scripture and the Use of Scripture*. Edited by W. S. Vorster. Pretoria: Unisa, 1978.

De la Croix, P. M. *God and the Soul*. Spirituality of the Old Testament. Volume 1. St. Louis: Herder, 1961.

———. *Divine Love*. Spirituality of the Old Testament. Volume 2. St. Louis: Herder, 1962.

———. *Divine Pathways*. Spirituality of the Old Testament. Volume 3. St. Louis: Herder, 1963.

Derrida, J. *Of Grammatology*. Baltimore: Johns Hopkins University Press, 1976.

Donahue, J. "The Quest for Biblical Spirituality." Pages 73–97 in *Exploring Christian Spirituality. Essays in Honor of Sandra M. Schneiders, IHM*. Edited by B. Lescher and E. Liebert. Mahwah: Paulist Press, 2006.

Fee, G. "History as Context for Interpretation." Pages 15–32 in *The Act of Bible Reading. A Multi-Disciplinary Approach to Bible Interpretation*. Edited by E. Dyck. Downer's Grove: InterVarsity, 1996.

Fensham, C. "The Treaty between Israel and the Gibeonites." *The Biblical Archaeologist Reader* 3 (1970): 121–26.

Gabler, J. P. *De iusto discrimine theologiae biblicae et dogmaticae regundisque recte utriusque finibus*. Altdorf, 1787.

Gadamer, H.-G. *Wahrheit und Methode. Grundzuge einer philosophischen Hermeneutik*. Tübingen: Mohr, 1975.

Goldsworthy, G. "A Biblical-Theological Perspective on Prayer." *The Southern Baptist Journal of Theology* 10, no. 4 (2006): 14–25.

Graf, F. W. "Protestantischer Fundamentalismus und liberaler Rechtsstaat." Pages 15–26 in *Köktendincilik ve Çogulculuk. Fundamentalismus und Pluralismus*. Edited by C. San. Schriftenreihe des türkisch-deutschen Kulturbeirats, 10. Ankara, 1996.

Habermas, J. *Theorie des kommunikativen Handelns* (Bd.1: *Handlungsrationalität und gesellschaftliche Rationalisierung*, Bd. 2: *Zur Kritik der funktionalistischen Vernunft*). Frankfurt am Main: Suhrkamp Verlag, 1981.

Haykin, M. "'Draw Nigh unto my Soul': English Baptist Piety and the Means of Grace in the Seventeenth and Eighteenth Centuries." *The Southern Baptist Journal of Theology* 10, no. 4 (2006): 54–73.

Houston, J. "Toward a Biblical Spirituality." Pages 167–73 in *The Act of Bible Reading. A Multi-Disciplinary Approach to Bible Interpretation*. Edited by E. Dyck. Downer's Grove: InterVarsity, 1996.

Johnson, P. "What's New with the New Age? Why Christians Need to Remain on Guard against the Threat of New Age Spirituality." *The Southern Baptist Journal of Theology* 10, no. 4 (2006): 74–83.

Kuhn, T. S. *The Structure of Scientific Revolutions*. Chicago: University of Chicago Press, 1962.

Le Marquand, G. "Siblings or Antagonists? The Ethos of Biblical Scholarship from the North Atlantic and African Worlds." Pages 61–85 in *Biblical Interpretation in African Perspective*. Edited by D. Adamo. Lanham, Md.: University Press of America, 2006.

Le Roux, J. H. "A Story of Two Ways. Thirty Years of Old Testament Scholarship in South Africa." Pages 114–40 in *Old Testament Essays* Supplement Number 2. Pretoria: Verba Vitae, 1993.

———. "The Nature of Historical Understanding" (or: "Hermeneutics and History"). *Studia Historiae Ecclesiasticae* XIX, no. 1 (1993): 35–63

Lessing, G. E. "Über den Beweis des Geistes und der Kraft." In *Werke, 8. Bd.: Theologiekritische Schriften III, Philosophische Schriften*. Edited by H. Göpfert. München, 1777.

Lombaard, C. J. S. "Spirituality: Sense and Gist. On Meaning, God and Being." Pages 94–107 in *The Spirit That Empowers: Perspectives on Spirituality*. Edited by P. G. R. de Villiers, C. Kourie and C. J. S. Lombaard. *Acta Theologica* Supplementum 11. Bloemfontein: University of the Free State Press, 2008.

———. "Genealogies and Spiritualities in Genesis 4:17–22, 4:25–26, 5:1–32." Pages 146–64 in *The Spirit That Moves. Orientation and Issues in Spirituality*. Edited by P. G. R. de Villiers, C. Kourie and C. J. S. Lombaard. *Acta Theologia* Supplementum 8. Bloemfontein: University of the Free State Press, 2006.

———. "Four Recent Books on Spirituality and the Psalms: Some Contextualising, Analytical and Evaluative Remarks." *Verbum et Ecclesia* 27, no. 3 (2006): 909–29

——— "Teks en Mens. J. H. le Roux se Lees van die Bybel binne die Konteks van Hoofstroom-Eksegese in Suid-Afrika." *Old Testament Essays* 19, no. 3 (2006 [Special Edition]): 912–25.

———. "The Relevance of Old Testament Science in/for Africa: Two False Pieties and Focussed Scholarship." *Old Testament Essays* 19, no. 1 (2006): 144–55.

———. "The Old Testament between Diachrony and Synchrony: Two Reasons for Favouring the Former." *Journal for Semitics/Tyskrif vir Semitistiek* 15, no. 1 (2006): 18–31.

———. "Four South Africans' Proposals for a Central Theme to 'Scriptural Spirituality.'" *Scriptura* 88, no. 1 (2005): 139–50.

———. "The Old Testament in Christian Spirituality: Perspectives on the Undervaluation of the Old Testament in Christian Spirituality." *HTS Teologiese Studies/Theological Studies* 59, no. 2 (2003): 433–50.

———. "Geloof en Geskiedenis. *Vox Voetianorum* 26, no. 1 (2002): 43–45.

———. "Wat Dateer Ons? Enkele Opmerkings rondom die Datering van Bybelse Tekste." *HTS Teologiese Studies/Theological Studies* 58, no. 4 (2002): 1859–63.

———. "The Bible in the Apartheid Debate." Pages 69–87 in *1948 + 50 Years. Theology, Apartheid and Church: Past, Present and Future*. Edited by J. W. Hofmeyr, C. S. J. Lombaard and P. J. Maritz. Perspectives on the Church/Perspektiewe op die Kerk, Series 5: Vol. 1. Pretoria: IMER (Institute for Missiological and Ecumenical Research), University of Pretoria, 2001.

Maimela, S. *Proclaim Freedom to My People. Essays on Religion and Politics*. Braamfontein: Skotaville Publishers, 1987.

Maluleke, T. "The Bible among African Christians: A Missiological Perspective." Pages 87–112 in *To Cast Fire upon the Earth. Bible and Mission Collaborating in Today's Multicultural Global Context*. Edited by T. Okure. Pietermaritzburg: Cluster Publications, 2000.

Ollenburger, B. *Old Testament Theology: Flowering and Future*. Revised edition. Winona Lake: Eisenbrauns, 2004.

Otto, E. "A Hidden Truth behind the Text or the Truth of the Text: At a Turning Point of Biblical Scholarship Two Hundred Years after De Wette's *Dissertatio Critico-Exegetica*." Pages 19–28 in *South African Perspectives on the Pentateuch between Synchrony and Diachrony*. Edited by J. H. le Roux and E. Otto. New York: T&T Clark, 2007.

Plummer, R. "Are the Spiritual Disciplines of 'Silence and Solitude' Really Biblical?" *The Southern Baptist Journal of Theology* 10, no. 4 (2006): 4–12.

Popper, K. *Conjectures and Refutations: The Growth of Scientific Knowledge*. London: Routledge, 1989.

Preuß, H. D. *Theologie des Alten Testaments, Band 1: JHWHs erwählendes und verpflichtendes Handeln*. Stuttgart: Kohlhammer, 1991.

Rossouw, H. W. *Klaarheid en Interpretasie. Enkele Probleemhistoriese Gesigspunte in verband met die Leer van die Duidelikheid van die Heilige Skrif.* D.Th. proefskrif, Vrije Universiteit. Amsterdam: Drukkerij en uitgeverij Jacob van Campen N.V., 1963.

Schaeffer, F. *True Spirituality.* Wheaton: Tyndale House, 1971.

Schleiermacher, F. *Hermeneutik und Kritik. Mit einem Anhang sprachphilosophischer Texte Schleiermachers.* Hrsg. Manfred Frank. Frankfurt am Main: Suhrkamp Verlag, 1977.

Sheriffs, D. *The Friendship of the Lord. An Old Testament Spirituality.* Repr., Eugene, Ore.: Wipf & Stock, 2004.

———. "Empire and the Gods: Mesopotamian Treaty Theology and the Sword in the First Millennium B.C." D.Litt. diss., University of Stellenbosch, 1976.

"The *SBJT* Forum: Thinking about True Spirituality (including interviews with D. A. Carson, Mark Coppenger, Joel Beeke and Pierre Constant)." *The Southern Baptist Journal of Theology* 10, no. 4 (2006): 84–96.

Thiselton, A. C. *New Horizons in Hermeneutics.* Grand Rapids: Zondervan, 1992.

Troeltsch, E. *Über historische und dogmatische Methode in der Theologie. Gesammelte Schriften, II.* Tübingen: JCB Mohr, 1922.

Von Rad, G. *The Problem of the Hexateuch and Other Essays.* Edinburgh: Oliver & Boyd, 1966.

Wellum, S. "Editorial: 'Spirituality'—*Caveat Emptor.*" *The Southern Baptist Journal of Theology* 10, no. 4 (2006): 2–3.

Wogaman, J. P. *Christian Ethics. A Historical Introduction.* Louisville: John Knox, 1993.

Wright, S. "The Reformation Piety of Theodore Beza." *The Southern Baptist Journal of Theology* 10, no. 4 (2006): 38–53.

Betwixt Text and Nature, God and Evolution: Biblical Reception and Creationism at the Creation Museum in Cultural-Anthropological Perspective[*]

ABSTRACT
Based on a survey of academic and popular literature, a personal visit, a number of interviews, and comments on an initial draft of this essay, this study seeks to understand the hermeneutics associated with the Creation Museum in Petersburg, Kentucky, just outside Cincinnati, Ohio, United States of America. Meant neither as a critique nor as a defence of these hermeneutics, a thick description in cultural-anthropological sense is offered here of the reception of the biblical text—primarily the Genesis creation accounts—reflected within this institution, as it reacts against its dominant cultural and natural-scientific environments in which the explanatory framework of evolution, in the tradition of Charles Darwin, is generally accepted.

1. An Introductory Note on Methodology

The genesis of this chapter lies in a two-month research visit during 2008 to St. Paul University, Ottawa, Canada, for a project on the Mass Media and Spirituality.[1] This visit included some time in the United States in order, among other reasons, to visit the Creation Museum (www.creationmuseum.org) in Petersburg,

---

[*] This essay was initially presented as a paper at the *Mystical Readings of the Bible* conference of the Spirituality Association of South Africa, in April 2009, at the Santa Sophia Centre, Pretoria, South Africa.

[1] The first paper from this project, "Fleetingness and Media-ted Existence. From Kierkegaard on the Newspaper to Broderick on the Internet", was read at the *Media, Spiritualities and Social Change* conference, 4–7 June 2008, Center for Media, Religion and Culture, School of Journalism and Mass Communication, University of Colorado, Boulder); cf. C. J. S. Lombaard, "Fleetingness and Media-ted Existence. From Kierkegaard on the Newspaper to Broderick on the Internet," *Communicatio* 35, no. 1 (2009): 17–29.

Kentucky, just outside Cincinnati, Ohio. The purpose of this visit, as had been arranged with its proprietors and staff beforehand, was to come to a first-hand understanding of the Museum and the message(s) it seeks to convey; to adapt Marshall McLuhan's famous phrase: a museum is a message.[2] Museums too are a form of mass communication, set up with great effort in order to say something.[3] They are more static and with a more limited direct range of contact than the popular mass media of our time, such as the newspaper and television, but as cultural deposits they are more durable[4] and are certainly more imposing during direct personal contact, which explains the continued existence of this mass medium in a culture given to economy and fleetingness.

To come to an understanding of the message(s) of the Creation Museum and the way it conveys such was, in the mode of the anthropologist,[5] the purpose of my visit. Based on extensive prior reading which resulted in a loosely structured interview schedule of open questions, meetings were held with managerial, creative, and academic staff members employed at the Museum, with further impressions gained from impromptu informal discussions with visitors to the Museum. Extensive notes were taken of the milieu, the Museum's official personal and video presentations, and of the bookstore, with copies of the DVDs, reading material and a regular newsletter distributed by the Creation Museum (or more accurately, by its parent company, Answers in Genesis—www.answersingenesis.org) further informing my observations.

---

[2] M. McLuhan, *Understanding Media: The Extensions of Man* (2d ed.; Toronto: Signet Books, 1964); cf. J. Marchessault, *Marshall McLuhan. Cosmic Media* (London: SAGE, 2005), 164.
[3] Cf. A. L. Jones, "Exploding Canons: The Anthropology of Museums," *Annual Review of Anthropology* 22 (1993): 201–20; J. Haas, "Power, Objects, and a Voice for Anthropology," *Current Anthropology* 37 (1996): 1–22.
[4] Cf. Lombaard, "Fleetingness and Media-ted Existence," 17–29.
[5] Cf. B. Morris, *Religion and Anthropology. A Critical Introduction* (Cambridge: Cambridge University Press, 2006), 1–13.

It is these sources that form the basis of the broadly interpretative essay offered here. This interpretation is, however, offered within the context of the broader sensitivities of North American culture around the creationism-evolutionism dispute (see below). In fact, one cannot escape the observation that the Creation Museum is part of an intense cultural values contestation within the United States of America. Within a broad cultural-anthropological perspective, better sense can be made of the intent of the Creation Museum as a form of religious mass communication. Although the Museum understands itself primarily as an expression of faith, this expression (that is: argued confession) is certainly not offered in a socio-spiritual void, but is to a significant extent both a product of and contributor to North American cultural dynamics.

The next step in the research process was to present the substance of this essay as a paper at the *Mystical Readings of the Bible* conference of the Spirituality Association of South Africa in April 2009 in Pretoria. Input from discussions of this paper at this conference was then incorporated, after which the essay was sent to a number of critical readers, particularly with a view to judging whether a critical distance had been maintained in my writing. Upon completion of that round of consultation, the paper was sent to Mr. Mark Looy, one of those in the leadership of the Creation Museum, to request—as had previously been arranged—comments on two matters: whether the information conveyed in the essay is indeed accurate, and whether the evaluations offered are, in his view, balanced and fair.[6] In this way, this essay is able to present

---

[6] The only response received was the suggestion that the term "fundamentalist" may be substituted with "evangelical," a suggestion not followed in this essay, because the latter term is too broad to properly characterise the religious views encountered at the Creation Museum. I must emphasise though that I do not use the term "fundamentalist" pejoratively, which was possibly the concern underlying Mr. Looy's suggestion.

here an interpretation that is as informed and even-handed as possible, though clearly still a personal one.[7]

2. An Aspect of Cultural Conflict within the United States of America

Complex and diverse as the North American religio-politico-cultural (RPC[8]) scene is, it remains interesting to observe how American Christianity (and wider, for it certainly affects at least the Jewish scene too) persists in continually dividing itself into two camps: "liberal" and "conservative."[9] Church denominations,

---

[7] Cf., however, M. E. Marty, *Modern American Religion, Volume 2: The Noise of Conflict, 1919–1941* (Chicago: The University of Chicago Press, 1991), 7–10.
[8] Intellectually to separate religion, politics, and cultural aspects of personal and group identities is possible, as the modernist project in the West has shown; however, as postmodernism has had to teach us again, such divisions remain rather artificial. When it comes to the natural business of living, rather than socio-philosophical analyses of life, religio-politico-cultural (RPC) impulses mix inextricably in the psyches of individuals, in the senses of identities of groups, and in the vague self-awarenesses of societies and their cultural streams.
[9] For a reaction against how the moral relativism implied by this kind of "dualism" is played out in United States politics, see A. Huffington, "The Torture Moment," *The Huffington Post*, 24 April 2009. Online: www.huffingtonpost.com/arianna-huffington/the-torture-moment_b_190687. html; cf. C. J. S. Lombaard, "Report: Mission to the USA (April-May 1999)" (Presbyterian Church USA, 1999); so too R. Wuthnow, "Old Fissures and New Fractures in American Religious Life," in *Religion and American Culture. A Reader* (ed. D. G. Hackett. 2d ed.; Routledge: New York, 2003), 361–63.

For fuller descriptions of the complexities running across the United States religious sphere, cf. e.g., W. H. Conser, "Mainstream or Any Streams? Diversity and Its Limits," in *Religion in America. European and American Perspectives* (ed. H. Krabbendam and D. Rubin; Amsterdam: VU University Press, 2004), 19–28; P. Jenkins, "The Center and the Fringe: America's Religious Futures," in *Religion in America. European and American Perspectives* (ed. H. Krabbendam and D. Rubin; Amsterdam: VU University Press, 2004), 51–66; Wuthnow, "Old Fissures and New Fractures," 363–71; P. Jenkins, *Mystics and Messiahs. Cult and New Religions in American History* (Oxford: Oxford University Press, 2000), 227–39.

synodal regions within denominations, parishes/congregations, and individuals self-identify themselves, often strongly, in such terms. These fault lines in the contemporary United States run not, as in the European churches from the eighteenth century onwards, along issues such as the historical probability of the occurrence of divine miracles or the virgin birth and resurrection of Jesus,[10] but along contentious current questions such as abortion, the death penalty, and homosexuality. Although in both cases the nature of the authority of the church's Scriptures stand central,[11] the debates are constituted in quite different ways. Whereas in the European context these debates were conditioned by the problems of a historical cultural awareness[12]—and hence critical exegesis was practiced for the use of the Bible as a source for spiritual nourishment[13]—the US is characterised more by a divergence on socio-political viewpoints.

As an arm's length observer, one of course has a different perspective of a culture/society than people who daily live in it do; however, both the "insider" and "outsider" perspectives are valid interpretative stances—cf. M. E. Rabe, "Revisiting 'Insiders' and 'Outsiders' as Social Researchers," *African Sociological Review/Revue Africaine de Sociologie* 7, no. 2 (2003), 149–61.

My thanks particularly to Mrs. Marian Seagren-Hall and the adult education group of the First Presbyterian Church, Wausau, Wisconsin, United States of America, for offering critical remarks.

[10] Initially, though, these were also the issues against which American conservatism reacted; see e.g., J. G. Melton, "Critiquing Cults: An Historical Perspective," in *Introduction to New and Alternative Religions in America, Volume 1: History and Controversies* (ed. E. V. Gallager and W. M. Ashcraft; Westport, Conn.: Greenwood Press, 2006), 127; Jenkins, *Mystics and Messiahs*, 25–69; C. H. Lippy, *Being Religious, American Style: A History of Popular Religiosity in the United States* (Westport, Conn.: Praeger, 1994) 167–68.

[11] W. S. Hudson, *Religion in America* (4th ed.; New York: Macmillan, 1987), 250–52.

[12] Cf. J. H. le Roux, "The Nature of Historical Understanding" (or: "Hermeneutics and History"), *Studia Historiae Ecclesiasticae* XIX, no. 1 (1993): 35–63.

[13] Usually when a statement to this effect is made, its intent is to criticise historical-critical exegesis. That is in no way the purpose here. On the contrary, I

Interesting is the way in which these American culture wars[14] groups of "values" (that is, of opinions held on these controversial questions) seem usually to cluster together. To keep to two of the above examples: although it is common in the US RPC climate to be either in favour of abortion and opposed to the death penalty (= a "liberal" cluster of values) or the opposite (= a "conservative" cluster of values), a position that opposes both these issues (a traditional Catholic outlook) would be more difficult to find public acceptance, and one that favours both is hardly imaginable, for the latter two options transgress the neat lines that separate in broad US cultural politics the conservative and liberal clusters of values. In the United States, the two main RPC clusters of values mix as well as oil and water.

Literary and cultural critic Harold Bloom has further characterised the "American way" of being religious as inherently gnostic.[15] That is, faith is found not primarily in a direct relationship with God, but in a set of beliefs which are to be held as correct.[16] What one knows and "feels" (less or unargued views) about these important matters is what brings salvation, which is experienced most directly in acceptance by one's peers in faith.

---

am strongly in favour of historical criticism as an exegetical endeavour, precisely for reasons of spiritual nourishment (see C. J. S. Lombaard, "The Old Testament between Diachrony and Synchrony: Two Reasons for Favouring the Former," in *The Pentateuch between Synchrony and Diachrony* [ed. J. H. le Roux and E. Otto; New York: T&T Clark, 2007], 61–70; see also C. J. S. Lombaard, "What Is Biblical Spirituality?—Perspectives from a Minor Genre of Old Testament Scholarship," in *Seeing the Seeker. Explorations in the Discipline of Spirituality* [ed. H. Blommestijn et al.; Festschrift for Kees Waaijman; *Studies in Spirituality* Supplement 19. Louvain, Belgium: Peeters, 2008], 139–53).

[14] Cf. Marty, *Modern American Religion*, 4, 184, 188, 193.

[15] H. Bloom, *The American Religion. The Emergence of a Post-Christian Nation* (New York: Simon & Schuster, 1992), 49.

[16] This is a position which as a whole is very close to classic European liberalism, in which the value of religion was relegated to morality only. The horizontal dimension of faith thus completely suppressed the vertical.

Not God, but one's view of how God is and the way in which this view should be given expression (e.g. Bible study or—at times, almost *versus*—social action), determines one's self-concept of faith and faith alliances. Waaijman's earlier definition of spirituality as that which happens between the self and one's ultimate value is precisely accurate here.[17] This is, furthermore, not an apophatic faith, willing to consider God only in the negative; rather, it is decidedly kataphatic, drawing, however, directly on what is, surprisingly, typically mystic: it asserts certain truths firmly, because—the mystic element[18]—this is the knowledge, or at least the way, that has been revealed. However, here the result is not a contemplative discernment. Rather, secure knowledge elicits decisive action; formulated more broadly: public religion in the United States calls forth competition for social dominance.[19]

This same two-fold division mentioned above also rules the RPC scene as far as the "creationism versus evolution" social fracture in the United States is concerned. To summarise this partition all too briefly: creationism is adhered to by "conservatives" only, whereas evolution is, typically, its "liberal" alternative.

---

[17] See O. Steggink and K. Waaijman, *Spiritualiteit en Mystiek I: Inleiding* (Nijmegen: Gottmer, 1985), 79–100; for the fullest available description of spirituality, cf. P. Nissen, "Kees Waaijman, *Doctor Dialogicus*," in *Seeing the Seeker. Explorations in the Discipline of Spirituality* (ed. H. Blommestijn et al.; Festschrift for Kees Waaijman; *Studies in Spirituality* Supplement 19; Louvain, Belgium: Peeters, 2008), 5; cf. also K. Waaijman, *Spirituality: Forms, Foundations, Methods* (trans. John Vriend; Dudley, Mass.: Peeters, 2002).
[18] Cf. J. S. Krüger, *Sounding Unsound. Orientation into Mysticism* (Pretoria: Aurora Press, 2006); C. Wessinger, "New Religious Movements and Violence," in *Introduction to New and Alternative Religions in America, Volume 1: History and Controversies* (ed. E. V. Gallager and W. M. Ashcraft. Westport, Conn.: Greenwood Press, 2006), 195.
[19] Marty, *Modern American Religion*, 9–10; Lippy, *Being Religious, American Style*, 196; Hudson, *Religion in America*, 107–26.

However, what precisely is meant by these two terms, "creationism" and "evolution"?

3. What Is Creationism?

Creationism is a view on how all that exists has come into being, taking most particularly the First Testament/Old Testament/Hebrew Bible account of Gen 1 (although a more precise demarcation would be Gen 1:1–2:4a[20]) as a literal, "eye witness" description (captured in text by means of divine inspiration of the Scriptures[21] and always associated with a Mosaic authorship of the Pentateuch[22]) of how God created everything.

Though now most often related to religious conservatism, most particularly the tenet in its Christian fundamentalist guise of the inerrancy of the Scriptures in all respects,[23] the creationist view far predates "fundamentalism" (taking the formal date of the latter's beginnings as the Dixon-edited 1910–1915 12-volume book series titled *The Fundamentals*).[24] Ascribing logical

---

[20] The abbreviation "Genesis 1*" will forthwith be used to refer to Gen 1:1–2:4a. Cf. e.g. C. Westermann, *Genesis 1–11* (Biblischer Kommentar Altes Testament 1/1; Neukirchen-Vluyn: Neukirchener Verlag, 1975), 104–244.

[21] Cf., however, J. Liebenberg, "The Use of the Bible in the Science-Theology Debate," in *Nature, God and Humanity* (ed. C. W. du Toit; Pretoria: University of South Africa, 1996), 123, drawing on J. Barr, *Fundamentalism* (London: SCM, 1977), 40.

[22] Cf. for a history in this regard, C. Houtman, *Der Pentateuch. Die Geschichte seiner Erforschung neben einer Auswertung* (Kampen: Kok, 1994).

[23] Cf. Marty, *Modern American Religion,* 191, 205–14.

[24] See A. C. Dixon, ed., *The Fundamentals. A Testimony to the Truth* (12 vols.; Chicago: The Testimony Publishing Company, 1910–1915); cf. H. Munson, "Fundamentalism," in *The Blackwell Companion to the Study of Religion* (ed. R. A. Segal; Oxford: Blackwell, 2006), 255–70.

 This book series reacted not only to secular modernism in the United States which became influential from the 1800s, but also against a range of smaller new religious movements/cults—see D. E. Cowan, "Evangelical Christian Countercult Movement," in *Introduction to New and Alternative*

inconsistencies in the Genesis 1* text[25] either to the fallibility of human understanding or the omnipotence of God, the ancient Near Eastern cultural situatedness along with the modern broad scholarly acceptance of the apologetic nature of this text (namely as an answer to the Babylonian creation myth of the Enuma Elish[26] which thus dates the Genesis 1* text to the exile of the Judean upper social strata to Babylon, *c.* 586–539 B.C.E.[27]) are either refuted or glossed over by creationists. In addressing its adversary, common strategies are to downplay the strength of the theory of evolution, to seek aspects of nature which seem not to be explained by evolution (e.g. random mutations, or the mystery that life exists at all), and to stress the authority of the Bible (as interpreted by creationists).[28]

Viewed broadly, it seems clear that firm, modern(ist) versions of ideas on the nature of truth, an ancient Greek category of thought thoroughly entrenched across more than two millennia of Western(ised) culture, and on the nature of biblical authority, an article of faith which has behind it two millennia of Christian-

---

Religions in America, Volume 1: History and Controversies (ed. E. V. Gallager and W. M. Ashcraft; Westport, Conn.: Greenwood Press, 2006), 146.

For overviews of fundamentalism, cf. G. L. Priest, "A. C. Dixon, Chicago Liberals, and *The Fundamentals*," *Detroit Baptist Seminary Journal* 1 (1996), 113–34; Marty, *Modern American Religion*, 184–214; Hudson, *Religion in America*, 337–42.

[25] For instance, the creation of light (day 1) before the creation of the sun (day 4)—respectively verses 3–5 and 14–19 of Gen 1.

[26] Cf. Westermann, *Genesis 1–11*, 39–65.

[27] Cf. J. M. Miller and J. H. Hayes, *A History of Ancient Israel and Judah* (Philadelphia: Westminster, 1986), 416–20.

[28] Cf. G. M. Branch, "The Theory of Evolution: A Review of Its Current Scientific Status," in *Nature, God and Humanity* (ed. C. W. du Toit; Pretoria: University of South Africa, 1996), 222–23. Further examples from history are mentioned by J. F. Durand, "Evolution and Fundamentalism," in *Nature, God and Humanity* (ed. C. W. du Toit; Pretoria: University of South Africa, 1996), 249–50.

dogmatological development,[29] are combined here to form the basis of the intellectual and pisteological construct of creationism. The context that dominates in assembling this construct is, however, not most directly the ancient Near Eastern, Greek, or earlier Christian-Western ages, but modern America (roughly post-1900), with its RPC battle for the hearts and minds of the North-American populace.

This is equally true of the newest form of creationism,[30] called the theory of intelligent design.[31] This theory argues in typically Greek-philosophical mode from the orderliness of the universe, from which is deduced a creator of nature, whereupon this conclusion is, even if by implication only, applied to the Judeo-Christian concept of divinity. This is the rhetorical strategy of intelligent design within the North American RPC terrain of struggle in this regard, to offer an essentially creationist alternative to evolution as an explanatory model for how the universe came into being and forms of life came to be as they are.[32]

Interestingly, even though arguments from proponents of intelligent design are found frequently and in different ways in the Creation Museum, the terminology "intelligent design" is carefully avoided. The reason for this is that the confession offered by the Creation Museum is more direct: not by deduction may creation be attributable to God, but by direct proclamation from the Bible. A theologically motivated, more direct approach can thus be observed here.

---

[29] Cf. J. Buitendag, "'God met Ons': Gelowig Nagedink oor die Skrif," *HTS Teologiese Studies/Theological Studies* 64, no. 3 (2008): 1131–54.

[30] Cf. the differentiation between creationists in I. G. P. Gous, "Meaning—Intelligently Designed. Keeping the Bible in (a Modern) Mind," *Old Testament Essays* 20, no. 1 (2007): 36–37.

[31] Cf. C. W. du Toit, *Viewed from the Shoulders of God: Themes in Science and Theology* (Pretoria: Research Institute for Theology and Religion, University of South Africa, 2007), 297–316.

[32] Cf. Gous, "Meaning—Intelligently Designed," 335–36.

4. What Is Evolution?

When Charles Darwin a century and a half ago took up and extended earlier antecedent ideas[33] in his *The Origin of Species by Natural Selection*, he provided natural science with an explanatory model and a vocabulary which has proven to be, albeit by now at times in adapted forms,[34] one of the most successful theories of modern science. Further upsetting the pre-Enlightenment's broad and foundational Greek-philosophical acceptance of the ideal stability of all things, along with its influence on Judeo-Christian theological thought, leading it to regard God as being not only the ultimate, but also the immediate cause of all events/change,[35] this novel descriptive framework has been one of a series of proposals, along with, for example, the big bang theory and the theory of continental drift, which have advanced natural science tremendously in recent times and, as a corollary, have put non-scientific understandings of such matters which cast themselves as, still, more valid alternatives, under great pressure.[36]

---

[33] Cf. for a summary: P. van Dyk, "So-called Intelligent Design in Nature. A Discussion with Richard Dawkins," *Old Testament Essays* 20, no. 3 (2007): 851–52; for a more extensive treatment: J. H. Swanepoel, "Bydraes van Darwin se Voorgangers tot die Ewolusieteorie," *SA Tydskrif vir Natuurwetenskap en Tegnologie* 10, no. 1 (1991): 11–17.

[34] See Branch, "The Theory of Evolution," 218–21; P. van Dyk, "Evolusie: die Misverstand tussen Teologie en Biologie," *Hervormde Teologiese Studies* 49, no. 1 and 2 (1993): 286–88.

[35] Van Dyk, "So-called Intelligent Design in Nature," 848–51; cf. Marty, *Modern American Religion,* 186–87.

[36] Cf. P. J. Bowler, *Monkey Trials and Gorilla Sermons: Evolution and Christianity from Darwin to Intelligent Design* (Cambridge, Mass.: Harvard University Press, 2007); P. J. Croce, "Is Life Worth Living?" in *Religions of the United States in Practice* (vol. 1; ed. C. McDannell; Princeton: Princeton University Press, 2001), 237; C. W. du Toit, "The Contribution of Arthur Peacocke to the Science-Theology Debate," in *Nature, God and Humanity* (ed. C. W. du Toit. Pretoria: University of South Africa, 1996), 84–85.

The essentials of the Darwinian proposal, that the adaptation (or Darwin's formulation, so as to escape the idea of progress: "descent with modification")[37] of plant and animal species to their environments are at once random (natural deviances, we now know from genetic origins) and selectively successful in nature (hence heightening the chance of survival for that nonstandard strain of that species in that terrain),[38] have often been popularly misunderstood.[39] Within non-popular, that is, the broad scientific community, evolution has become normal science (in the sense of Kuhn),[40] forming a paradigm of understanding and explanation that, though not perfect,[41] has been of value far beyond its original biological parameters.

5. A More Common Creationism-Evolution Omelette

Quite naturally, attempts have been made to combine a literal interpretation of Genesis 1* with evolution theory. In Christian circles, by calling on 2 Pet 3:8,[42] and in Jewish circles, by calling on the Talmud,[43] the most popular strategy has been to redefine the יוֹם of Genesis 1* as a very lengthy period of time, even though the text itself does not give any such indications. In this way, even

---

[37] Cf. Van Dyk, "Evolusie: die Misverstand tussen Teologie en Biologie," 286.
[38] Van Dyk, "So-called Intelligent Design in Nature," 853–56; Branch, "The Theory of Evolution," 212–18.
[39] Cf. J. W. van Huyssteen, *Alone in the World? Human Uniqueness in Science and Theology* (Grand Rapids: Eerdmans, 2006), 60–67; summarised in C. J. S. Lombaard, "Wetenskap en Bybel Saamgeweef," *Beeld* (*By*-bylaag) 4 Junie 2007: 13.
Online: http://152.111.1.88/argief/berigte/beeld/2007/06/04/B1/13/gvadam.html.
[40] T. S. Kuhn, *The Structure of Scientific Revolutions* (Chicago: University of Chicago Press, 1962).
[41] Van Dyk, "Evolusie: die Misverstand tussen Teologie en Biologie," 281–82.
[42] "ὅτι μία ἡμέρα παρὰ κυρίῳ ὡς χίλια ἔτη καὶ χίλια ἔτη ὡς ἡμέρα μία".
[43] Cf. e.g. N. Aviezer, *In the Beginning... Biblical Creation and Science* (Hoboken, N.J.: KTAV, 1990), 1–2.

billions of years of development may be fit into a "day" of the Genesis 1* account. (Interestingly, this interpretative strategy is rejected by staff at the Creation Museum, since it is at odds with their literal interpretation of the Genesis creation account/s).

However, this apologist strategy (namely to salvage the credibility of Genesis 1* for a scientific age) never quite satisfies—apart from the fact that the "fit" between nature and text soon becomes forced, with a regular "aha!"-experience on rhetorical display (to reinterpret here somewhat the psychological dimensions of this phenomenon by, originally, Bühler[44]): the ancient contextually argumentative intent of the Genesis 1* text, namely as a priestly, that is, Israelite confession over against the Babylonian Enuma Elish creation account, is never taken into consideration. Genesis 1* as ancient, historically datable literature of religious type is turned into a contemporary kind of natural-scientific report. Moreover, rather than a concrete ancient Near Eastern confession with clearly traceable and comprehensible intertextual play, Genesis 1* now becomes a magical document, with the "real" (= natural-scientific) creation events as its "hidden" meaning (the mode of the mystic or of the Gnostic interpreter), to be unlocked only now, by means of the most modern insights from a completely unrelated source (the mode of the allegorist, or the heretic), namely natural science. The "key and lock" do not match.[45]

The nature of the text is distorted when viewed through such modernist lenses.[46] While both science and religion offer understanding, the former relates this to knowledge; the latter, to

---

[44] See K. Bühler, *Tatsache und Probleme zu einer Psychologie der Denkvorgänge. Über Gedanken* (Archiv für die gesamte Psychologie, 9; Leipzig: Wilhelm Engelmann, 1907), 14.

[45] See H. W. de Knijff, *Sleutel en Slot: Beknopte Geschiedenis van de Bijbelse Hermeneutiek* (Kampen: Kok, 1980); so, too, Du Toit, "The Contribution of Arthur Peacocke to the Science-Theology Debate," 90–91.

[46] Van Dyk, "Evolusie: die Misverstand tussen Teologie en Biologie," 286–88.

meaning. Although intellect and existentialism do mingle, exerting their respective influences in both directions, they are not identical.[47] Hence, both can equally, and inter-dynamically, be valid: *cogito ergo sum* and *credo ergo sum*.

At the Creation Museum, a different communicative strategy is, however, followed.

6. Creationism and Evolution at the Creation Museum

I had a number of my preconceptions challenged about those associated with the Creation Museum soon after arriving on the premises. Chief among these was my expectation to find a staunchly anti-intellectualist climate; the dissolution of this expectation I employ as a structuring aid for my description below of the Museum. This is namely done in four parts: geography, staff, interior architecture, and displays. Some of the T-shirts and peak hats on display for sale initially fed my scepticism about what I would find, with emblazoned slogans such as "Creation museum. Prepare to believe." This was, after all, a religious theme park, in the fashion that had developed in post-World War II America as tourist attractions.[48] That the Creation Museum fit this mould well was clear from the way it was marketed and from the way visitors described themselves. For some groups, such as the Amish, dressed in distinctive clothing from yesteryear, this has even become something of a prized holiday destination. "This is our thinking," one such patron, who had brought his family for the day, responded with quiet confidence. However, surprising to me was the catchphrase found on as many items of clothing merchandise: "Science is awesome." This, I had yet to realise, stood in a firm

---

[47] Gous, "Meaning—Intelligently Designed," 40, drawing on H. W. Rossouw, *Die Sin van die Lewe* (Kaapstad: Tafelberg, 1981).
[48] Cf. Lippy, *Being Religious, American Style*, 224, 227–28.

tradition within creationism of not wanting to be (seen as) anti-scientific.[49]

6.1 Geography of the Creation Museum

The Creation Museum, which had been in operation for about a year at the time of my June 2008 visit, is to a significant extent aimed at the heart of middle America. Not only is it sociologically an outflow of the heyday of mid-twentieth century US Christian fundamentalism; in addition, it is intended to speak to the vast American middle class. It is also deliberately situated in its current, very central location. Mr. Mark Looy, Chief Communications Officer of Answers in Genesis/The Creation Museum, was happy to recount the deliberate choice of geography: rather than the initially considered other localities, including Orlando, Florida (home to Disney World, among other tourist attractions), which would not be placed centrally enough, and with the Orlando location having too many connotations of superficial entertainment for their tastes, the vicinity of Cincinnati, Ohio was a reasoned choice. It is close to the predominantly eastward placement of the US population. This translates directly to the demographic actuality that 190 million Americans, that is roughly two-thirds of the American populace, can drive by motor vehicle to the Creation Museum within one day. It is also within relatively easy reach of the Canadian province of Ontario. Moreover, the flight connections to Cincinnati are excellent, with the nearby airport being one of the important North American hubs for Delta Airlines. In addition, when in 1994 the parent company of the Creation Museum, Answers in Genesis, decided on Cincinnati, the city had just been chosen by the 1993 *Almanac*, a magazine for entrepreneurs, as the most desirable city out of three hundred in the United States in which to live. In many respects, thus, Cincinnati is a choice

---

[49] Marty, *Modern American Religion*, 188.

location, and this contributes strongly to the Creation Museum attracting between 3,000 and 4,000 visitors a day during its summer season—much more than any similar sites, such as a smaller creation museum in San Diego, (www.icr.org/discover/index/discover_museum), and a fossil museum in Germany with a similar creationist disposition (cf. www.nwcreation.net/museums.html).

Though a tongue-in-cheek assertion would hold that creationists, given their partiality to a strictly circumscribed placement of all things on earth and in time, could be expected to choose their prime site wisely, at the very least the choice of this location was a well-considered business decision. However, there clearly is more to this choice of geography. Here a deliberate selection was made for a specific place (rather than a non-place)[50] that is integrally meaningful to the mission of the Creation Museum. The Cincinnati region itself holds no symbolic currency for creationists as would, for instance, Salt Lake City, Utah, for Mormons; however, it is not a holy site that the founders of the Creation Museum sought. The RPC debate in which this museum is engaged regards the entire American populace (and wider) as its site of struggle. The spirituality it seeks to promote is regarded by its proponents as both timeless and borderless (in geographical sense). Therefore, openness and convenience are the main criteria for such an engagement.[51] This is communicated not only by the extensive travels to speaking engagements of the leadership of the Creation Museum/Answers in Genesis, but also by the deliberate

---

[50] Cf. D. Perrin, *Studying Christian Spirituality* (New York: Routledge, 2007), 63–68, drawing on M. Augé, *Non-places: Introduction to an Anthropology of Supermodernity* (London: Verso, 1995).

[51] This general impression of openness was somewhat belied by the imposing security in the form of armed guards with police dogs at the facility. This was however ascribed to "post 9/11" vigilance, an atmosphere which was (not surprisingly) most evident at United States airports. Still, I retained a sense of unease that the reason given may not have been all that was behind these security measures.

accessibility of the terrain at which its message is presented most imposingly.

6.2 Staff of the Creation Museum

According to Mr. Looy, the Creation Museum employs three hundred staff members, which includes creative[52] and library staff, and a small number of scholars. The latter is of particular interest. A small group of about six academics are in the fulltime employ of the Creation Museum, all qualified with advanced degrees in the natural sciences. Their tasks comprise research, including the publication of scholarly articles, public speaking engagements, and answering questions on the Answers in Genesis webpage. Naturally, all these activities take place from the vantage point of creationism, with two main thrusts: pointing out problems they perceive with evolution as a model of science, and presenting alternative explanations, often in the vein of intelligent design. Being published in mainstream scientific journals, however, presents particular difficulties.

In an interview with David Menton, holder of a Ph.D. in Biology from the ivy league Brown University, these aspects were discussed quite frankly. His expectation, he said, was that the

---

[52] A South African note: Very early on during my visit to the Museum's premises, waiting for my first appointment, I was surprised to be greeted in my home language, Afrikaans. During two conversations it became clear that this was an ex-South African, now resident in Cincinnati, who was one of the seven employees involved with the design of the Creation Museum's webpages. She had been engaged as a graphic artist, while still living in Pretoria, at the Transvaal Museum (www.gauteng.com/content.php?page=Transvaal%20Museum; it has since been renamed the National Museum of Natural History), which has a substantial collection of ancient fossils on prominent display, with the thinking behind it, however, as would be expected, the acceptance of current scientific consensus, also as regards evolution. On my prompt, the respondent affirmed that she felt at home within the ideological climate at the Creation Museum.

156 *The Old Testament and Christian Spirituality*

human body would make sense—that is why he studied it. Hence, too, his interest in vestigial organs such as the coccyx, long a debating point between evolutionists and their opponents,[53] with the former ascribing the now obsolete status of such organs to humans having evolved past their use. The logical retort from creationists is to put forward a continued use for such organs, among other strategies.

Another interesting decision by the Creation Museum was to employ Hollywood-quality set designers to take care of the interior of the buildings. Mr. Patrick Marsh, Museum Design Director, who had earlier been responsible for the set design of motion pictures such as *Jaws* and *King Kong*, and had been involved in a similar capacity with the 1984 Olympic Games, sees his role as that of telling a story inside the Museum. Rather than simply presenting a collection, he would like to engage the visitor, he points out. Interpreting a script written by Mr. Ken Ham (the most public face of Answers in Genesis/the Creation Museum, with a long-running weekly radio show "Answers… with Ken Ham," broadcast on nine hundred radio stations[54]), which is based on the "7 C's" (a traditional salvation historical overview, here given a mnemonic twist: Creation, Corruption, Catastrophe, Confusion, Christ, Cross, Consummation), Mr. Marsh's exhibition track leads visitors to meander through this traditional salvation history.

Within the usual media triad of information-entertainment-education, the emphasis is here on the latter, namely to show patrons the archaeological "truth" of the Bible, for "it is good science." In the work of Mr. Marsh, thus, Bible interpretation,

---

[53] Cf. J. Bergman and G. Howe, *Vestigial Organs Are Fully Functional* (Kansas City: Creation Research Society Books, 1990).
[54] It was Ham's book (see K. Ham, *The Lie: Evolution* [Green Forest, Ark.: Master Books, 1987]) that had led to Looy's conversion to Christianity-and-creationism; in his words: "When I became a Christian and a creationist…" (cf. Liebenberg, "The Use of the Bible," 123, drawing on Barr, *Fundamentalism,* 1).

(creation/ist) science and art meet. Multi-media presentations are used, because people do not read much, he indicates. Therefore a visual drama is created "through each one of the spaces, to bring thought to the message." Taking great pleasure in and care with his art, he wants to satisfy the senses, for him here though in a more meaningful way than in Hollywood, he says, because it brings greater and deeper happiness.

It is to the way in which Mr. Marsh does this that we turn next.

6.3 Interior architecture of the Creation Museum

Mr. Marsh deliberately creates at the Museum settings and experiences which "support the Bible," as a service to the churches, namely to help them "defend their message." "The spaces must do something; affect the people," and his hope is that "each space conveys the message." Drawing on eleven years of studying Zen gardens and temples in Japan, a meandering flow of corridors leading to exhibition rooms have been installed within the space of the 6,500 square meters of museum building. The corridors first lead downhill, symbolising society going downhill. From sin, in the nether regions of the building, the corridors lead upwards, with aspects of traditional Christian salvation history exhibited next to the walkways and in dedicated exhibition rooms. The corridors end at the highest point in exhibits calling for the glorification of God, since it is God who is the inspiration of all greatness.

Next, brief descriptions are given of the displays along this (what may be called) symbolic salvation history walkway, and of some of the presentations on offer.

6.4 Displays and presentations in the Creation Museum

A clear juxtaposition is created in the displays between "God's word" and "human reason," with the implicit subtext being: which is the more trustworthy? In the intended rhetoric, piety predictably will lead most patrons to choose the first option (that is, if one is to accept the proposed alternatives). This is related, by means of multicoloured plaques and big-screen televised videos, to examples such as fossil remains and the formation of canyons—matters of contested dating in the creationism-evolution debate.

On the problem of the dinosaurs, the paucity of evidence in some respects is employed to question the stability of all interpretations of the skeletal remains, with the choice offered again: "I think, therefore I am" *versus* "I am that I am"—that is, Descartes *versus* Yahweh; reason *versus* revelation; humanity *versus* God. One senses here almost a mystic drift in the argument of the proposed choice: it is as if the observer should leave the world behind, in order to find unity of purpose with God (here with a firm emphasis on the divinity as Creator), again to return to the earth, now viewing it "anew," in a certain way.

In the same manner, the understanding of the coming into being of the universe, plants, animals, and humans are placed under this dualism, with a big display evidencing a beginning date for everything as "4004 B.C." Martin Luther's *sola scriptura* principle and his famous Wittenberg act of 1517 are employed too, to cast doubt on the churches that have—following the logic of the Creation Museum displays—accepted reason over Bible, with a dramatic installation room exhibiting scenes and sounds of urban decay as examples of a culture that has grown loose from the Bible. Video displays, large plaques, and posters continually underline such ideas in different ways throughout the exhibits.

A particular logical difficulty is to make acceptable the co-existence of humans and dinosaurs. This difficulty receives greater attention in a special, elevated "Dinosaur Den," reiterating many points made elsewhere in the Museum. By calling on Gen 1:30's seemingly vegetarian world and Gen 2:9's view of the abundance of such food (thus not making anything of the textual fissure between Gen 2:4a and b), the problem of dinosaurs feeding on humans is solved. By plus-minus life-sized puppet displays and accompanying plates with Bible verses and explanatory notations, it is made explicit that God created the first humans, and that they did not evolve. Marriage and innocent nudity, the latter rather coyly inferred, are shown in the displays in a paradise setting. Adorably, dinosaurs frolic in the undergrowth close by.

The above is juxtaposed harshly in the following installations with depictions of pain, injustice and suffering—the result of the serpent, sin, and curse. Clothes, sacrifice, death, illness, carnivores, burdensome work, poison, weeds, suffering, murder all become part of life, as does, interestingly, the aging of the earth.

The narrative of Noah's ark receives ample attention, with a range of displays and life-like depictions of scenes, some in miniature form, some through interactive video games, some through life-sized installations. Here too the problem of dinosaurs rears its head: how would such fierce, large animals fit in a real ark? However, in a cut-away miniature model of the ark, as in some of the children's books on sale in the Museum's bookstore, a brilliantly creative solution is offered: dinosaurs were of course included among the pairs of animals on Noah's ark. Only, they were youngsters.

The flood associated with Noah's ark in addition becomes a hermeneutical key to understanding the fossil record. "The Bible is the key to help us understand geological features," a video voice-over reiterates. Similarly, the tower of Babel explains the existence of different peoples. The next major point on display is the coming of a Messiah, namely Jesus. Throughout these displays, frequent use of Hebrew audio-phrases and the Hebrew alphabet on stone inscriptions (such as the tables of the Decalogue) and decorated wall areas contribute to creating a sense of authenticity for the observer.

Not only in such displays, but also in multi-dimensional presentations (public speakers, high quality video and slide shows, on the foreground of which are life-like installations) the same message is carried. Titled "Men in white" (the ironic allusion to a popular motion picture should not escape one), two angels, Mike and Gabe (a thoroughly American abbreviation of angelic names), in one such triple-screened video presentation in a mid-sized movie theatre, debate God's role in the universe. With vibrating cinema-house chairs and light water spouts in viewers' faces, the experience is most entertaining. Both this and the rhetoric of the film dialogue intend clearly to warn against what children in particular are taught, specifically at school, namely evolution.[55]

In another such presentation, Mr. Carl Kerby, a very dynamic speaker, argues with much humour the case for creationism. Part of his presentation includes recounting how he had recently been refused the pulpit in a congregation where he had been invited to preach, when it was realised by his hosts that his wife is Japanese. Mr. Kerby's firm rejection of such racism had for sceptics in the audience the rhetorical effect of strengthening a great deal his credibility as a trustworthy source.

The latter is further fortified by his strategy of communication against evolutionism. A series of beautiful slides are shown of perplexing occurrences in plant and animal life, with each occurrence briefly described. The question is then posed by Mr. Kerby whether such cases can be explained by mere happenstance (implying evolution), leaving open the inference (a typical intelligent design oratory technique) that there must be a Higher Power behind all things. However, in each instance a subsequent question is posed, on whether this on its own is enough proof for God creating these things directly, to which the audience is then prompted to respond, "Not even close!" After a number of repetitions of this rhetorical circle, the final answer is given.

---

[55] For an overview of the South African situation in this regard, cf. J. J. F. Durand, "The Influence of Religion and Politics on the Teaching of Evolution in South Africa," *Ekklesiastikos Pharos*, New Series 13/85, no. 1 and 2 (2003): 203–23.

Evolution is wrong, simply and finally, because the Bible tells us so.

Here, science is "reinterpreted in the light of the Bible" (to twist here the intention of the words of Du Toit).[56]

6.5 Taken together

Mr. Kerby has a number of other points he makes during his presentation, described above; indeed, in all of the above, only certain highlights have been included. A section on the bookstore at the Creation Museum could, for instance, have been added here, making in another way the same points. The case is already made well enough that in the different personal and video presentations, in the "language" of the interior lay-out of the Museum, with the academic staff and through the broader geography of the Creation Museum, its argument has been perfectly honed to communicate strongly one central message:[57] the theological and scientific, and thus logical priority of creationism over evolution—to a culture which is to a large extent open to such argumentation.

Certainly, in all respects, the Creation Museum is thus a case of highly intelligent design. Even though many, amongst whom I count myself, view the Bible in a very different way, and many—again, I am included here—still insist no less on its authority as the Word of God, yet have no qualms with the theory of evolution, the cogency of the message of the Creation Museum ought to be recognised. That there is a great degree of personal integrity and

---

[56] See Du Toit, "The Contribution of Arthur Peacocke to the Science-Theology Debate," 85; cf. Liebenberg, "The Use of the Bible," 125.

[57] Apart from the already mentioned security measures, the Zen garden outside the museum does not sing along with this well-directed choir. However, its serenity and beauty is such that one ought to ascribe this, positively, to tolerance towards other spiritual traditions.

honesty behind this is beyond any doubt.[58] It is for precisely this reason that the Creation Museum makes such a fascinating object of study, particularly from a somewhat distanced religio- and cultural-anthropological observer's perspective as was followed here.

7. The Creation Museum and Spirituality

Given the model of Biblical Spirituality with which I operate,[59] which includes analysis on the one hand of spiritualities encountered *in* the Bible and on the other hand of spiritualities *from* the Scriptures, the Creation Museum is an engaging example of the latter. It offers us an instance of a very specific and—considering that museums are a form of mass communication—a highly institutionalised, and in the case of this Museum, an obviously purposefully unified reception and expression of the Genesis 1* text. It is an interpretation of a particular kind we find here, though: the Bible plays an "evidential role,"[60] providing us with the final proof of what reality is, also as far as the natural sciences are concerned.

The Creation Museum is also a good example of the high degree of influence of broad culture upon spirituality: this museum is in many respects a very American phenomenon, conditioned by a century's history of the negative reception of Darwin, and playing out within the sphere of North American RPC debates during the twentieth century and now, viewing itself, as involved in a battle for "true" Christianity, or for a "true" Christian culture, over against (government-forced) cultural "liberalism."[61]

---

[58] I am not, however, blind to the potential and actual conflictednesses within that context, which is of course natural and to be expected. Such considerations lie, however, beyond the scope here.
[59] Lombaard, "What Is Biblical Spirituality?" 139–53.
[60] Liebenberg, "The Use of the Bible," 133–34.
[61] Cf. Marty, *Modern American Religion*, 190.

Spirituality never stands detached from, and is in this sense also conditioned by, the culture or society in which it is expressed.

In both these interpretative contexts, an intensely-experienced personal conviction, interpreted as a revelation of God's true intent, lies at the heart of at least the leadership of the Creation Museum, but certainly also of most of its patrons and supporters. This is an orientation that for its adherents lies outside the terrain of contestation from either normal science or human reasoning; it is a hermeneutical world that is inward-looking,[62] and critical only in the sense that such intellectual work would feed the premises of the already accepted (world)views. This may well be described, from a social-scientific perspective, as a mythological worldview of sorts;[63] from the side of natural science, as a mystifying take on reality; and from the discipline of Spirituality, as approaching in many respects the mode of the mystic.

---

[62] C. J. S. Lombaard, "South African Perspectives on the Communication of the Bible in Church and Society" (Ph.D. diss., North-West University, Potchefstroom Campus, 2004), 5–8.

[63] Cf. P. van Dyk, "Mythical Linkage and Mythical Frameworks," *Old Testament Essays* 18, no. 3 (2005): 863–78.

BIBLIOGRAPHY

Augé, M. *Non-places: Introduction to an Anthropology of Supermodernity*. London: Verso, 1995.
Aviezer, N. *In the Beginning... Biblical Creation and Science*. Hoboken, N.J.: KTAV, 1990.
Barr, J. *Fundamentalism*. London: SCM, 1977.
Bergman, J. and G. Howe. *Vestigial Organs Are Fully Functional*. Kansas City: Creation Research Society Books, 1990.
Bloom, H. *The American Religion. The Emergence of a Post-Christian Nation*. New York: Simon & Schuster, 1992.
Bowler, P. J. *Monkey Trials and Gorilla Sermons: Evolution and Christianity from Darwin to Intelligent Design*. Cambridge, Mass.: Harvard University Press, 2007.
Branch, G. M. "The Theory of Evolution: A Review of Its Current Scientific Status." Pages 210–25 in *Nature, God and Humanity*. Edited by C. W. du Toit. Pretoria: University of South Africa, 1996.
Bühler, K. *Tatsache und Probleme zu einer Psychologie der Denkvorgänge. Über Gedanken*. Archiv für die gesamte Psychologie, 9. Leipzig: Wilhelm Engelmann, 1907.
Buitendag, J. "'God met Ons': Gelowig Nagedink oor die Skrif." *HTS Teologiese Studies/Theological Studies* 64, no. 3 (2008): 1131–54.
Conser, W. H. "Mainstream or Any Streams? Diversity and Its Limits." Pages 19–28 in *Religion in America. European and American Perspectives*. Edited by H. Krabbendam and D. Rubin. Amsterdam: VU University Press, 2004.
Cowan, D. E. "Evangelical Christian Countercult Movement." Pages 143–64 in *Introduction to New and Alternative Religions in America, Volume 1: History and Controversies*. Edited by E. V. Gallager and W. M. Ashcraft. Westport, Conn.: Greenwood Press, 2006.

Croce, P. J. "Is Life Worth Living?" Pages 234–52 in *Religions of the United States in Practice*. Volume 1. Edited by C. McDannell. Princeton: Princeton University Press, 2001.
Darwin, C. *On the Origin of Species by Means of Natural Selection, or the Preservation of Favoured Races in the Struggle for Life*. London: John Murray, 1859.
De Knijff, H. W. *Sleutel en Slot: Beknopte Geschiedenis van de Bijbelse Hermeneutiek*. Kampen: Kok, 1980.
Dixon, A. C., ed. *The Fundamentals. A Testimony to the Truth*. 12 volumes. Chicago: The Testimony Publishing Company, 1910–1915.
Durand, J. F. "The Influence of Religion and Politics on the Teaching of Evolution in South Africa." *Ekklesiastikos Pharos*, New Series 13/85, no. 1 and 2 (2003): 203–23.
———. "Evolution and Fundamentalism." Pages 244–58 in *Nature, God and Humanity*. Edited by C. W. du Toit. Pretoria: University of South Africa, 1996.
Du Toit, C. W. *Viewed from the Shoulders of God: Themes in Science and Theology*. Pretoria: Research Institute for Theology and Religion, University of South Africa, 2007.
———. "The Contribution of Arthur Peacocke to the Science-Theology Debate." Pages 84–101 in *Nature, God and Humanity*. Edited by C. W. du Toit. Pretoria: University of South Africa, 1996.
Gous, G. P. "Meaning—Intelligently Designed. Keeping the Bible in (a Modern) Mind." *Old Testament Essays* 20, no. 1 (2007): 34–52.
Haas, J. "Power, Objects, and a Voice for Anthropology." *Current Anthropology* 37 (1996): 1–22.
Ham, K. *The Lie: Evolution*. Green Forest, Ark.: Master Books, 1987.
Houtman, C. *Der Pentateuch. Die Geschichte seiner Erforschung neben einer Auswertung*. Kampen: Kok, 1994.

Hudson, W. S. *Religion in America*. Fourth edition. New York: Macmillan, 1987.

Huffington, A. "The Torture Moment." *The Huffington Post*, 24 April 2009. Online: www.huffingtonpost.com/arianna-huffington/the-torture-moment_b_190687.html

Jenkins, P. "The Center and the Fringe: America's Religious Futures." Pages 51–66 in *Religion in America. European and American Perspectives*. Edited by H. Krabbendam and D. Rubin. Amsterdam: VU University Press, 2004.

Jenkins, P. *Mystics and Messiahs. Cult and New Religions in American History*. Oxford: Oxford University Press, 2000.

Jones, A. L. "Exploding Canons: The Anthropology of Museums." *Annual Review of Anthropology* 22 (1993): 201–20.

Krüger, J. S. *Sounding Unsound. Orientation into Mysticism*. Pretoria: Aurora Press, 2006.

Kuhn, T. S. *The Structure of Scientific Revolutions*. Chicago: University of Chicago Press, 1962.

Le Roux, J. H. "The Nature of Historical Understanding" (or: "Hermeneutics and History"). *Studia Historiae Ecclesiasticae* XIX, no. 1 (1993): 35–63.

Liebenberg, J. "The Use of the Bible in the Science-Theology Debate." Pages 120–49 in *Nature, God and Humanity*. Edited by C. W. du Toit. Pretoria: University of South Africa, 1996.

Lippy, C. H. *Being Religious, American Style: A History of Popular Religiosity in the United States*. Westport, Conn.: Praeger, 1994.

Lombaard, C. J. S. "Fleetingness and Media-ted Existence. From Kierkegaard on the Newspaper to Broderick on the Internet." Paper read at the *Media, Spiritualities and Social Change* Conference, 4–7 June 2008. Center for Media, Religion and Culture, School of Journalism and Mass Communication, University of Colorado, Boulder, United States of America; *Communicatio* 35, no. 1 (2009): 17–29.

———. "What Is Biblical Spirituality?—Perspectives from a Minor Genre of Old Testament Scholarship." Pages 139–53 in *Seeing the Seeker. Explorations in the Discipline of Spirituality.* Edited by H. Blommestijn et al. Festschrift for Kees Waaijman; *Studies in Spirituality* Supplement 19. Louvain, Belgium: Peeters, 2008.

———. "The Old Testament between Diachrony and Synchrony: Two Reasons for Favouring the Former." Pages 61–70 in *The Pentateuch between Synchrony and Diachrony.* Edited by J. H. le Roux and E. Otto. New York: T&T Clark, 2007.

———. "Wetenskap en Bybel Saamgeweef." *Beeld* (*By*-bylaag) 4 Junie 2007: 13. Online: http://152.111.1.88/argief/berigte/beeld/2007/06/04/B1/13/gvadam.html.

———. "South African Perspectives on the Communication of the Bible in Church and Society." Ph.D. diss., North-West University, Potchefstroom Campus, 2004.

———. "Report: Mission to the USA (April-May 1999)." Presbyterian Church United States of America, 1999.

Marchessault, J. *Marshall McLuhan. Cosmic Media.* London: SAGE, 2005.

Marty, M. E. *Modern American Religion, Volume 2: The Noise of Conflict, 1919–1941.* Chicago: The University of Chicago Press, 1991.

McLuhan, M. *Understanding Media: The Extensions of Man.* Second edition. Toronto: Signet Books, 1964.

Melton, J. G. "Critiquing Cults: An Historical Perspective." Pages 126–42 in *Introduction to New and Alternative Religions in America, Volume 1: History and Controversies.* Edited by E. V. Gallager and W. M. Ashcraft. Westport, Conn.: Greenwood Press, 2006.

Miller, J. M. and J. H. Hayes. *A History of Ancient Israel and Judah.* Philadelphia: Westminster, 1986.

Morris, B. *Religion and Anthropology. A Critical Introduction.* Cambridge: Cambridge University Press, 2006.

Nissen, P. "Kees Waaijman, *Doctor Dialogicus*." Pages 1–7 in *Seeing the Seeker. Explorations in the Discipline of Spirituality.* Edited by H. Blommestijn et al. Festschrift for Kees Waaijman; *Studies in Spirituality* Supplement 19. Louvain, Belgium: Peeters, 2008.

Perrin, D. *Studying Christian Spirituality.* New York: Routledge, 2007.

Priest, G. L. "A. C. Dixon, Chicago Liberals, and *The Fundamentals*." *Detroit Baptist Seminary Journal* 1 (1996): 113–34.

Rabe, M. E. "Revisiting 'Insiders' and 'Outsiders' as Social Researchers." *African Sociological Review/Revue Africaine de Sociologie* 7, no. 2 (2003): 149–61.

Rossouw, H. W. *Die Sin van die Lewe.* Kaapstad: Tafelberg, 1981.

Steggink, O. and K. Waaijman. *Spiritualiteit en Mystiek I: Inleiding.* Nijmegen: Gottmer, 1985.

Swanepoel, J. H. "Bydraes van Darwin se Voorgangers tot die Ewolusieteorie." *SA Tydskrif vir Natuurwetenskap en Tegnologie* 10, no. 1 (1991): 11–17.

Munson, H. "Fundamentalism." Pages 255–70 in *The Blackwell Companion to the Study of Religion.* Edited by R. A. Segal. Oxford: Blackwell, 2006.

Van Dyk, P. "So-called Intelligent Design in Nature. A Discussion with Richard Dawkins." *Old Testament Essays* 20, no. 3 (2007): 847–59.

———. "Mythical Linkage and Mythical Frameworks." *Old Testament Essays* 18, no. 3 (2005): 863–78.

———. "Evolusie: die Misverstand tussen Teologie en Biologie." *Hervormde Teologiese Studies* 49, no. 1 and 2 (1993): 281–95.

Van Huyssteen, J. W. *Alone in the World? Human Uniqueness in Science and Theology.* Grand Rapids: Eerdmans, 2006.

Vorster, J. N. "The Use of Scripture in Fundamentalism." Pages 155–75 in *Paradigms and Progress in Theology*. Edited by J. Mouton, J. G. van Aarde and W. S. Vorster. Pretoria: HSRC, 1988.

Waaijman, K. *Spirituality: Forms, Foundations, Methods.* Translated by John Vriend. Dudley, Mass.: Peeters, 2002.

Wessinger, C. "New Religious Movements and Violence." Pages 165–205 in *Introduction to New and Alternative Religions in America, Volume 1: History and Controversies.* Edited by E. V. Gallager and W. M. Ashcraft. Westport, Conn.: Greenwood Press, 2006.

Westermann, C. *Genesis 1–11.* Biblischer Kommentar Altes Testament 1/1. Neukirchen-Vluyn: Neukirchener Verlag, 1975.

Wuthnow, R. "Old Fissures and New Fractures in American Religious Life." Pages 357–71 in *Religion and American Culture. A Reader*. Edited by D. G. Hackett. Second edition. Routledge: New York, 2003.

Exegesis and Spirituality*

ABSTRACT
Many of the problems underlying the tension between faith and scholarship, church and academia, piety and Bible scholarship concern the way exegesis and spirituality have either been combined or separated. Often, the ways in which exegesis and spirituality are either combined or separated create more problems than solutions. In this paper, reasoned from within the emerging discipline of Biblical Spirituality, these problems are argued, and some proposals made.

1. Hear Ye, Hear Ye?

Scholars of religion in general and of the Bible in particular are all too aware of the reality that the relationship between the Scriptures and faith is not an easy one;[1] nor has it ever been—contrary to recurring calls that we "return" to the "biblical" faith.[2] Whereas popular ideas in society on this topic hold to a simplistic relationship, namely that Christianity draws its faith rather directly from the Bible—a view that is to a significant extent also fed by church catechisms, which tend to keep to unhistorical approaches—scholars know that the concepts of "faith" or "Scripture" are not simple; nor, certainly, is the relationship

---

* Some ideas in this essay were, after our initial cooperation, presented as a discussion paper by my doctoral student, Daniel Nae, at the Research Sharing Conference, Adventist Theological Institute, Cernica, Romania, in May 2007 (see bibliography). This essay was then developed from those initial impulses, and was presented by me at the fiftieth congress of the Old Testament Society of South Africa in August 2007 at the University of Pretoria, South Africa.
[1] Cf. e.g. G. le Marquand, "Siblings or Antagonists? The Ethos of Biblical Scholarship from the North Atlantic and African Worlds," in *Biblical Interpretation in African Perspective* (ed. D. Adamo; Lanham, Md.: University Press of America, 2006), 62–63.
[2] Cf. P. Zimmerling, *Evangelische Spiritualität. Wurzeln und Zugänge* (Göttingen: Vandenhoeck & Ruprecht, 2003), 32.

between these two. For instance, in Old Testament studies much research has focussed on the internal debate within and between the different books of the Hebrew Bible, which reflect diverse and competing theological strands within ancient Israel. Thus, within the Hebrew Bible itself, rival notions stand at odds with one another.[3] The same may be said of the New Testament, even though it had a much shorter gestation period and consists of a more limited literary scope.[4] Not surprisingly, therefore, attempts at writing a biblical theology comprising both Testaments have shown quite clearly the difficulties in tracing consistencies within all the dissimilarities both within and between the Semitic and Hellenistic parts of the Bible.[5]

The complications involved with interpreting such a diffusion of textual deposits within Scripture have given rise to many of the dogmatological controversies and even to ecclesial schisms throughout two millennia of church history.[6] In the wake of the modern period's almost instinctive drive towards specialisation and compartmentalisation, these same interpretative problems are evidenced in the varied ways in which the different disciplines of

---

[3] Cf. R. Albertz, *Religionsgeschichte Israels in alttestamentlicher Zeit* (vols. 1 and 2; Göttingen: Vandenhoeck & Ruprecht, 1992).

[4] Cf. e.g. P. Balla, *Challenges to New Testament Theology. An Attempt to Justify the Enterprise* (Tübingen: Mohr Siebeck, 1997), 147–209.

[5] Cf. e.g. the essays collected in S. E. Porter, ed., *Hearing the Old Testament in the New Testament* (Grand Rapids: Eerdmans, 2006); Old Testament theologies such as those by Preuß and Brueggemann try to solve the diversity by playing concepts off against one another, as the central approach to their work; see H. D. Preuß, *Theologie des Alten Testaments, Band 1: JHWHs erwählendes und verpflichtendes Handeln* (Stuttgart: Kohlhammer, 1991), and W. Brueggemann, *Theology of the Old Testament: Testimony, Dispute, Advocacy* (Minneapolis: Fortress, 1997). K. Nürnberger proposes an evolutionary approach (in *Theology of the Biblical Witness. An Evolutionary Approach* [Theologie: Forschung und Wissenschaft, Band 5; Münster: LIT Verlag, 2002]).

[6] Cf. F. L. Canale, *Understanding Revelation-Inspiration in a Postmodern World* (Berrien Springs: Andrews University Lithotech, 2001), 25.

the theological encyclopaedia employ the Bible. Not infrequently, Bible scholars find themselves aghast at what for instance Practical Theologians, Missiologists or Systematic Theologians do with, or perhaps, to the Bible. On their part, scholars of these disciplines may well express their bewilderment at the extent of exegetical controversy related to almost every verse of the Bible, not to mention the technical expertise required to make an informed judgement call on, for example, the composition of the "Big Five" of the Old Testament, namely the Moses-books,[7] or on the authenticity of the Jesus-words within the "Big Five" of the New Testament, namely the four Gospels and the Pauline corpus.

Within the biblical sciences themselves, the diversity of deliberate reading strategies—what Barton terms "'advocacy' readings"[8]—in order to interpret the Bible *for* or *with* the politically suppressed and the marginalised in societies,[9] the under-recognised gender,[10] the abused environment,[11] *et cetera*, also indicate the plurality of ways in which the Bible speaks, or is brought to speak, to modern socio-ethical concerns. What is more, on many of these approaches so much has already been written, that it requires more than the usual dedication just to become at home within an approach as it relates to one section of Scripture related to a single modern issue. Truly comparative readings in this

---

[7] Cf. C. J. S. Lombaard, "What is Isaac Doing in Amos 7?" *Old Testament Essays* 17, no. 3 (2004): 435.

[8] See J. Barton, "Biblical Studies," in *The Blackwell Companion to Modern Theology* (ed. G. Jones; Oxford: Blackwell, 2004), 25.

[9] Cf. e.g. G. West, *Biblical Hermeneutics of Liberation. Modes of Reading the Bible in the South African Context* (Pietermaritzburg: Cluster Publications/2d edition: Pietermaritzburg: Cluster Publications and Maryknoll: Orbis, 1991/1995²).

[10] Cf. e.g. K. Vorster, "Christian Attitude and the Human Dignity of Women," *Studia Historiae Ecclesiasticae* XXXII, no. 2 (2006): 229–68.

[11] Cf. e.g. S. McFague, *Life Abundant: Rethinking Theology and Economy for a Planet in Peril* (Minneapolis: Fortress, 2001).

respect are almost impossible. Gaining a sense of clear orientation through the biblical literature and its applications, the more so.

It is not unexpected, therefore, that this diversity of approaches is often experienced as a cacophony of sorts, in which everything but faith finds a place: there is "no room for God" in exegesis.[12] Bible scholars may experience a tension, at least, if not a dichotomy, between exegesis and spirituality; that is, between the scientific approach to the biblical text and the experience of their faith. These are seen as two different, even antagonistic worlds (with perhaps most famously, Linnemann).[13] In many such cases,

---

[12] D. A. Hagner, "The Place of Exegesis in the Postmodern World," in *History and Exegesis. New Testament Essays in Honor of Dr. E. Earle Ellis for His 80th Birthday* (ed. S.-W. Son; New York: T&T Clark, 2006), 307.

[13] See E. Linnemann, *Historical Criticism of the Bible: Methodology or Ideology?* (Grand Rapids: Baker, 1990); cf. G. D. Fee, "To What End Exegesis? Reflections on Exegesis and Spirituality in Philippians 4:10–20," *Bulletin for Biblical Research* 8 (1988): 75–88; cf. also D. Nae, "Presentation," at the Research Sharing Conference (Adventist Theological Institute, Cernica, Romania, 2007).

Protestant and Catholic exegetes tend to differ in this respect. Because of a different theology of church, and more importantly, because of a greater awareness and practice of spirituality, Catholic exegetes show to a greater degree "continuing attempts to relate historical criticism to theological interpretation" (see J. R. Donahue, "Between Jerusalem and Athens: The Changing Shape of Catholic Biblical Scholarship," in *Hermes and Athena: Biblical Exegesis and Philosophical Theology* [ed. E. Stump and T. P. Flint; Notre Dame, Ind.: University of Notre Dame Press, 1993], 294; cf. 293–99). *Vaticanum II* has aided much in this (cf. e.g. J. A. Fitzmyer, *The Biblical Commission's Document "The Interpretation of the Bible in the Church": Text and Commentary* (Subsidia Biblica 18; Roma: Editrice Pontificio Instituto Biblico, 1995).

Protestant theologians to a greater degree tend to fail in two respects: they lose their faith in the face of historical exegetical findings, and they seem to have more limited gifts in applying these findings to modern situations, à la e.g., C. Stuhlmueller (*The Spirituality of the Psalms* [Collegeville, Minn.: Liturgical Press, 2002]) or J. F. Craghan (*Love and Thunder. A Spirituality of the Old Testament* [Collegeville, Minn.: The Order of St. Benedict, Inc., 1983]). This certainly has to do with more than the legacy of the classical distinction by

this tension results in a longing for the (perceived) simplicity, the harmony of the early church within which the Bible was read, by allegorical means, as directly nourishing a relationship with God. For a range of reasons, Bible and faith were (experienced to be) at one; exegesis and spirituality, a duet in harmony.

Could it be that critical Bible reading has cost us our faith? Has contextual exegesis (for all scholarly methods reflect either implicitly or purposively the context of their origins and uses) come to mean the end of spirituality? Can we read the Bible and at the same time find ourselves being read by the Bible; that is, can a literary encounter lead to an existential/spiritual encounter?[14] Put in more explicit terms of faith:[15] can we still hear a word from God from the Word of God?[16]

Gabler (1787) between dogmatic and historical theology; perhaps Protestant exegetes are more inclined to be influenced by the presuppositions of modernism because of a less developed sense of explicit spiritual identity?—cf. Zimmerling, *Evangelische Spiritualität*, 15–21; Nae, "Presentation." Different presuppositions thus inform the theological matrix of the exegetes concerned. The way in which the *Sola Scriptura* concept has come to be interpreted in post-Reformation Protestantism may well add to the difficulties exegetes from this tradition (in which I also find myself) experience; cf. C. J. S. Lombaard, "The Old Testament between Diachrony and Synchrony: Two Reasons for Favouring the Former," *Journal for Semitics/Tyskrif vir Semitistiek* 15, no. 1 (2006): 22–23, drawing on F. E. Deist, Witnesses to the Old Testament (The Literature of the Old Testament, vol. 5; Pretoria: NG Kerkboekhandel, 1988), 1–7, 199, and H. W. Rossouw, *Klaarheid en Interpretasie. Enkele Probleemhistoriese Gesigspunte in verband met die Leer van die Duidelikheid van die Heilige Skrif* (D.Th. proefskrif, Vrije Universiteit; Amsterdam: Drukkerij en uitgeverij Jacob van Campen N.V., 1963).

[14] Cf. K. Stendahl, "The Bible as a Classic and the Bible as Holy Scripture," in *Beyond Form Criticism. Essays in Old Testament Literary Criticism* (ed. P. R. House; Winona Lake: Eisenbrauns, 1992), 39–46.

[15] Cf. C. J. Wethmar, *Dogma en Verstaanshorison: 'n Histories-Sistematiese Ondersoek in verband met die Hermeneutiese Funksie van die Kerklike Dogma met Besondere Verwysing na die Teologie van Gerhard Ebeling* (Amsterdam: Rodopi, 1977), 159–200; M. Schneiders, "Biblical Foundations of Spirituality,"

2. A Simple Life?

Naturally, we should guard against oversimplification. Clearly, the reading of the Bible in the early church was no simple act of faith. Both the church controversies and the exegetical turns the interpreters had to make in order to find a useful meaning in the text (the unfolding development of the fourfold sense of Scripture, for instance) indicate that a romanticised view of the unity of exegesis and spirituality would fit those contexts poorly. Equally, as I have argued elsewhere,[17] a simple change in exegetical methods in our times would neither bring clarity of theological understanding nor unity of research findings.[18] As with the princes of Pss 118:9 and 146:3, our trust should not be placed in method.[19]

---

in *Scripture as the Soul of Theology* (ed. E. J. Mahoney; Collegeville, Minn.: Liturgical Press, 2000), 4–12.

[16] It seems ever more clearly that the topic of revelation-interpretation (see Schneiders, "Biblical Foundations of Spirituality," 9–22) or revelation-inspiration (see F. L. Canale, *Back to Revelation-Inspiration: Searching for the Cognitive Foundation of Christian Theology in a Postmodern World* [Lanham, Md.: University Press of America, 2001]; Nae, "Presentation") is being placed on the agenda of Bible scholars.

[17] See Lombaard, "The Old Testament between Diachrony and Synchrony," 18–31.

[18] I have argued my preference for the historical methodologies as the most suitable among the exegetical approaches, because these fit the historical nature of the Christian faith best; see C. J. S. Lombaard, "What Is Biblical Spirituality?—Perspectives from a Minor Genre of Old Testament Scholarship," in *Seeing the Seeker. Explorations in the Discipline of Spirituality* (ed. H. Blommestijn et al.; Festschrift for Kees Waaijman; Studies in Spirituality Supplement 19; Louvain, Belgium: Peeters, 2008), 139–53; C. J. S. Lombaard, "The Old Testament between Diachrony and Synchrony: Two Reasons for Favouring the Former," in *The Pentateuch between Synchrony and Diachrony* (ed. J. H. le Roux and E. Otto; New York: T&T Clark, 2007), 61–70.

For examples of the latter approach, cf. e.g. C. J. S. Lombaard, "Genealogies and Spiritualities in Genesis 4:17–22, 4:25–26, 5:1–32," in *The Spirit That Moves. Orientation and Issues in Spirituality* (ed. P. G. R. de

If we seek simplicity, or unity, we should not seek such outcomes in either a romanticised view of the early church or in the solution of a changed methodology, but rather, I would propose, in what is by now a millennia-old tradition:

Already during the time of the post-exilic reconstruction of the Israelite community, the reading of the biblical texts had become part of the practice of faith—that is, the spirituality—of ancient Israel. In Neh 7:72b–8:18 we see the beginnings of an expression of faith in which the reading of Scripture and its exposition is at once transposed back to a mythologically idealised time of Moses *and* instituted as part of the festival culture of Israel, to be maintained in perpetuity. In the Torah, past and present, text explication and sense application are combined, in order to bestow on the faithful their (re)new(ed) religious identity.

Even though the character of the Bible, the identity of the faith concerned, the manner of reading, and a host of other factors have changed much over the intervening two and a half millennia, the essence of this spirituality has remained.[20]

Villiers, C. Kourie and C. J. S. Lombaard; *Acta Theologia* Supplementum 8; Bloemfontein: University of the Free State Press, 2006), 146–64; Stuhlmueller, *The Spirituality of the Psalms*; K. Berger, *Hermeneutik des Neuen Testaments* (Gütersloh: Gütersloher Verlagshaus Gerd Mohn, 1988), 430–37; Craghan, *Love and Thunder*. Studies such as those in Bowe (see B. E. Bowe, *Biblical Foundations of Spirituality. Touching a Finger to the Flame* [Lanham, Md.: Rowman & Littlefield Publishers, Inc., 2003], 23–176), offer more thematic, rather than historical, deliberations (cf. Zimmerling, *Evangelische Spiritualität*, 40).

[19] H.-G. Gadamer, *Wahrheit und Methode. Grundzuge einer philosophischen Hermeneutik* (Tübingen: Mohr, 1975); cf. J. H. le Roux, "Hans-Georg Gadamer en die Ou Testament," *Verbum et Ecclesia* 23, no. 2 (2002), 383–92; C. J. S. Lombaard, "Teks en Mens. J. H. le Roux se Lees van die Bybel binne die Konteks van Hoofstroom-Eksegese in Suid-Afrika," *Old Testament Essays* 19, no. 3 (2006 [special ed.]): 916–20.

[20] Quote from Lombaard, "What Is Biblical Spirituality?" 148.

Put differently: if we do seek some kind of sense of belonging within an unbroken continuity, a sense of firmness, if you will, we need seek no further than the tradition of which we are but the newest generation. For this very tradition is the line of interpreters of the biblical texts beginning with Second Temple Judaism, then, for Christian exegetes, running through the New Testament and early church, *via* the patristic interpreters and their interpreters in the Middle Ages, and from the Reformation and the Enlightenment with their rational-existential turns, through modernism up to early post-modernism,[21] within which we find ourselves at present.[22] As with all scholarship, we are part of a social group, of a guild, even, within which certain norms exist. We are not alone,[23] even though we may feel ourselves at times cast adrift within a veritable sea of interpretations. As with prayer, the value of biblical scholarship lies not in the sense of accomplishment or meaningfulness we may experience, or fail to experience. Rather, again, as with prayer, the act itself, in this instance of studying the Bible, is a spiritual exercise, giving personal expression to what the Christian faith tradition has given us, and it is an act of engagement with our context—not necessarily because some form of relevance is demanded of us, but simply because we are children of our time,

---

[21] For selections on biblical interpretation, from Origen's allegory to modern pragmatism, see the essays collected in J. M. Court, ed., *Biblical Interpretation. The Meanings of Scripture—Past and Present* (London: T&T Clark, 2003).

[22] The fear of post-modernism with respect to exegesis, expressed recently by Hagner (in "The Place of Exegesis in the Postmodern World," 296–302), is in my view somewhat overstated. Post-modernism is no more than the current phase of modernism, though with the harsher edges of the latter now—more realistically, and more humanely—softened, so that greater space is left for, among other matters, spirituality; cf. e.g. Zimmerling, *Evangelische Spiritualität*, 127–34.

[23] With acknowledgement to Van Huyssteen (see J. W. van Huyssteen, *Alone in the World? Human Uniqueness in Science and Theology* (Grand Rapids: Eerdmans, 2006).

and we render results that in various direct and indirect ways interact with our contexts.[24] Studying the Word of God is a godly act—not in the sense of personal and communal Bible study for devotional purposes only, but in the hard academic sense as well.[25]

Naturally, the means of interpretation, that is, the backdrop against which the text is placed in order to elucidate its meaning(s), has changed throughout the centuries—a dynamic which should not be unexpected. The point is, however, that for the most part, the interpreters throughout Christian history were faithfully trying to read the biblical texts for their time, and can therefore to a significant extent be regarded as apologists for the Bible within their contexts.[26] The fact that much of the earlier intentions and methods are at times poorly reviewed nowadays has much to do with changes in, precisely, context; certainly, it has less to do with their neglect of intellectual rigour and faith commitment than it has with ours (a point in some ways parallel to that made by Barton[27]).

3. No Easy Answers

The above paragraph begs the question, though, whether a "simple life" as it is understood here, referring to an unproblematic

---

[24] Cf. C. J. S. Lombaard, "The Relevance of Old Testament Science in/for Africa: Two False Pieties and Focussed Scholarship," *Old Testament Essays* 19, no. 1 (2006): 151–52.

[25] Osborne, for instance, mentions that biblical hermeneutics has three essential aspects: scientific, artistic and spiritual, which may be translated into "What it meant?" (exegesis), "What it means for me?" (devotional), and "How to share with you what it means for me?" (sermonic); see G. R. Osborne, *The Hermeneutical Spiral* (Downers Grove: InterVarsity, 1991), 5.

[26] Cf. Barton, "Biblical Studies," 23–25; R. Gill, "The Practice of Faith," in *The Blackwell Companion to Modern Theology* (ed. G. Jones; Oxford: Blackwell, 2004), 4–5; Balla, *Challenges to New Testament Theology*, 215–50.

[27] See J. Barton, "Reading Texts Holistically: The Foundation of Biblical Criticism," in *Congress Volume Ljubljana 2007* (ed. A. Lemaire; *Vetus Testamentum* Supplement 133; Leiden: Brill, 2010), 367–80.

relationship between Bible and believer, is really to be desired. Is it realistic to long for an easy relationship between Bible and faith, or exegesis and spirituality? Or would such an easy relationship amount to oversimplification? I suggest the latter, for two reasons:

- On the one hand, the fact is that reading the Bible is no mean feat. There are good sociological reasons for Christianity bringing forth in Western(ised) cultures the institution of the university: the intellectual demands of theology were such that it required an institution of relative autonomy within which the truth of the church could be subjected to intellectual scrutiny, to the benefit of humanity.[28] In addition, the concentrated tradition of hermeneutical reflection within modern Christianity (over Schleiermacher,[29] Heidegger,[30] Gadamer,[31] and others) gives evidence of great effort being made to do justice to the intense, and existential, difficulties of biblical interpretation.[32]
- On the other hand, spirituality itself is not a simple matter: although *homo sapiens* certainly has had a spiritual dimension, since at least its earliest cultural deposits,

---

[28] Cf. C. J. S. Lombaard, "There is Rebellion Afoot, and Revelry—The Nascent Reformation of Intellectual Integrity within South African Universities," *Education as Change* 10, no. 1 (July 2006): 81; Zimmerling, *Evangelische Spiritualität*, 18.
[29] F. Schleiermacher, *Hermeneutics and Criticism and Other Writings* (trans. and ed. Andrew Bowie; Cambridge: Cambridge University Press, 1998).
[30] M. Heidegger, *Sein und Zeit* (10. unveränderte Auflage; Tübingen: Niemeyer, 1963).
[31] H.-G. Gadamer, *Wahrheit und Methode. Grundzuge einer philosophischen Hermeneutik* (Tübingen: Mohr, 1975).
[32] Cf. also A. C. Thiselton, *Thiselton on Hermeneutics: Collected Works with New Essays* (Grand Rapids: Eerdmans, 2006); idem, New Horizons in Hermeneutics (Grand Rapids: Zondervan, 1992).

namely rock drawings,[33] to define that human reality with any precision is a task we must by now accept cannot be accomplished conclusively.[34] Though we can gain a substantive understanding of the dimensions of human spirituality in general and of Christian spirituality in particular, any attempt at capturing in words some definitive sense of those aspects, or of the whole, ends in futility.[35]

In the to and fro of both public/popular and theological/ intellectual debate on the relationship between exegesis and

---

[33] Cf. Van Huyssteen, Alone in the World?
[34] C. J. S. Lombaard, "Spirituality: Sense and Gist. On Meaning, God and Being," in *The Spirit That Empowers: Perspectives on Spirituality* (ed. P. G. R. de Villiers, C. Kourie, and C. J. S. Lombaard; *Acta Theologica* Supplementum 11; Bloemfontein: University of the Free State Press, 2008), 94–107; cf. C. Kourie, "What Is Christian Spirituality?" in *Christian Spirituality in South Africa* (ed. C. Kourie and L. Kretzschmar; Pietermaritzburg: Cluster Publications, 2000), 9–33; K. Waaijman, "Toward a Phenomenological Definition of Spirituality," *Studies in Spirituality* 3 (1993): 5–57; D. J. Smit, "Kan Spiritualiteit Beskryf Word?" *Ned. Geref. Teologiese Tydskrif* 30 , no. 1 (1989): 83–94.
[35] Lombaard's table tries to give some structure to the different more common usages of the term "spirituality" (see C. J. S. Lombaard, "The Old Testament in Christian Spirituality: Perspectives on the Undervaluation of the Old Testament in Christian Spirituality," *HTS Teologiese Studies/Theological Studies* 59, no. 2 [2003]: 450). As a definition-in-brief, that of Schneiders (in "Biblical Foundations of Spirituality," 2) serves well: "The fundamental meaning of 'Christian spirituality' is the lived religious experience of believers as they attempt, over time, to integrate their life within the framework of the ultimate values of Christianity, namely, a developing relationship to the Trinitarian God of Jesus Christ within the community called Church in service to the Reign of God in the world."; cf. also Bowe, *Biblical Foundations of Spirituality,* 10–20. However, the emphases of modernism and post-modernism on individualism and their a- or anti-institutional impulses draw the emphasis on church in a definition such as this into question; cf. Zimmerling, *Evangelische Spiritualität,* 133–38.

spirituality, these complexities have a confounding effect. Not only do simple answers prove elusive; the questions keep becoming more complex. This does not mean that the issues should not be analysed, teased out, and debated; it does mean, however, that we should not expect to reach any point of finality. Such a point is precluded by the inescapable interrelationship between individual and community, and the irreducible intricacy of this interrelationship,[36] in both understanding the Bible and in understanding and expressing one's faith. The diversity of spiritualities within the Bible,[37] and the dialogically-critical engagement with such a Bible from within latter-day spiritualities,[38] are therefore not to be ignored; in fact, such diversity nourishes faithful reading.[39]

Any attempt at finding a spiritual "Mitte" to the Bible is therefore bound to say more about the spirituality of the individual interpreter than it does about the Bible as a whole.[40] It is for precisely this reason too that it becomes unacceptable that, when Christian biblical spirituality is written on, more often than not the

---

[36] Cf. C. J. S. Lombaard, "Four South Africans' Proposals for a Central Theme to 'Scriptural Spirituality,'" *Scriptura* 88, no. 1 (2005): 148.

[37] Preferable to speaking of "the spirituality that comes to expression in the Bible" remains the acknowledgement "that within the Christian Bible there is a plurality of spiritualities" (see Schneiders, "Biblical Foundations of Spirituality," 3).

[38] Cf. Lombaard, "Four South Africans' Proposals," 140–41.

[39] Craghan, *Love and Thunder,* 7–15; cf. ix, 195–211.

[40] Cf. e.g. Lombaard, "Four South Africans' Proposals," 139–50, on: S. D. Snyman, "Spiritualiteit—'n Perspektief uit die Ou Testament," *In die Skriflig* 31, no. 4 (1997): 375–87; A. B. du Toit, "Lewensgemeenskap met God as Essensie van Bybelse Spiritualiteit," *Skrif en Kerk,* 14, no. 1 (1993): 28–46; D. J. Louw, "Spiritualiteit as Bybelse Vroomheid in die Teologie en die Gemeentelike Bediening," *Praktiese Teologie in Suid-Afrika* 4, no. 2 (1989): 1–17; A. Nolan, *Biblical Spirituality* (Springs: The Order of Preachers [Southern Africa], 1982).

emphasis is strongly on the New Testament.[41] Clearly, the full, contradictory richness of the whole of the Bible must be drawn on by those interested in engaging in a critical, yet in different ways engaged, biblical spirituality. This would to a significant extent encourage theologies built in humility. Moreover, the ever-changing contexts in the flow of history within which successive generations of Bible scholars find themselves, along with intellectual and other developments, will continually prevent to the question of the relationship between exegesis and spirituality an "amen".

---

[41] Cf. S. Rakoczy, "Spirituality in Cross-Cultural Perspective and Mission Studies," in *To Cast Fire upon the Earth. Bible and Mission Collaborating in Today's Multicultural Global Context* (Pietermaritzburg: Cluster Publications, 2000), 74–76; Lombaard, "The Old Testament in Christian Spirituality," 433–50.

BIBLIOGRAPHY

Albertz, R. *Religionsgeschichte Israels in alttestamentlicher Zeit*. Vol. 1 and 2. Göttingen: Vandenhoeck & Ruprecht, 1992.

Balla, P. *Challenges to New Testament Theology. An Attempt to Justify the Enterprise*. Tübingen: Mohr Siebeck, 1997.

Barton, J. "Reading Texts Holistically: The Foundation of Biblical Criticism." Pages 367–80 in *Congress Volume Ljubljana 2007*. Edited by A. Lemaire. *Vetus Testamentum* Supplement 133. Leiden: Brill, 2010.

———. "Biblical Studies." Pages 18–33 in *The Blackwell Companion to Modern Theology*. Edited by G. Jones. Oxford: Blackwell, 2004.

Berger, K. *Hermeneutik des Neuen Testaments*. Gütersloh: Gütersloher Verlagshaus Gerd Mohn, 1988.

Bowe, B. E. *Biblical Foundations of Spirituality. Touching a Finger to the Flame*. Lanham, Md.: Rowman & Littlefield Publishers, Inc., 2003.

Brueggemann, W. *Theology of the Old Testament: Testimony, Dispute, Advocacy*. Minneapolis: Fortress, 1997.

Canale, F. L. *Back to Revelation-Inspiration: Searching for the Cognitive Foundation of Christian Theology in a Postmodern World*. Lanham, Md.: University Press of America, 2001.

———. *Understanding Revelation-Inspiration in a Postmodern World*. Berrien Springs: Andrews University Lithotech, 2001.

Craghan, J. F. *Love and Thunder. A Spirituality of the Old Testament*. Collegeville, Minn.: The Order of St. Benedict, Inc., 1983.

Court, J. M. ed. *Biblical Interpretation. The Meanings of Scripture—Past and Present*. London: T&T Clark, 2003.

Donahue, J. R. "Between Jerusalem and Athens: The Changing Shape of Catholic Biblical Scholarship." Pages 285–313 in *Hermes and Athena: Biblical Exegesis and Philosophical Theology*. Edited by E. Stump and T. P. Flint. Notre Dame, Ind.: University of Notre Dame Press, 1993.

Deist, F. E. *Witnesses to the Old Testament*. The Literature of the Old Testament. Volume 5. Pretoria: NG Kerkboekhandel, 1988.

Du Toit, A. B. "Lewensgemeenskap met God as Essensie van Bybelse Spiritualiteit." *Skrif en Kerk*, 14, no. 1 (1993): 28–46.

Gabler, J. G. *De iusto discrimine theologiae biblicae et dogmaticae regundisque recte utriusque finibus*. Altdorf, 1787.

Fee, G. D. "To What End Exegesis? Reflections on Exegesis and Spirituality in Philippians 4:10–20." *Bulletin for Biblical Research* 8 (1988): 75–88.

Fitzmyer, J. A. *The Biblical Commission's Document "The Interpretation of the Bible in the Church". Text and Commentary*. Subsidia Biblica 18. Roma: Editrice Pontificio Instituto Biblico, 1995.

Gadamer, H.-G. *Wahrheit und Methode. Grundzuge einer philosophischen Hermeneutik*. Tübingen: Mohr, 1975.

Gill, R. "The Practice of Faith." Pages 3–17 in *The Blackwell Companion to Modern Theology*. Edited by G. Jones. Oxford: Blackwell, 2004.

Hagner, D. A. "The Place of Exegesis in the Postmodern World." Pages 292–308 in *History and Exegesis. New Testament Essays in Honor of Dr. E. Earle Ellis for His 80th Birthday*. Edited by S.-W. Son. New York: T&T Clark, 2006.

Heidegger, M. *Sein und Zeit*. 10. unveränderte Auflage. Tübingen: Niemeyer, 1963.

Kourie, C. "What Is Christian Spirituality?" Pages 9–33 in *Christian Spirituality in South Africa*. Edited by C. Kourie and L. Kretzschmar. Pietermaritzburg: Cluster Publications, 2000.

Le Marquand, G. "Siblings or Antagonists? The Ethos of Biblical Scholarship from the North Atlantic and African Worlds." Pages 61–85 in *Biblical Interpretation in African Perspective*. Edited by D. Adamo. Lanham, Md.: University Press of America, 2006.

Le Roux, J. H. "Hans-Georg Gadamer en die Ou Testament." *Verbum et Ecclesia* 23, no. 2 (2002): 383–92.

Linnemann, E. *Historical Criticism of the Bible: Methodology or Ideology?* Grand Rapids: Baker, 1990.

Lombaard, C. J. S. "Spirituality: Sense and Gist. On Meaning, God and Being." Pages 94–107 in *The Spirit That Empowers: Perspectives on Spirituality*. Edited by P. G. R. de Villiers, C. Kourie and C. J. S. Lombaard. *Acta Theologica* Supplementum 11. Bloemfontein: University of the Free State Press, 2008.

———. "What Is Biblical Spirituality?—Perspectives from a Minor Genre of Old Testament Scholarship." Pages 139–53 in *Seeing the Seeker. Explorations in the Discipline of Spirituality*. Edited by H. Blommestijn et al. Festschrift for Kees Waaijman; *Studies in Spirituality* Supplement 19. Louvain, Belgium: Peeters, 2008.

———. "The Old Testament between Diachrony and Synchrony: Two Reasons for Favouring the Former." Pages 61–70 in *The Pentateuch between Synchrony and Diachrony*. Edited by J. H. le Roux and E. Otto. New York: T&T Clark, 2007.

———. "The Old Testament between Diachrony and Synchrony: Two Reasons for Favouring the Former." *Journal for Semitics/Tyskrif vir Semitistiek* 15, no. 1 (2006): 18–31.

———. "There is Rebellion Afoot, and Revelry—The Nascent Reformation of Intellectual Integrity within South African Universities." *Education as Change* 10, no. 1 (July 2006): 71–84.

———. "The Relevance of Old Testament Science in/for Africa: Two False Pieties and Focussed Scholarship." *Old Testament Essays* 19, no. 1 (2006): 144–55.

———. "Genealogies and Spiritualities in Genesis 4:17–22, 4:25–26, 5:1–32." Pages 146–64 in *The Spirit That Moves. Orientation and Issues in Spirituality.* Edited by P. G. R. de Villiers, C. Kourie and C. J. S. Lombaard. Acta Theologia Supplementum 8. Bloemfontein: University of the Free State Press, 2006.

———. "Teks en Mens. J. H. le Roux se Lees van die Bybel binne die Konteks van Hoofstroom-Eksegese in Suid-Afrika." *Old Testament Essays* 19, no. 3 (2006 [Special Edition]): 912–25.

———. "Four South Africans' Proposals for a Central Theme to 'Scriptural Spirituality'." *Scriptura* 88, no. 1 (2005): 139–50.

———. "What is Isaac Doing in Amos 7?" *Old Testament Essays* 17, no. 3 (2004): 435–42.

———. "The Old Testament in Christian Spirituality: Perspectives on the Undervaluation of the Old Testament in Christian Spirituality." *HTS Teologiese Studies/Theological Studies* 59, no. 2 (2003): 433–50.

Louw, D. J. "Spiritualiteit as Bybelse Vroomheid in die Teologie en die Gemeentelike Bediening." *Praktiese Teologie in Suid-Afrika* 4, no. 2 (1989): 1–17.

McFague, S. *Life Abundant: Rethinking Theology and Economy for a Planet in Peril.* Minneapolis: Fortress, 2001.

Nae, D. "Presentation." At the Research Sharing Conference, Adventist Theological Institute, Cernica, Romania, 2007.

Nolan, A. *Biblical Spirituality.* Springs: The Order of Preachers (Southern Africa), 1982.

Nürnberger, K. *Theology of the Biblical Witness. An Evolutionary Approach.* Theologie: Forschung und Wissenschaft, Band 5. Münster: LIT Verlag, 2002.

Osborne, G. R. *The Hermeneutical Spiral.* Downers Grove: InterVarsity, 1991.

Porter, S. E. ed. *Hearing the Old Testament in the New Testament.* Grand Rapids: Eerdmans, 2006.

Preuß, H. D. *Theologie des Alten Testaments, Band 1: JHWHs erwählendes und verpflichtendes Handeln.* Stuttgart: Kohlhammer, 1991.

Rakoczy, S. "Spirituality in Cross-Cultural Perspective and Mission Studies." Pages 73–86 in *To Cast Fire upon the Earth. Bible and Mission Collaborating in Today's Multicultural Global Context.* Pietermaritzburg: Cluster Publications, 2000.

Rossouw, H. W. *Klaarheid en Interpretasie. Enkele Probleemhistoriese Gesigspunte in verband met die Leer van die Duidelikheid van die Heilige Skrif.* D.Th. proefskrif, Vrije Universiteit. Amsterdam: Drukkerij en uitgeverij Jacob van Campen N.V., 1963.

Schleiermacher, F. *Hermeneutics and Criticism and Other Writings.* Translated and edited by Andrew Bowie. Cambridge: Cambridge University Press, 1998.

Schneiders, M. "Biblical Foundations of Spirituality." Pages 1–22 in *Scripture as the Soul of Theology.* Edited by E. J. Mahoney. Collegeville, Minn.: Liturgical Press, 2000.

Smit, D. J. "Kan Spiritualiteit Beskryf Word?" *Ned. Geref. Teologiese Tydskrif* 30, no. 1 (1989): 83–94.

Snyman, S. D. "Spiritualiteit—'n Perspektief uit die Ou Testament." *In die Skriflig* 31, no. 4 (1997): 375–87.

Stendahl, K. "The Bible as a Classic and the Bible as Holy Scripture." Pages 39–46 in *Beyond Form Criticism. Essays in Old Testament Literary Criticism.* Edited by P. R. House. Winona Lake: Eisenbrauns, 1992.

Stuhlmueller, C. *The Spirituality of the Psalms.* Collegeville, Minn.: Liturgical Press, 2002.

Thiselton, A. C. *Thiselton on Hermeneutics: Collected Works with New Essays.* Grand Rapids: Eerdmans, 2006.

———. *New Horizons in Hermeneutics.* Grand Rapids: Zondervan, 1992.

Van Huyssteen, J. W. *Alone in the World? Human Uniqueness in Science and Theology.* Grand Rapids: Eerdmans, 2006.

Vorster, K. "Christian Attitude and the Human Dignity of Women." *Studia Historiae Ecclesiasticae* XXXII, no. 2 (2006): 229–68.

———. "Toward a Phenomenological Definition of Spirituality." *Studies in Spirituality* 3 (1993): 5–57.

West, G. *Biblical Hermeneutics of Liberation. Modes of Reading the Bible in the South African Context.* Pietermaritzburg: Cluster Publications/Second edition: Pietermaritzburg: Cluster Publications and Maryknoll: Orbis, 1991/1995²

Wethmar, C. J. *Dogma en Verstaanshorison: 'n Histories-Sistematiese Ondersoek in verband met die Hermeneutiese Funksie van die Kerklike Dogma met Besondere Verwysing na die Teologie van Gerhard Ebeling.* Amsterdam: Rodopi, 1977.

Zimmerling, P. *Evangelische Spiritualität. Wurzeln und Zugänge.* Göttingen: Vandenhoeck & Ruprecht, 2003.

About the Author

Christo Lombaard is Professor of Christian Spirituality at the University of South Africa. Educated in South Africa, he holds two doctorates: the Ph.D. in Communication Studies from the North-West University, Potchefstroom Campus, and the D.D. in Old Testament Studies from the University of Pretoria. His research interests include Biblical Spirituality, Pentateuch Theory, Spirituality Theory, Spirituality and Sexuality, and aspects of Journalism. His other interests include writing and performing blues, folk and rock music, and authoring literary pieces.

He may be contacted at ChristoLombaard@gmail.com.

www.ingramcontent.com/pod-product-compliance
Lightning Source LLC
Chambersburg PA
CBHW021810220426
43662CB00006B/251